Pat and Betty's
No-Fuss Cooking

Pat and Betty's
No-Fuss Cooking

More than 200 Delicious,

Time-Saving, and Easy

Recipes from the

Reynolds Kitchens

Patricia A. Schweitzer and Betty T. Morton

New York

LIBRARY OF CONGRESS CATALOGING-IN-PUBLICATION DATA

Schweitzer, Patricia A.
    Pat and Betty's no fuss cooking: more than 200 delicious, time-saving, and easy recipes from the Reynolds Kitchens/Patricia A. Schweitzer and Betty T. Morton.—1st ed.
        p. cm.
    Includes index.
    ISBN 1-4013-0060-X
    1. Cookery. 2. Quick and easy cookery. 3. Aluminum foil.
    I. Morton, Betty T. II. Reynolds Kitchens (Firm)
    III. Title.
    TX652.S42 2003
    641.5'55—dc 21

                                                                    2003044976

Hyperion books are available for special promotions and premiums.
For details contact Hyperion Special Markets, 77 West 66th Street, 11th floor, New York, New York 10023-6298, or call 212-456-0133.

Book design by Richard Oriolo

FIRST EDITION

1   3   5   7   9   10   8   6   4   2

Contents

Introduction **Who We Are and What We Do**

IF YOU KNOW US AS those two ladies who represent Reynolds products on TV, radio, and the Internet, or recognize us when we appear at major food events or as talk show guests, you'd be right. But you might be surprised to know that we do it not because we are actresses, but because we are home economists in the Reynolds Kitchens.

It's a great job when you think about it. We spend many days in a fully equipped kitchen, developing and taste-testing recipes. If you like to cook as much as we do, nothing could be better. If you like to solve problems for consumers as much as we do, it's even more rewarding.

Betty has been working for Reynolds for over twenty years, and Pat for nearly fourteen. During that time, we have seen the Reynolds product line expand and become more innovative. We've learned a lot along the way, and while we're both trained home economists, our backgrounds are quite different.

Betty arrived in the Reynolds Kitchens after having worked in two major food company test kitchens in the Midwest and as product development manager for a sandwich company in Norfolk, Virginia.

Pat worked as an extension home economist for the University of Minnesota and then moved to Florida, where she worked for the Florida Department of Natural Resources. Prior to joining the Reynolds Kitchens she was a food writer and restaurant critic for a Richmond newspaper.

Our Jobs

No single day is the same as the one before, but every day is dedicated to increasing demand for our products. Luckily, this is a painless task, since we believe so deeply in Reynolds products and how they can make life easier for the home cook.

The flagship product, Reynolds Wrap Aluminum Foil, is the one most folks associate with Reynolds. The foil product line includes standard weight foil, heavy duty foil, extra heavy duty foil, pop-up foil sheets, extra heavy duty foil bags, holographic aluminum foil, and, one of our newer products, nonstick aluminum foil.

We also develop recipes that use plastic wrap, parchment paper, paper and foil baking cups, oven bags, wax paper, and disposable plastic cookware.

This allows us great scope. Unlike working in the test kitchen for a food brand, we can develop recipes for a wide variety of foods. As you will find on the following pages, we create snacks, salads, casseroles, roasts, grilled dishes, desserts, cakes, cookies, and more. They are all easy and fast, perfect for today's busy lifestyle, which is why we want to share so many of them in a cookbook.

The kitchen itself is fitted with the same everyday appliances you are likely to find in any home kitchen. We have well-known brands of stoves, ovens, refrigerators, and freezers, but none is fancy or of restaurant caliber. Our mission is to make our recipes work in home kitchens, and to accomplish this, we use the equipment and utensils anyone might have at home.

Life in the Test Kitchen

All of our recipes are developed for specific uses. For example, a recipe might be shown in a television commercial, used in a magazine ad, or featured in a photo in the coupon section of the newspaper. When we receive a request for a recipe, we often schedule a meeting with marketing managers and folks from the advertising department. During the meeting, we discuss the purpose of the recipe, the theme of the promotion, and any special requirements the recipe should fill. We might discuss some concepts for recipes. Then we go back to the kitchens and brainstorm ideas. The ideas might be based on a newly popular ingredient, a food trend, a dish we have noticed recently in restaurants, or something we gleaned from magazine and newspaper food stories.

As we consider ideas, we think about flavors, textures, ease of preparation, and how well a dish will photograph. Uppermost in our minds is developing recipes that meet the needs of today's consumer. We also know that speed and convenience are our consumers' number-one concern.

Once we decide on a recipe idea, we draft the recipe on our computers. We then prepare it, adjusting it as we go along if necessary. We conduct taste panels to evaluate and rate each round of recipe tests. When we are satisfied that the criteria have been met, we convene a taste panel of the people at the original meeting to show the recipe and have a final evaluation. If the recipe passes, we add it to our ever-growing recipe database.

From start to finish, the process may take two to three weeks or longer, depending on how many recipes are needed, and because projects overlap, we never work on just one recipe. Our criterion is to test a recipe a maximum of three times. If an original idea needs significant improvement after three tries, we reject it and move on to another idea.

The result of this system is a wonderful collection of accessible, delicious, and realistic recipes designed to make the best use of our products but also of our consumers' time.

Lights! Camera! Action!

In the mid- '90s we started hearing rumors that the new ad campaign was going to feature home economists, so we joked between ourselves about "who would play us." When the creative team from the advertising agency arrived for a meeting with the campaign presentation, they had a blow-up photograph of us as part of the pitch. We couldn't believe they were serious!

As it turns out, the agency's strategy was right and we've been helping make commercials ever since. The reason it seems to work so well is probably because of our role in the Reynolds Kitchens. We work with a product throughout the entire developmental process. By conducting performance testing and recipe development, we really get to know a product's benefits.

When a commercial is being developed we also become consultants regarding the food and recipes that would be most appropriate. Therefore, it just seems to make sense that we should also be sharing what we know directly with our consumers. So when the director says "Action!" we don't need to act. We just need to be Pat and Betty.

Pat and Betty's
No-Fuss Cooking

Stock Your Kitchen Right

I have been known to peer into people's cabinets and even inspect the shelves in other test kitchens. If they don't have our products, I make sure they get them!
—Betty

When we travel, Betty is the tireless promoter. She strikes up conversations and shares brochures with everyone, from waiters to fellow passengers on the airplane!
—Pat

WE ALWAYS SAY THAT A well-stocked kitchen makes cooking efficient and easy. When equipment and ingredients are at your fingertips, you can enjoy the process of getting a meal on the table more.

Just about everyone has space limitations, so it's sensible to outfit your kitchen with essentials. Then, if you have room, add those items you especially like or want. If you have good sharp knives, the right size pans, and an assortment of herbs, spices, pastas, rice, and baking supplies on hand, for example, cooking becomes a pleasure rather than a frantic chore.

Reynolds Staples

We think all our products fall under the category of staples. If you have space to store them, you'll be happy to have them close by. They save time and cleanup, and speed up cooking. Without question, Reynolds products fit today's busy lifestyles.

For instance, an everyday meal cooked in a Reynolds Oven Bag is a significant time and energy saver. Cooking times are reduced and there's no stirring or pot watching. The turkey size Reynolds Oven Bag is a bonus during the holidays or anytime you want to cook a turkey, ham, or roast.

We make a number of different foil products and we want to help you learn when to use them. Follow the recommendations in our recipes, but also understand these basics. Standard weight Reynolds Wrap Aluminum Foil is terrific for covering casseroles or wrapping sandwiches, and if doubled, can be used for packet cooking. Wrappers Pop-Up Foil Sheets, which are standard weight foil, are convenient for quick snacks on the go and large sandwiches that won't fit into plastic bags. Turn to Release Non-Stick Foil when baking or grilling cheesy or sticky foods and for freezing. Use Reynolds Wrap Heavy Duty Foil for lining pans, tenting turkeys, and packet cooking, and Extra Heavy Foil for cooking on the grill. Reynolds Foil Bags, made with extra heavy duty foil, are handy for oven or grill cooking complete meals.

Reynolds Plastic Wrap—clear or color—serves myriad uses. It stretches over dishes and bowls to seal in freshness, is great for wrapping food for storage, and the color plastic wraps make food marvelously festive. And of course we love the seasonal printed plastic wrap during the holidays.

Cut-Rite Wax Paper celebrated its seventy-fifth anniversary in 2002, and although most home cooks have a roll of it in the kitchen, it's an underused product. We hear from consumers that they use it most often to line bottoms of cake pans, and this is an excellent use. But it does so much more. Line your countertops with it for easy cleanup, especially when you're performing messy tasks such as rinsing or breading chicken pieces, measuring dry ingredients, or decorating cookies or cupcakes. It's also fabulous for the microwave. Wax paper self vents to avoid excessive steam buildup. It holds in moisture, though, and prevents splattering to keep the microwave clean. Wax paper is less expensive than paper towels and contains no inks or dyes. Like parchment paper, it is convenient for combining dry ingredients and then funneling them into the mixing bowl. Look for wax paper sandwich size bags, too. They are great for lunchbox snacks.

Reynolds Parchment Paper is being used more and more by home bakers to line cookie sheets and bottoms of cake pans and to sandwich cookie and pie crust dough when it's being rolled. Parchment paper is readily available in supermarkets and other stores, so if you haven't tried it, it's easy to find.

Reynolds Baking Cups are wonderful for cupcakes and muffins. Muffin pans stay clean and the baked product is neatly contained. Foil baking cups stand on their own without a muffin pan. Our extra-large foil baking cups are designed for jumbo muffins and shortcakes. Mini baking cups are available in paper and foil, and they're great for candies and party favors. Look for seasonal and fun designs to use throughout the year to make your baked goods a little more special.

Pot Lux cookware was introduced in 2000 and comes in three sizes. These oven-safe containers are superb for lasagna and other casseroles, salads, brownies, and cakes. Use them in the microwave as well as the oven, but remember the lid should only be used in the microwave, not the oven. We use Pot Lux cookware time and again in our test kitchen and at home for baking and taking foods away from home. They're great for storing and reheating leftovers, too. To clean, just place the cookware on the top rack of the dishwasher!

Finally, Reynolds Freezer Paper with the plastic coating is essential for those who do a lot of freezing, such as hunters and anyone who lives miles from a supermarket and likes to "stock up." Freezer paper is also handy for lining countertops to prevent meat juices from leaking through, and it's great for crafts. Speaking of crafts, we know that quilters love it: They use it to make stencils and appliqués. How gratifying to know that our products have uses outside of the kitchen!

Kitchen Equipment

The following list is inclusive enough to cover the equipment you'll need for our recipes, although many home cooks will want to augment it with other products. It pays to buy the best quality pots and pans you can afford—they last longer and cook more evenly. The same can be said about knives. Buy good ones, take good care of them, and they will last a lifetime.

1. Good set of knives
2. Set of pots and pans
   a. Two or three saucepans with lids ranging from 1- to 4-quart capacities
   b. 6, 10-, and 12-inch non-stick skillets
   c. 6- to 8-quart stock pot

3. Baking pans or dishes (metal and glass or ceramic)
   a. 9-by-13-inch and 8-inch square
   b. 9-inch round cake pans
   c. Round and square casserole dishes
   d. Cookie sheets
   e. 12-cup muffin pans
   f. Large roasting pan, at least two inches deep
   g. 9- or 10-inch round glass pie plate
   h. 10-inch tube or bundt pan
   i. 9-inch loaf pan
4. Microwave-safe dishes
5. Electric mixer (standing or hand)
6. Food processor and/or blender
7. Wire cooling racks

Utensils

1. Instant-read and standard meat thermometers
2. Measuring cups
3. Measuring spoons
4. Hand can opener or electric can opener
5. Set of mixing bowls
6. Assorted cutting boards
7. Heat-proof rubber spatula
8. Metal spatula
9. Kitchen scissors
10. Whisks
11. Vegetable peeler
12. Box-shape grater
13. Rolling pin
14. Tongs
15. Kitchen timer
16. Wooden spoons

17. Slotted spoon
18. Pizza cutter
19. Oven mitts and pot holders
20. Ruler for measuring accurately
21. Pastry brush and pastry blender
22. Various sized strainers
23. Colander
24. Salad spinner
25. Apple corer and/or melon baller
26. Citrus juicer

Pantry

The foods listed here all keep well in a cool, dark pantry or cupboard. Store oils, spices, and herbs away from heat and light, and flour and sugar away from moisture. Date the products you don't use very often and replace them regularly. These might include herbs, spices, baking powder and soda, and bread crumbs.

1. All-purpose flour
2. Granulated sugar
3. Brown sugar
4. Salt
5. Pepper
6. Vegetable oil
7. Olive oil
8. Sesame oil
9. Vinegar
10. Baking powder
11. Baking soda
12. Pure vanilla extract and other flavored extracts you like (almond, lemon, orange, rum)
13. Dried bread crumbs

14. Dried herbs and spices
    a. Ground cinnamon
    b. Whole nutmeg
    c. Ground nutmeg
    d. Basil
    e. Oregano
    f. Thyme
    g. Rosemary
    h. Italian seasoning
    i. Garlic powder
    j. Ground ginger
    k. Seasoned salt
    l. Creole seasoning
    m. Seasoning blends such as jerk, Cajun, and taco
15. Assorted pastas
16. Rice
17. Canned goods
    a. Seasoned tomatoes
    b. Black, red, and white beans
    c. Soups and broth
18. Coffee and tea
19. Bread and/or tortillas
20. Tortilla chips
21. Crackers
22. Cookies
23. Peanut butter
24. Onions
25. Potatoes
26. Cake and brownie mixes
27. Cornstarch

Refrigerator

It's easy to let condiments and other foods accumulate on the refrigerator door and the backs of shelves. Clean out the refrigerator periodically and use up or discard half-empty and outdated jars of mustard, marinades, and other products. Line the vegetable bins with wax paper or freezer paper to keep them fresh and easy to clean.

1. Condiments
   a. Mustard
   b. Salad dressings
   c. Mayonnaise
   d. Ketchup
   e. Salsa
   f. Jellies, jams, or preserves (We like the all-fruit brands, too.)
   g. Pickles
   h. Worcestershire sauce
   i. Soy sauce
   j. Teriyaki sauce and marinade
   k. Hot pepper sauce
2. Fruits and vegetables
3. Hard cheese (such as Cheddar), cream cheese, and cottage cheese
4. Sour cream or yogurt
5. Milk
6. Eggs
7. Butter
8. Juice
9. Bacon and lunch meat (including turkey bacon)

Freezer

Wrap foods in non-stick heavy duty foil for freezer storage. Foil contours to the shape of the food and eliminates air pockets that can cause freezer burn. Freezer paper is economical when freezing large amounts of meat. Be sure to label the food in the freezer and eat meat and poultry within a sensible time. (Look on our website at reynoldskitchens.com for our Freezer Storage Time Chart.)

1. Meats, poultry, and fish
2. Vegetables
3. Fruits
4. Ice cream or frozen yogurt
5. Bread, rolls
6. Juice
7. Ice

Shopping Tips

Finally, follow these few tips and you'll always have food on hand for a quick and easy meal direct from the Reynolds Kitchens, courtesy of Pat and Betty! We find these to be useful, and money- and time-saving. We think you will, too.

1. Plan meals ahead of time.
2. Shop with a list to prevent over-shopping and forgetting items.
3. Don't shop when you're hungry. (You'll buy more than you need.)
4. Use coupons.
5. Watch for advertised specials.
6. Buy staples in bulk if you have room to store them.
7. Buy seasonal fruits and vegetables. They generally are better and fresher.

a well-stocked kitchen

makes cooking efficient

and easy

Appetizers, Snacks, and Salads

Tortilla Pinwheel Appetizers

Honey-Sesame Chicken Drummettes

Jalapeño Beef and Cheese Roll-Ups

Santa Fe Chicken and Black Bean Dip

Cranberry-Chili Smoked Sausage Bites

Feta Cheese Ball

Fruit Tray with Pineapple Cream Dip

Vegetable Platter with Cheesy Italian Dip

Marinated Vegetable Salad

Spinach Bites

Easy Sweet-and-Spicy Meatballs

Watermelon Boat

Romaine Salad with Orange Vinaigrette

Tomato-Basil Pasta Salad

Easy Coleslaw

Honey-Almond Fruit Salad

Fruit Salad with Strawberry Dressing

Greek Pasta Salad

Tex-Mex Layered Salad

BLT Salad

Potluck Pasta Salad

Grilled Jamaican-Style Chicken Salad

California Chicken Salad

Turkey and Wild Rice Salad

Cheesy Chicken Nachos

Mexican Pita Snack

Pizza Quesadilla

California Grilled Pizza

Super-Stuffed Subs

Easy Grilled S'Mores

Crunchy Snack Mix

Smiley Face Snack Holders with Crunchy Snack Mix

Crispy Caterpillar Bookworms

Caramel Treat Cups

PBJ Puzzle Sandwich

Eating snacks instead of sitting down to a more formal meal is a trend on the rise. And why not? Snacks are fun finger foods to share with your kids and friends.

—Pat

When my husband was growing up, a snack before bedtime was a ritual, and it's a habit he has carried into adulthood. I think it's great because while a snack can be healthful, it's always a treat.

—Betty

OVER THE YEARS, WE'VE NOTICED trends as we've come up with recipes in the Reynolds Kitchens. Home cooks prepare more chicken and leaner cuts of meat. They eat smaller portions of red meat and know that they should increase their weekly intake of fish. Most folks recognize immediately how they, themselves, have changed their eating habits in these ways. But another trend we've noticed is an increase in snacking.

Snacks

Americans eat more often than in days gone by. Many of us munch all day long. This may sound excessive but doesn't have to be, because there's nothing wrong with getting your daily caloric intake from five or six small meals rather than three large ones. The trick is to recognize that this is what you're doing.

Some days are just too packed to find time to sit down to a meal. Teenagers and small children rely on snacks, too, to fuel their growing bodies. Stroll down the frozen food aisle of the supermarket and check out all the frozen snacks. While these are handy to have available, we offer recipes for Super

Stuffed Subs, Pizza Quesadilla, PBJ Puzzle Sandwiches, and Mexican Pita Snack—all easy enough for your kids to make and wholesome enough for you to feel good about them. (Best of all, after your kids make these with our products, you won't be left with a sinkful of dirty pots and pans. Cleanup is so easy, they'll do much of it themselves!)

Some of the more whimsical snacks in this chapter derive from winning recipes submitted in a contest we held in our home city of Richmond, Virginia. We asked local crafters and homemakers to form teams and create recipes and crafts using Reynolds Color Plastic Wrap. Talk about creativity! We got some incredible ideas.

We took the best ideas back to the Kitchens and refined them. Both our Crispy Caterpillar Bookworms and Smiley Face Snack Holders were inspired by that contest—and are among our favorites.

We came up with our Cheesy Chicken Nachos for the introduction of Reynolds Wrap Release Non-Stick Aluminum Foil. We traveled around the country demonstrating how even the gooiest cheese snack doesn't stick to the foil. The crowds loved it!

Appetizers

What's the difference between appetizers and snacks? It depends how and when you serve them. Appetizers are those tasty little dishes we prepare for family and friends when we entertain; snacks are more casual fare. Among the recipes on these pages, there is plenty of room for crossover. Because we recognize how busy everyone is these days, none of our appetizers are difficult or time consuming, and using our products makes their preparation extra easy.

For instance, the Feta Cheese Ball and the Spinach Bites work at any kind of party, even a casual weekend get-together. Both the Honey-Sesame Chicken Drummettes and the Santa Fe Chicken and Black Bean Dip are hearty, filling, and perfect for an evening grilling party, tailgating, or better yet, when you have a few guests over to watch the game.

Salads

We also include salads in this chapter. Simply put, we love them! Both of us like to eat a wide variety of fresh foods, but because of our job, we don't always have time to plan ahead. This might be why we are so devoted to salads—they're easy, quick, creative, and can include almost anything you especially like.

Betty comes from North Carolina, where vinegar-based barbecue is king and coleslaw is its natural partner. Check out our recipe for Easy Coleslaw and then serve it with ribs, grilled hamburgers, or tucked into a sandwich. Like so many of our recipes, it's so easy, you'll make it all the time.

It's difficult to choose a favorite salad in this chapter. The Turkey and Wild Rice Salad is a natural with leftover turkey any time of year, but the dried

cherries or cranberries make it lovely during the holidays. And then there's our Grilled Jamaican-Style Chicken Salad, which happily serves as a main course, or our Romaine Salad with Orange Vinaigrette, an easy yet sophisticated side salad.

A fair number of the salads here were developed to show off the benefits of our Reynolds Pot Lux Disposable Cookware. The Tomato-Basil Salad and the Greek Pasta Salad, for example, are full of good flavors and seasonal ingredients. Use the best vine-ripened tomatoes, if you can, and carry the salad to a picnic or potluck dinner in the same container in which you make it. The ruffled pasta we use in the Greek salad is great with the feta cheese, cherry tomatoes, cucumber slices, and salty, black Kalamata olives. These bold ingredients cling to the pasta's nooks and crannies, so you get a burst of flavor with every bite.

Words of Wisdom

With just a little planning, many of these snacks and appetizers can be made ahead of time so you and your kids have easy access to them. Wrap them well in plastic wrap or foil, refrigerate or freeze, and enjoy the freshness of your own home cooking. If you use our color plastic wrap, even your refrigerator will look more inviting!

Disposable Pot Lux cookware is a fantastic product for make-ahead salads. You can mix, store, transport, and serve all in the same dish and don't have to worry about leaving it behind at a party.

Tortilla Pinwheel Appetizers

Four 8-inch flour or whole wheat tortillas

¼ cup soft pineapple cream cheese

4 spinach leaves

12 thin slices baked ham

PREP TIME
10 minutes

CHILL TIME
30 minutes

MAKES
24 appetizers

1 Lay a sheet of plastic wrap on the countertop. Place a tortilla on the plastic wrap. Spread a tablespoon of cream cheese over the tortilla.

2 Center a spinach leaf in the middle of the tortilla. Arrange 3 slices of ham in a single layer on top of the spinach. Cut the ham to fit, if necessary. Roll up the tortilla to enclose the filling, wrapping the plastic wrap around the tortilla. Twist the ends of the plastic wrap to seal. Repeat with the remaining 3 tortillas. Refrigerate until ready to serve.

3 Unwrap the tortillas and cut each one into 6 disks. The ham, spinach leaves, and cream cheese form a pinwheel design.

> **REYNOLDS KITCHENS TIP**
>
> *Reynolds plastic wrap stretches tight to seal food so that it stays fresh in the refrigerator until you are ready to eat it— a perfect covering for appetizers and snacks.*

. . .

Honey-Sesame Chicken Drummettes

1 cup honey

¼ cup soy sauce

3 tablespoons dark sesame oil

2 tablespoons all-purpose flour

2 teaspoons garlic powder

½ to 1 teaspoon crushed red pepper flakes (optional)

24 chicken wing drummettes

1 tablespoon sesame seeds

PREP TIME
10 minutes

GRILL TIME
20 minutes

MAKES
6 servings

1 Prepare a charcoal or gas grill so that the coals are medium-hot or preheat the oven to 450°F. Put a large extra heavy duty foil bag in a 1-inch-deep pan and set aside.

2 In a shallow glass, ceramic, or plastic bowl, whisk together the honey, soy sauce, sesame oil, flour, garlic powder, and red pepper flakes, if using. Add the chicken

and turn gently to coat. Spoon the chicken and any excess sauce into the bag, making sure the chicken is in a single, even layer inside the bag. Double fold the open end of the bag.

3 Slide the bag onto the grill or leave it in the pan and place in the oven. Grill for 20 to 25 minutes in a covered grill or bake for 30 minutes.

4 Hold the bag with oven mitts and cut it open with a knife. Do not rip the bag, as the chicken will have to continue cooking in it. Carefully fold back the top of the bag so that steam can escape. Using a long-handled wooden spoon or long tongs, turn the wings in the sauce to coat them.

5 Sprinkle the chicken with sesame seeds. Grill or bake for 10 to 20 minutes longer or until the chicken is browned and cooked through.

> **REYNOLDS KITCHENS TIP**
>
> *Use crumpled pieces of aluminum foil as scouring pads to clean grill racks. It's an easy way to keep your grill clean between uses.*

. . .

Jalapeño Beef and Cheese Roll-Ups

<table>
<tr><td>PREP TIME
5 minutes</td></tr>
<tr><td>COOK TIME
1 ¼ minutes</td></tr>
<tr><td>MAKES
2 servings</td></tr>
</table>

Two 8-inch flour tortillas	½ cup shredded Monterey jack cheese with hot peppers
Four thin 1-ounce slices cooked roast beef	2 tablespoons chunky salsa

1 Fold a piece of wax paper in half. The wax paper should be large enough when folded to enclose two flour tortillas. Insert the tortillas between the halves of the wax paper. Fold the edges closed to seal the packet. Microwave on high power for 15 to 35 seconds, or until softened.

2 Put 2 slices of roast beef on each tortilla. Sprinkle the cheese evenly over the beef. Spoon 1 tablespoon of salsa evenly down the center of each tortilla. Roll up the tortillas, enclosing the filling.

3 Place each filled tortilla diagonally in the center of a sheet of wax paper. Wrap burrito-style by folding the bottom and sides of the wax paper over the tortillas. Roll each tortilla toward the corner of the wax paper. Place seam-side down on a microwave-safe plate.

4 Microwave on high power for 1¼ to 1½ minutes, or until the cheese melts. Serve immediately.

REYNOLDS KITCHENS TIP

Wax paper is perfect for heating tortillas in the microwave. It prevents them from drying while wrapping them loosely enough so that they vent naturally.

Jalapeño Beef and Cheese Roll-Ups

Santa Fe Chicken and Black Bean Dip

PREP TIME
10 minutes

GRILL TIME
10 minutes

MAKES
8 servings

One 15½-ounce can black beans, rinsed and drained

One 16-ounce jar chunky salsa

2 tablespoons drained and chopped canned jalapeño slices

2 tablespoons all-purpose flour

1 tablespoon Santa Fe–style spice blend

1 pound skinless, boneless chicken breast tenders, cut into ½-inch-thick pieces

1½ cups shredded Mexican-style cheese blend

Tortilla chips

1 Prepare a charcoal or gas grill so that the coals are medium-hot or preheat the oven to 450°F. Put a large extra heavy duty foil bag in a 1-inch-deep pan and set aside.

2 In a large bowl, combine the beans, salsa, jalapeños, flour, and spice blend. Stir in the chicken and then spoon the chicken into the bag, making sure the chicken is in a single, even layer inside the bag. Double fold the open end of the bag.

3 Slide the bag onto the grill or leave it in the pan and place in the oven. Grill for 10 to 12 minutes in a covered grill or bake for 25 to 30 minutes, or until heated through.

4 Hold the bag with oven mitts and cut it open with a knife. Do not rip the bag. Carefully fold back the top so that steam can escape. Using a long-handled wooden spoon, stir the chicken to break it apart.

5 Spoon the chicken mixture into a serving bowl. Sprinkle with the cheese and serve immediately with the tortilla chips.

Cranberry-Chili Smoked Sausage Bites

PREP TIME
10 minutes

GRILL TIME
12 minutes

MAKES
8 to 10 servings

One 1-pound can whole berry cranberry sauce

One 12-ounce bottle chili sauce

2 tablespoons flour

1 tablespoon yellow mustard

Two 14- to 16-ounce packages smoked sausage, cut diagonally in ¹/₂-inch pieces

1 medium onion, cut in 12 wedges and separated

1 medium green bell pepper, cut into large dice

1 Prepare a charcoal or gas grill or preheat the oven to 450°F. The coals should be medium-hot. Put a large extra heavy duty foil bag in a 1-inch-deep pan.

2 In a large bowl, mix together the cranberry sauce, chili sauce, flour, and mustard. Add the sausage, onion, and green pepper. Spoon into bag and spread in an even layer. Double fold the bag to seal.

3 Slide the bag onto the grill or leave it in the pan and place in the oven. Grill for 12 to 15 minutes in a covered grill or bake for 30 to 35 minutes, or until heated through.

4 Hold the bag with oven mitts and cut it open with a knife. Carefully fold back the top of the bag so that steam can escape. Stir before serving.

> **REYNOLDS KITCHENS TIP**
>
> *Line the inside of a charcoal grill with aluminum foil for easy cleanup. Puncture the foil at the grill vent openings before lighting the charcoal.*

···

Feta Cheese Ball

PREP TIME
10 minutes

CHILL TIME
6 hours

MAKES
16 servings

8 ounces light cream cheese, softened

8 ounces feta cheese with basil and tomato, crumbled

¹/₂ cup chopped walnuts

Assorted crackers

1 In the bowl of an electric mixer set on medium-high speed, beat the cream cheese until smooth. Add the feta cheese and beat until well blended.

2 Lay a large sheet of plastic wrap on the countertop. Spoon the cheese mixture in the center of the plastic wrap.

3 Roll and shape the cheese into a ball using the plastic wrap as a guide. Twist the plastic wrap closed so that the cheese ball is well wrapped. Refrigerate for at least 6 hours or overnight.

4 Before serving, spread the walnuts on a sheet of plastic wrap large enough to enclose the cheese ball.

5 Unwrap the cheese ball, discard the plastic wrap it was enclosed in, and roll the cheese ball in the nuts so that it is evenly coated. Wrap the nut-coated ball in plastic wrap. Set aside to come to room temperature before serving.

6 Unwrap the cheese ball and serve it with assorted crackers.

Feta Cheese Ball

Fruit Tray with Pineapple Cream Dip

PREP TIME
15 minutes

CHILL TIME
30 minutes

MAKES
3 cups of dip

FRUIT

1 fresh pineapple

Assorted fresh fruit, such as strawberries, grapes, sliced apples, peaches, or pears, kiwi, and melon chunks

DIP

One 3-ounce package cream cheese, softened

One 15¼-ounce can crushed pineapple

One 3.3-ounce package vanilla or white chocolate instant pudding and pie filling mix

1 cup frozen whipped topping, thawed

1 Slice the pineapple in half from top to bottom. Hollow out the core and carefully slice and cut the pineapple from one half of the shell, keeping the shell intact. Set aside. Cut the shell away from the remaining pineapple half. Cube all the pineapple flesh for dipping.

2 Place the reserved half pineapple shell in the center of a large serving platter. Arrange the pineapple cubes and other fresh fruit around the shell.

3 Cover the platter with extra-wide plastic wrap and refrigerate until serving.

4 To make the dip, beat the cream cheese in the bowl of an electric mixer set on medium-high speed until smooth. Drain the crushed pineapple and reserve the juice. Add the juice and the instant pudding mix to the cream cheese and beat until blended.

5 Stir the crushed pineapple and the whipped topping into the cream cheese mixture. Cover the bowl with plastic wrap and refrigerate for about 30 minutes to give the flavors time to blend.

6 When ready to serve, spoon the dip into the reserved pineapple half. Serve with the fresh fruit.

> **REYNOLDS KITCHENS TIP**
>
> *Extra-wide plastic wrap is excellent for covering large trays and platters of sliced fruit. Unlike other plastic wraps, it stretches to fit tightly over the platter so that the fruit stays in place as you arranged it. Even if you travel, it does not slide around, so you arrive at your destination with a pretty display.*

Vegetable Platter with Cheesy Italian Dip

PREP TIME
10 minutes

CHILL TIME
1 hour

MAKES
8 to 10 servings

1 cup light sour cream

$1/2$ cup light mayonnaise

$1/2$ cup grated Parmesan cheese

One .7-ounce package dry Italian salad dressing mix

$1/4$ cup milk

2 tablespoons lemon juice

Assorted fresh raw vegetables, such as carrots, zucchini, mushrooms, broccoli, celery, and cherry tomatoes

1 In a serving bowl, combine the sour cream, mayonnaise, Parmesan cheese, Italian salad dressing mix, milk, and lemon juice, and stir until well mixed.

2 Cover with plastic wrap and refrigerate for at least 1 hour to allow the flavors to blend.

3 Slice or otherwise prepare the vegetables. Arrange them on a 12-inch round glass platter. Cover with plastic wrap and refrigerate until ready to serve.

4 Serve the dip with the vegetables for dipping.

REYNOLDS KITCHENS TIPS

- *Use precut vegetables from the grocery produce section or a salad bar to make a beautiful platter with no chopping.*

- *Reynolds plastic wrap forms a tight seal that will keep the vegetables perfectly arranged on the platter until serving time. Center a sheet over the platter. Press both ends under the platter to seal. To cover an open side, grab the plastic wrap about 2 to 3 inches from the edge; push out and stretch over the rim of the platter with your thumbs. Repeat with remaining plastic wrap.*

Vegetable Platter with Cheesy Italian Dip

Marinated Vegetable Salad

Marinated Vegetable Salad

PREP TIME
15 minutes

COOK TIME
3 minutes

CHILL TIME
4 hours

MAKES
6 servings

3 cups broccoli florets

3 cups cauliflower florets

3 medium carrots, sliced

2 tablespoons water

1/4 cup coarsely chopped red onion

1 large red pepper, roasted and cut into strips

1/2 cup light Caesar salad dressing

1 Put the broccoli, cauliflower, and carrots in a 3-quart microwave-safe baking dish. Sprinkle with water. Cover the dish with plastic wrap and turn back one edge to vent.

2 Microwave on high power for 3 to 4 minutes, or until the vegetables are crisp-tender. Stir after 1½ minutes.

3 Transfer the hot vegetables to a colander and rinse with cold water. Drain well.

4 Put the vegetables in a serving bowl. Add the onion, pepper strips, and salad dressing. Cover with plastic wrap and refrigerate for at least 4 hours or overnight.

> **REYNOLDS KITCHENS TIP**
>
> To roast peppers, preheat the broiler. Cut the peppers in half lengthwise. Remove the stems, membranes, and seeds. Line a baking sheet with non-stick aluminum foil, non-stick (dull) side facing up. Place the peppers, cut-side down, on the foil-lined baking sheet. Flatten the peppers with the palm of your hand. Broil for 10 to 12 minutes about 3 inches from the heat source or until blackened and charred. Wrap peppers in the same sheet of foil used for roasting and let stand for 10 minutes. Unwrap and gently pull the blackened skin from the peppers.

• • •

Spinach Bites

PREP TIME
30 minutes

COOK TIME
12 minutes

MAKES
64 appetizers

Two 17¼-ounce packages frozen puff pastry sheets (4 sheets total)

One 10-ounce package frozen chopped spinach, cooked and drained

1 cup shredded Swiss cheese

1/2 cup chopped onion

1/2 cup lowfat cottage cheese

1/4 cup fine dry bread crumbs

3 eggs

1/2 teaspoon salt

1/4 teaspoon ground nutmeg

1 teaspoon water

Spinach Bites

1. Preheat the oven to 400°F. Line 2 or 3 cookie sheets with non-stick aluminum foil, non-stick (dull) side facing up.

2. Let the pastry sheets thaw at room temperature for about 20 minutes before unfolding them.

3. Meanwhile, in a bowl, mix together the spinach, Swiss cheese, onion, cottage cheese, bread crumbs, 2 eggs, salt, and nutmeg.

4. Unfold the puff pastry sheets and roll each one into a 12-inch square on a lightly floured sheet of parchment paper. Using a sharp knife, cut each square into sixteen 3-inch squares.

5. Whisk the remaining egg with the water to make an egg wash.

6. Spoon 1 teaspoon of the spinach mixture in the center of each square. Using a small pastry brush, brush two edges of each pastry square with egg wash. Fold the squares in half to form triangles. Press the edges together with a fork to seal.

7. Arrange the filled triangles on the cookie sheets. Brush the tops of the triangles with the remaining egg wash. (The Spinach Bites can be wrapped in heavy duty foil and frozen at this point.)

8. Bake for 12 to 14 minutes or until golden brown and puffed.

> **REYNOLDS KITCHENS TIP**
>
> *If baking frozen triangles, put the Spinach Bites in the oven without thawing and increase the baking time by 2 to 4 minutes.*

Easy Sweet-and-Spicy Meatballs

2 pounds frozen meatballs

One 9-ounce jar sweet and sour sauce

¼ cup packed brown sugar

3 tablespoons soy sauce

¾ teaspoon garlic powder

¼ to ½ teaspoon cayenne pepper

PREP TIME
10 minutes

COOK TIME
35 minutes

MAKES
72 meatballs

1 Preheat the oven to 350°F. Line a 9-by-13-by-2-inch pan with non-stick aluminum foil, non-stick (dull) side facing up.

2 Arrange the meatballs in a single layer in the pan.

3 In a bowl or large glass measuring cup, stir together the sweet and sour sauce, brown sugar, soy sauce, garlic powder, and cayenne pepper. Pour over the meatballs and stir gently to coat them. Take care not to break the meatballs.

4 Bake the meatballs for about 35 minutes, or until they are heated through and the sauce is bubbling. Check the meatballs after 15 minutes and spoon sauce over them.

5 Serve the meatballs immediately with toothpicks or small cocktail forks.

To line pans with Release Foil, flip pan upside down. Press a sheet of foil around pan with non-stick side down.

Remove foil. Flip pan upright and drop foil inside with non-stick side toward food. Crimp edges of foil to rim of pan.

Watermelon Boat

1 large watermelon

Fresh fruit, such as cantaloupe cubes, honeydew melon cubes, pineapple chunks, strawberry halves, and grapes

PREP TIME
15 minutes

MAKES
1 watermelon boat

1 Cut the watermelon in half lengthwise. Lift off top half of the watermelon. Cover one half with extra-wide plastic wrap and refrigerate for later use.

2 Cut out the center of the remaining watermelon half and cut the melon into large cubes.

3 Use a sharp knife to carve "V" shapes around edge of hollowed-out watermelon rind. This will make a decorative watermelon boat.

4 Fill the boat with watermelon cubes and other fresh fruit. Cover with extra-wide plastic wrap and refrigerate until ready to serve. This is best served ice cold.

REYNOLDS KITCHENS TIP

Extra-wide plastic wrap is ideal for wrapping large, oddly shaped and sometimes cumbersome foods such as watermelon.

Watermelon Boat

Romaine Salad with Orange Vinaigrette

PREP TIME
10 minutes

CHILL TIME
30 minutes

MAKES
4 servings

SALAD

5 ounces fresh Romaine lettuce leaves ($^1/_2$ of a 10-ounce package)

$^1/_2$ cup matchstick carrots

$^1/_2$ medium Red Delicious apple, cored and cut into large chunks

$^1/_2$ cup seedless red grapes

$^1/_2$ cup mandarin oranges, drained

$^1/_4$ cup pecan pieces

VINAIGRETTE

$^1/_4$ cup sweet orange marmalade

2 tablespoons white wine vinegar

1 tablespoon olive oil

$^1/_8$ teaspoon ground ginger

Salt and freshly ground black pepper (optional)

1 Toss the lettuce leaves, carrots, apple chunks, and grapes together in a disposable plastic cookware pan large enough to hold the salad. Gently arrange the orange slices on top of the salad. Cover the pan with its lid and refrigerate until serving time. This can be prepared up to 4 hours ahead of time. The lidded container makes it easy to transport, too.

2 To make the vinaigrette, whisk together the marmalade, vinegar, oil, and ginger. Season to taste with salt and pepper, if desired. Set aside until ready to serve.

3 Take the salad from the refrigerator. Toss gently to mix the orange slices with the other ingredients. Top with the pecans. Drizzle the vinaigrette over the salad and toss to mix. Serve immediately.

> **REYNOLDS KITCHENS TIP**
>
> *Disposable cookware is terrific for summer picnics and salads. It's lightweight, easy to transport (the lid stays in place!), and good-looking enough for serving.*

Tomato-Basil Pasta Salad

PREP TIME
18 minutes

CHILL TIME
1 hour

MAKES
8 servings

One 8-ounce package bowtie pasta, cooked and drained

1 pint cherry or grape tomatoes, halved

1 yellow bell pepper, seeded and cut into large dice

One 6-ounce jar marinated artichoke hearts, drained and coarsely chopped

4 large fresh basil leaves, cut into strips

2 tablespoons olive oil

2 tablespoons red wine vinegar or balsamic vinegar

1 clove garlic, minced

Salt and freshly ground black pepper

1 In a 1½-quart disposable plastic cookware pan, combine the pasta, tomatoes, bell pepper, artichoke hearts, and basil leaves.

2 In a small bowl, whisk together the olive oil, vinegar, and garlic, and season to taste with salt and pepper. Pour over the pasta salad, toss until well mixed, cover the pan with its lid, and refrigerate for at least 1 hour.

3 Serve chilled.

> **REYNOLDS KITCHENS TIP**
>
> *To cut basil into strips easily, stack the leaves and then roll them lengthwise into a tight roll. Slice crosswise into thin strips.*
>
> *For a pretty touch, use small cookie cutters to cut the yellow bell pepper into interesting shapes.*

. . .

Easy Coleslaw

PREP TIME
10 minutes

CHILL TIME
1 hour

MAKES
10 to 12 servings

One 16-ounce package coleslaw mix (cabbage and carrots)

⅔ cup mayonnaise, or more as needed

2 tablespoons sugar

2 tablespoons cider vinegar

2 teaspoons celery seed

½ teaspoon salt

Dash hot pepper sauce

1 Put the coleslaw mixture into a bowl or disposable plastic cookware pan large enough to hold the coleslaw.

2 In a small bowl, whisk together the mayonnaise, sugar, vinegar, celery seed, and salt. Add a little more mayonnaise if necessary. Season to taste with hot pepper sauce. Pour over the coleslaw and toss to mix.

3 Cover the pan with its lid. Refrigerate for at least 1 hour and up to 4 hours to give the flavors time to blend.

. . .

Honey-Almond Fruit Salad

PREP TIME
30 minutes
CHILL TIME
3 hours
MAKES
8 servings

One 20-ounce can pineapple chunks in juice

2 tablespoons honey

1/2 teaspoon almond extract

2 pints strawberries, halved

4 kiwi, peeled and sliced

2 mangoes, peeled and cubed

1 cup red seedless grapes

1 Drain the pineapple and reserve 1/3 cup of juice. Add the honey and almond extract to the reserved juice and stir to mix to make dressing.

2 In a large bowl, mix the pineapple chunks with the strawberries, kiwi, mangoes, and grapes.

3 Drizzle the dressing over the fruit. Cover with plastic wrap and refrigerate for 3 hours before serving.

Fruit Salad with Strawberry Dressing

PREP TIME
20 minutes

CHILL TIME
30 minutes

MAKES
8 to 10 servings

SALAD

1 pint strawberries, sliced

1 pint blueberries

4 peaches or nectarines, peeled and sliced

$\frac{1}{2}$ honeydew melon, cut into chunks

DRESSING

$\frac{1}{3}$ cup light cream cheese, softened

2 tablespoons sugar

One 8-ounce carton low-fat strawberry yogurt

1 teaspoon grated lemon peel

1 teaspoon fresh lemon juice

1 In an 8-by-8-inch disposable plastic cookware pan, combine the strawberries, blueberries, peaches, and melon. Cover and refrigerate for at least 30 minutes or until cold.

2 In a medium bowl, stir together the cream cheese and sugar until smooth. Add the yogurt, lemon peel, and lemon juice, and stir until well blended. Cover and refrigerate.

3 Serve the fruit salad with the dressing on the side or drizzle the dressing over the fruit and stir gently to coat.

REYNOLDS KITCHENS TIP

Disposable cookware pans are so handy for recipes such as this one. Chill the fruit right in the cookware and then toss it with the creamy, sweet dressing just before serving. The different types of berries and fruit taste best when allowed to mingle for 30 minutes or so—and it looks so pretty in the attractive white container.

Fruit Salad with Strawberry Dressing

Greek Pasta Salad

PREP TIME
15 minutes

CHILL TIME
2 hours

MAKES
6 servings

2 cups cooked ruffled pasta or ziti

1 cup cubed cooked chicken

½ pint cherry tomatoes, halved

1 medium cucumber, halved lengthwise and sliced

½ red onion, coarsely chopped

3 tablespoons fresh lemon juice

1 to 2 teaspoons salt

⅓ cup olive oil

1½ teaspoons dried oregano

One 4-ounce container crumbled feta cheese

½ cup sliced Kalamata olives

1 Stir together the pasta, chicken, tomatoes, cucumber, and onion in a large bowl.

2 In a small bowl, whisk the lemon juice with 1 teaspoon of salt until the salt dissolves. Add the olive oil and oregano, and stir to blend. Taste and adjust for seasoning and add more salt if desired. Pour over the pasta mixture and toss gently to blend. Add the feta cheese and olives and toss again.

3 Spoon the pasta salad into a 1½-quart disposable plastic cookware pan. Cover the pan with its lid and refrigerate for at least 2 hours. Serve chilled.

REYNOLDS KITCHENS TIP

Ruffled pasta, easy to find in the supermarket, is wonderful with the other ingredients. The feta and olives cling to it and lodge in the tiny nooks and crannies created by the ruffles.

Greek Pasta Salad

Tex-Mex Layered Salad

One 12-ounce package lettuce salad blend

Two 11-ounce cans corn with red and green peppers, drained

One 15-ounce can black beans, rinsed and drained

1 jalapeño pepper, seeded and minced (optional)

1 small onion, chopped

$\frac{1}{3}$ cup chopped fresh cilantro

$\frac{1}{2}$ cup ranch dressing

$\frac{1}{2}$ cup salsa

1 cup shredded Cheddar cheese

1 small avocado, cubed

1 medium tomato, diced

Tortilla chips, crushed

PREP TIME
15 minutes

CHILL TIME
2 hours

MAKES
12 to 16 servings

1 Layer the lettuce in a 9-by-12½-inch disposable plastic cookware pan.

2 In a large mixing bowl, combine the corn, black beans, jalapeño, if using, onion, and cilantro. Add the ranch dressing and salsa and toss to mix.

3 Spoon the corn and bean mixture over the lettuce. Sprinkle with cheese and top with avocado and tomato. Cover the pan with its lid and refrigerate for at least 2 hours to give the flavors time to blend.

4 Garnish with crushed tortilla chips before serving.

REYNOLDS KITCHENS TIP

This is a super salad to make for a neighborhood picnic or family reunion. It tastes better after a few hours, so it's a perfect travel companion. Pack it in a disposable plastic cookware pan, cover with the lid, let it get nice and cold in your refrigerator, and then transfer it to a cooler for travel. It's ready to serve when you get there—all you have to do is garnish it with crushed tortilla chips.

Tex-Mex Layered Salad

BLT Salad

1 cup ranch dressing (one 8-ounce bottle)

⅓ cup grated **Parmesan** cheese

¼ teaspoon freshly ground black pepper

4 cups torn **Romaine** lettuce leaves

2 cups cubed cooked potatoes

1 medium tomato, chopped

One 10-ounce package frozen green peas, thawed

⅓ cup chopped green onions

4 slices turkey bacon, cooked and coarsely crumbled

PREP TIME
10 minutes

CHILL TIME
4 hours

MAKES
6 to 8 servings

BLT Salad

1. In a small bowl, stir together the salad dressing, Parmesan cheese, and pepper.

2. Layer the lettuce, potatoes, tomato, and peas in a serving bowl. Spread the salad dressing over the salad and sprinkle with green onions.

3. Cover the bowl with plastic wrap and refrigerate for at least 4 hours or overnight.

4. Before serving, sprinkle with crumbled bacon. Serve chilled.

· · ·

Potluck Pasta Salad

2 cups uncooked rotini

2 cups broccoli florets

I cup sliced carrots

³/₄ cup light Caesar salad dressing

¹/₂ teaspoon coarsely ground black pepper

¹/₂ pound smoked turkey breast, cubed

2 medium zucchini, cut into strips

I cup cherry tomato halves

PREP TIME

15 minutes

CHILL TIME

2 hours

MAKES

8 servings

1. Cook the rotini in a large pot of boiling water for 10 minutes. Add the broccoli and carrots, and continue cooking for about 2 minutes longer until the pasta is tender. Drain and rinse with cold water to cool.

2. Transfer the pasta mixture to a bowl or baking dish. Toss with half the salad dressing and sprinkle with about ¹/₄ teaspoon pepper.

3. Layer the turkey, zucchini, and tomatoes on the pasta mixture. Drizzle with the remaining dressing and pepper. Cover with plastic wrap and refrigerate for at least 2 hours or overnight.

Potluck Pasta Salad

Grilled Jamaican-Style Chicken Salad

Grilled Jamaican-Style Chicken Salad

PREP TIME
25 minutes

CHILL TIME
30 minutes

MAKES
4 servings

MARINADE

¾ cup oil-and-vinegar salad dressing

2 tablespoons Jamaican pepper sauce or Caribbean-style steak sauce

1 teaspoon ground allspice

½ teaspoon dried thyme

4 green onions, sliced

SALAD

4 skinless, boneless chicken breast halves

One 10-ounce package salad mix or 8 cups torn lettuce

1 fresh mango, peeled and sliced

1 medium cucumber, sliced

¼ cup chopped cashews

1 In a small bowl, stir together the salad dressing, pepper sauce, allspice, thyme, and onions.

2 Put the chicken breasts in an 8-inch square baking dish. Pour half the marinade over the chicken and turn to coat. Cover the remaining marinade with plastic wrap and refrigerate to use as salad dressing.

3 Cover the chicken with plastic wrap and refrigerate for at least 30 minutes or for up to 8 hours.

4 Arrange the salad mix on 4 plates. Top each salad with mango and cucumber slices. Cover the plates with plastic wrap and refrigerate until serving.

5 Prepare a charcoal or gas grill so that the coals are medium-hot.

6 Lift the chicken from the marinade, letting most of the marinade drip back into the dish. Discard the marinade. Grill the chicken for 5 to 6 minutes on each side or until cooked through and the juices run clear when pierced with a fork. Cut the chicken into strips.

7 Remove the plastic wrap from the salad plates and arrange the hot chicken strips on the salads. Drizzle with the reserved salad dressing and sprinkle with cashews.

> **REYNOLDS KITCHENS TIP**
>
> *Serving a salad such as this is easy if you arrange the lettuce, mango, and cucumber slices on the plates ahead of time, cover the plates with plastic wrap, and chill. This way, when the chicken is grilled, all you need to do is unwrap the plates, add the hot chicken, and you're ready to go.*

California Chicken Salad

PREP TIME
20 minutes

CHILL TIME
2 hours

MAKES
4 to 6 servings

2½ cups (1¼ pounds) chopped cooked chicken or turkey

1½ cups light Italian salad dressing

1 teaspoon basil leaves

1 cup thinly sliced celery

Leaf lettuce

3 medium seedless oranges, peeled and sliced

1 pound red seedless grapes

2 medium ripe avocados

1 tablespoon fresh lemon juice

1 In a shallow baking dish, toss the chicken with 1 cup of the dressing and the basil and spread in an even layer. Cover with plastic wrap and refrigerate for at least 2 hours or overnight.

2 Remove from the refrigerator and stir in the sliced celery.

3 Line a large 16-by-12-inch oval platter with lettuce leaves. Arrange half the orange slices along each long side of the platter. Arrange the grapes on one end.

4 Peel and slice the avocados. Put them in a mixing bowl and toss with the lemon juice to coat evenly. Add the remaining ½ cup of the salad dressing and toss. Arrange the avocado slices on the opposite end of the platter from the grapes.

5 Using a slotted spoon, remove the chicken and celery from the marinade and place in the center of the platter on top of the lettuce. Cover with plastic wrap and refrigerate for up to 4 hours until ready to serve.

. . .

Turkey and Wild Rice Salad

PREP TIME
20 minutes

CHILL TIME
1 hour

MAKES
8 to 10 servings

3 cups cubed cooked turkey

2½ cups cooked wild rice

1 cup chopped carrots

¾ cup dried cherries or sweetened dried cranberries

½ cup sliced green onions

1 medium Granny Smith apple, cored and cubed

¼ cup orange juice

¼ cup apple cider vinegar

2 teaspoons Dijon mustard

½ cup vegetable oil

½ teaspoon salt

⅛ teaspoon black pepper

1 In a large bowl, combine the turkey, rice, carrots, cherries, green onions, and apple.

2 In a small bowl, whisk together the orange juice, vinegar, and mustard. Slowly add the oil, whisking constantly. Stir in the salt and pepper. Pour over the turkey mixture and toss to blend. Cover with plastic wrap and refrigerate for 1 to 2 hours. Serve chilled.

REYNOLDS KITCHENS TIP

If you want to make the dressing ahead of time or if you like to keep salad dressing already mixed and ready to use in the refrigerator, combine the ingredients for the dressing or vinaigrette in a glass drinking glass or glass jar (use glass, not plastic). Cover tightly with plastic wrap and shake. To sprinkle the dressing over salad, puncture the plastic with the tines of a fork.

Turkey and Wild Rice Salad

Cheesy Chicken Nachos

4 cups tortilla chips, about 4 ounces

2 cups Mexican-style shredded cheese

1 cup cooked, shredded chicken

1 cup salsa

1 small tomato, chopped

½ cup sliced black olives

2 green onions, sliced

PREP TIME
10 minutes

COOK TIME
8 minutes

MAKES
6 to 8 servings

1 Preheat the oven to 400°F. Line a 9-by-13-by-2-inch pan with non-stick aluminum foil, non-stick (dull) side facing up.

2 Spread the tortilla chips in the pan in an even layer. Sprinkle 1¾ cups of the cheese over the chips.

3 Stir the chicken and salsa together and spread on top of the chips. Top with the tomato, black olives, and green onions. Sprinkle with the remaining cheese.

4 Bake for 8 to 10 minutes or until the cheese melts. Serve immediately.

> **REYNOLDS KITCHENS TIP**
>
> *Using non-stick aluminum foil when you make nachos makes the whole process easy and practically mess-proof. The melted cheese is gooey and yummy, but doesn't stick to the foil, which makes these nachos easy to eat and easy to clean up.*

. . .

Mexican Pita Snack

One 6-inch pita bread

2 tablespoons chunky salsa

2 slices smoked turkey, torn into pieces

¼ cup shredded Cheddar cheese

PREP TIME
5 minutes

COOK TIME
8 minutes

MAKES
1 serving

1 Preheat the toaster oven to 400°F. Line the oven tray with a single pop-up foil sheet.

2 Put the pita bread on the toaster oven tray. Spread salsa on the pita bread, top with turkey, and sprinkle with the cheese.

3 Bake for 8 to 10 minutes or until the pita is crispy and the cheese melts.

Pizza Quesadilla

PREP TIME
5 minutes

COOK TIME
6 minutes

MAKES
I serving

One 8-inch flour tortilla

2 tablespoons pizza sauce

6 turkey pepperoni slices

$1/3$ cup shredded mozzarella cheese

1 Preheat the toaster oven to 400°F. Line the oven tray with a single pop-up foil sheet.

2 Put the flour tortilla on the tray. Spread pizza sauce on half of the tortilla. Arrange the pepperoni slices on the sauce and sprinkle with the cheese. Fold the tortilla in half.

3 Bake for 6 to 8 minutes or until the cheese melts and the tortilla is golden brown. Serve immediately.

REYNOLDS KITCHENS TIP

Single pop-up foil sheets are terrific for fast snacks, especially when you're making a quick treat for yourself. They're exactly the right size for one, and cleanup is a breeze.

...

California Grilled Pizza

PREP TIME
10 minutes

GRILL TIME
5 minutes

MAKES
4 servings

Two 8-inch pizza crusts

2 tablespoons olive oil

2 cloves garlic, finely chopped

$1/2$ medium red onion, cut into thin strips

2 plum tomatoes, thinly sliced

3 ounces marinated artichoke hearts, thinly sliced (half of a 6-ounce jar)

4 to 6 baby portobello mushrooms, thinly sliced

2 tablespoons chopped fresh basil

$1/2$ cup shredded mozzarella cheese

1 Prepare a charcoal or gas grill so that the coals are medium-hot.

2 Put each pizza crust on a single pop-up sheet of aluminum foil.

3 Heat the olive oil in a small skillet over medium heat and cook the garlic and onion for about 5 minutes or until softened.

4 Brush the pizza crusts with the olive oil mixture. Arrange the onion on the pizza.

Top with tomatoes, artichoke hearts, mushrooms, and basil. Brush the mushrooms with the marinade from the artichokes. Sprinkle with cheese.

5 Put the pizza on the foil sheet on the grill. Close the lid and grill for 5 to 7 minutes or until the cheese melts.

...

Super-Stuffed Subs

PREP TIME
20 minutes

GRILL TIME
12 minutes

MAKES
12 servings

6 sub rolls, sliced horizontally

½ cup Italian salad dressing

36 thin slices deli pepperoni (about 4 ounces)

12 thin slices deli ham (about ½ pound)

12 thin slices deli turkey (about ½ pound)

12 thin slices Provolone cheese (about ⅓ pound)

12 thin slices Swiss cheese (about ⅓ pound)

24 tomato slices (about 6 small tomatoes)

½ cup jarred sweet hot peppers, drained

1 Prepare a charcoal or gas grill for indirect grilling so that the coals are medium-hot or preheat the oven to 450°F. Put a large extra heavy duty foil bag in a 1-inch-deep pan and set aside.

2 Brush the cut sides of the sub rolls with Italian salad dressing. Layer the rolls with half the meat and half the cheese. Top with tomatoes and peppers. Layer the remaining meat and cheese on top of the peppers. Put the tops on the rolls and slice in half crosswise. Put the subs in the foil bag. Double fold the bag to seal.

3 Slide bag onto grill or leave it in the pan and put it in the oven. Grill for 12 to 15 minutes on covered grill or bake for 20 to 25 minutes.

4 Using oven mitts and a sharp knife, carefully cut the bag open. Fold it back for steam to escape. Serve immediately.

> **REYNOLDS KITCHENS TIP**
>
> *For indirect grilling, the heat source (coals or gas burner) is on one side of grill. Place foil bag on the opposite side of the grill, away from the heat source.*

Easy Grilled S'Mores

**4 whole graham crackers,
broken into 8 squares**

**Two 1.55-ounce milk chocolate
candy bars, halved crosswise**

4 regular marshmallows

PREP TIME
5 minutes

GRILL TIME
4 minutes

MAKES
4 servings

1 Prepare a charcoal or gas grill or preheat the oven to 450°F. The coals should be medium-hot.

2 For each s'more, top 1 graham cracker square with 1 candy bar half, 1 marshmallow, and then top with another graham cracker square. Repeat with remaining graham crackers, candy, and marshmallows.

3 Lay four 8-by-12-inch sheets of heavy duty aluminum foil on the countertop. Center a s'more on each one. Bring up the sides of the foil. Double fold the top and ends to seal the packets, leaving room for heat circulation inside. Repeat with the other s'mores. If using the oven, put the packets on a cookie sheet.

4 Grill for 4 to 5 minutes in a covered grill or bake for 4 to 5 minutes until the chocolate and marshmallows begin to melt and soften.

Easy Grilled S'Mores

Crunchy Snack Mix

PREP TIME

10 minutes

MAKES

4 servings

I cup small animal-shaped graham snacks

I cup candy-coated chocolate candies

I cup mini pretzels

I cup salted or dry roasted peanuts (optional)

Colorful sprinkles (optional)

In a mixing bowl, toss together the graham snacks, candy-coated chocolate candies, and pretzels. Mix in peanuts and sprinkles, if desired.

. . .

Smiley Face Snack Holders with Crunchy Snack Mix

PREP TIME

30 minutes

MAKES

4 snack holders

Eight 7½-inch paper plates

Pens or markers

Wiggle eyes (optional)

Crunchy Snack Mix, above

Invisible or clear tape

Curling ribbon (optional)

1 Draw a smiley face on back of a paper plate and attach the wiggle eyes, if desired. Fill the second plate with about 1 cup of the snack mix.

2 Put a smiley face plate on top of a filled plate and tape the edges together to secure. Wrap the plates between two 12-inch sheets of color plastic wrap. Gather the plastic wrap and twist at both sides of the face; tape to the back of the plates. Tape on additional plastic wrap or curling ribbon for hair, if desired. Repeat to make 4 snack holders.

. . .

Crispy Caterpillar Bookworms

PREP TIME

30 minutes

MAKES

4 treats

Crispy cereal treats

8 wiggle eyes

4 chenille stems

1 Prepare your favorite crispy cereal treat in a 9-by-13-by-2-inch pan and let it stand until firm.

2 Cut into eight 6½-by-2-inch bars. Stack two bars and press on them to round off the edges. Wrap the bars in clear or color plastic wrap.

3 Fold six 4-inch pieces of plastic wrap into ½-inch-wide strips. Evenly space and wrap 3 strips around each wrapped crispy treat to make caterpillar stripes. Attach 2 wiggle eyes to one end of each treat. Twist a chenille stem behind the eyes to form antennae. Gently twist treats to make caterpillars curvy, if desired.

REYNOLDS KITCHENS TIP

Here's another idea for the next time you make your favorite cereal treat: Crispy Cut-Outs. Give these cute cut-outs as party favors, lunchbox treats, or just an everyday gesture to make the day a little special.

To do so, press the cereal mixture into a greased pan. To prevent messy, sticky fingers, lay a sheet of plastic wrap over the pan and refrigerate for 10 to 15 minutes or longer until the mixture is firm. Remove the pan from the refrigerator and remove the plastic wrap. Using large star cookie cutters, cut out stars.

Cut star shapes from construction paper, about ¼ inch smaller than the Crispy Cut-Outs. Write a special message on each paper star.

Wrap each star cut-out in your favorite color of plastic wrap. Pinch any extra plastic wrap together at the top of the star. Place a paper message on the cut-out and overwrap with plastic wrap a second time. Tie the plastic wrap at the top with ribbon.

Crispy Caterpillar Bookworms

Caramel Treat Cups

PREP TIME
20 minutes

MAKES
18 treats

4 cups apple-cinnamon flavored cereal

1 cup mini chocolate-covered candies

1 cup dry-roasted peanuts

25 caramels, unwrapped

2 tablespoons milk

1 Put 18 foil baking cups in muffin pans or on a cookie sheet and set aside.

2 In a large bowl, stir together the cereal, candies, and peanuts, and set aside.

3 In a microwave-safe bowl, combine the caramels and milk. Microwave on high power for 1 minute and 35 seconds. Stir and microwave on high power for 40 seconds longer. Stir until smooth.

4 Pour the caramel mixture over the cereal mixture and stir to coat evenly. Spoon into the foil baking cups and set aside to cool.

5 Wrap each in color plastic wrap.

> **REYNOLDS KITCHENS TIP**
>
> *Foil baking cups are sturdy enough to stand on their own, even without muffin pans to support them. They are terrific for making individual candy snacks like these, which can then be packed or served easily in the foil cups. Wrapping each cup in pretty color plastic wrap makes it all the more festive and easy to transport.*

. . .

PBJ Puzzle Sandwich

PREP TIME
10 minutes

MAKES
4 sandwiches

1/2 cup creamy peanut butter

1/4 cup dried fruit bits or chopped dried fruit

1/4 cup apricot preserves or strawberry jam

8 slices white or whole wheat bread

1 Stir together the peanut butter, fruit bits, and preserves. Spread about one-fourth of the filling between 2 slices of bread.

2 Cut the center of the sandwich into a fun shape with a cookie cutter. Use a knife to

cut the remaining part of the sandwich into pieces to form a puzzle. Reassemble the sandwich.

3 Wrap the sandwich in a single pop-up aluminum foil sheet. Repeat to make 4 sandwiches.

PBJ Puzzle Sandwich

Fish and Seafood

Spicy Grilled Shrimp

Ginger-Shrimp and Broccoli

Sonoran Shrimp Packets

Shrimp Creole Packets

Caribbean Shrimp Packets

Shrimp with Confetti Rice Packets

Shrimp and Scallop Dinner

Scallops with Peanut Sauce

Honey-Glazed Salmon

Ginger-Sesame Salmon Packets

Salmon with Rainbow Peppers

Savory Salmon Provençal

Salmon with Asparagus and Sun-Dried Tomatoes

Ranch Salmon with Vegetables

Microwave Orange Roughy

Oriental Red Snapper

Lemon-Pepper Tilapia

Tuscan Halibut Packets

Swordfish with Corn and Salsa

Cajun Catfish with Potato Wedges

Fish Steaks with Herbed Vegetables

Fish with Lemon-Dill Butter Sauce

Lemon Fish with Rice Pilaf Packets

Parmesan-Baked Fish Packets

Herbed Fish and Vegetable Packets

Hawaiian Fish Packets

Dilled Fish and Garden Vegetable Packets

My husband and I eat crab legs, scallops, and other wonderful fish and seafood three or four times a week. Sometimes we have a seafood feast with numerous choices. It's better than eating out!
—Betty

Growing up on a farm in Minnesota, all I knew about fish was tuna in a can and frozen fish sticks. Now I love all kinds of seafood.
—Pat

Florida Department of Natural Resources Seafood Marketing Division for four years before moving to Virginia, is our resident expert on fish and seafood. But she wasn't always knowledgeable about the subject. Growing up on a farm in the Midwest, she rarely ate fresh fish. Pat thought she had done a great job bluffing through the interview for the Florida job until several years later when her boss told her, "I knew you didn't know a darn thing about fish!"

When we read the questions that come in through reynoldskitchens.com or look through our consumer mail, we don't notice nearly as much demand for fish as for meat and poultry, but interest is on the rise. Everyone is becoming more aware of its health benefits and wants to fit some kind of fish into their weekly meal plans.

We know fish and seafood can be intimidating to prepare, so our recipes are super easy to eliminate the guesswork. They're delicious, too. Some people worry that they will overcook or undercook the fish and it will be dry and tasteless or rubbery. They're also not sure what to buy.

This is where our products come to the rescue in a big way. Wrapping fish in foil, putting it in an extra heavy duty foil bag or cooking it in an oven bag guarantees moist, evenly cooked fish every time. With our recipes and products, you'll enjoy preparing seafood.

We love to cook fish. This chapter has some of our all-time favorite recipes. For instance, Betty's first choice is the Ginger-Sesame Salmon Packets. When you set the hot fish over the spinach leaves they wilt just enough for an elegant presentation. We both adore the Savory Salmon Provençal, which was developed from a winning contest recipe and is just wonderful for guests. The artichoke hearts, feta cheese, and Kalamata olives are a glorious combination with the salmon. Pat especially likes the Ginger-Shrimp and Broccoli, too, with its bold Asian flavors and vibrant red peppers.

Fish

Many home cooks get confused when buying fish. They're uncomfortable buying unfamiliar kinds and aren't sure what to look for when they get to the fish counter. They don't know whether to buy fresh or frozen fish.

The trick is to know that there are essentially two *types* of fish: lean and oily, which give fish its mild or full flavor. It's more important to buy fresh or high-quality frozen fish than to race around looking for a specific fish. Buy the *type* you prefer, and you'll be fine.

Lean fish, generally white-fleshed and mild, include cod, snapper, sole, and flounder. These benefit from moist cooking, such as steaming, poaching, or braising, and so lend themselves to foil packets, foil bags, and oven bags.

Oily fish include salmon, tuna, swordfish, trout, and bluefish, all of which are meaty enough to withstand dry heat cooking such as grilling and broiling. Catfish, monkfish, and sea bass are not especially oily, but are firm enough to withstand grilling. All of these denser, firmer fish can also be cooked in bags and foil or parchment packets. You can't find a more versatile source of protein!

This is why many of our recipes give you a choice. If you can't find good, fresh flounder, use cod or halibut. If you're tired of salmon, try tuna or swordfish.

We find that most of the frozen fish sold today is excellent quality. As Betty says, don't worry if you can't find good fresh fish, because frozen fish is a good alternative. It thaws quickly in cold water still in its wrapping—a three-quarter-inch thick fillet takes about 15 minutes to thaw—and once it's defrosted, it cooks exactly as fresh fish does.

When you cook any of these fish in bags or packets, there's no need for turning, rotating, or checking. Just let them cook as specified in the recipe, open the bag or packet, and enjoy the meal.

Seafood

You'll notice this chapter begins with seven recipes for shrimp and one for scallops. We love shrimp as much as anyone does and look for ways to cook it all year long.

 While you can buy fresh or frozen shrimp already shelled, it's far less expensive to buy it in the shell and peel it yourself. This is easy and surprisingly fast once you get the hang of it. The easiest way to peel and devein shrimp is with an inexpensive shrimp deveiner. It's a plastic tool that has a long, curved, pointed end. Remove the head of the shrimp with a knife. Then, just insert the pointed end of the shrimp deveiner into the top of the back where the sand vein is located. Push the deveiner all the way to the tail. In one swift motion, the shell is lifted and the back (outside curve) is cut to expose the sand vein. Just rinse the shrimp to remove the vein and you're done! Pat has taught this simple technique to everyone in the Reynolds Kitchens to save lots of time peeling shrimp.

Words of Wisdom

Whether you buy fresh or frozen fish or seafood, make sure you buy it from a reputable dealer. Stay away from those trucks along the road to the beach advertising "fresh caught." You never know where the fish was caught or if it was stored properly.

If you buy fresh fish, try to smell it first. It should have no odor or smell only faintly of the ocean. If you buy a whole fish, its scales should be wet and shiny and its eyes bright and clear. Stay away from anything that smells fishy!

Spicy Grilled Shrimp

PREP TIME
30 minutes

GRILL TIME
4 minutes

MAKES
4 servings

¼ cup fresh lemon juice

2 tablespoons Worcestershire sauce

4 teaspoons seafood seasoning

2 teaspoons lemon pepper

1 teaspoon dried basil

4 cloves garlic, minced

½ cup vegetable oil

1 pound medium raw shrimp, peeled and deveined

1 In a small bowl, whisk together the lemon juice, Worcestershire sauce, seafood seasoning, lemon pepper, basil, and garlic. Slowly add the oil, whisking until thickened. Pour half of the marinade into a shallow glass or plastic container. Reserve the rest for basting.

2 Add shrimp to shallow dish and stir to cover with marinade evenly. Cover with plastic wrap and refrigerate 30 minutes. Drain the shrimp and discard marinade.

3 Prepare a charcoal or gas grill. The coals should be medium-hot. Make holes for drainage in a sheet of non-stick aluminum foil and lay it on the grill rack with the non-stick (dull) side facing up. Arrange the shrimp on the foil.

4 Grill, uncovered, for 4 to 6 minutes, turning and basting once with the reserved marinade, or until the shrimp are firm and pink. Remove the shrimp from the foil sheet with tongs and serve immediately. Let the juices cool before handling and discarding the foil.

REYNOLDS KITCHENS TIP

The easy way to make drainage holes in the non-stick foil is to lay a sheet of foil over the rack of a cold grill, a broiler pan, or cooling rack. Make holes in some of the openings with a grilling or meat-carving fork. Place the sheet of foil on a preheated grill. This way, you create your own grilling grid so that small food, such as shrimp, won't fall through the rack or stick to the grill. And cleanup is a snap!

Ginger-Shrimp and Broccoli

2 pounds medium raw shrimp, peeled and deveined

4 cups broccoli florets

1 medium red bell pepper, cut in strips

2 cloves garlic, minced

1 tablespoon grated fresh ginger

2 tablespoons dark sesame oil

Soy sauce

PREP TIME
10 minutes

GRILL TIME
15 minutes

MAKES
5 to 6 servings

1 Prepare a charcoal or gas grill or preheat the oven to 450°F. The coals should be medium-hot. Put a large extra heavy duty foil bag in a 1-inch-deep pan.

2 Arrange the shrimp, broccoli, and red pepper in the bag in an even layer. Sprinkle with garlic and ginger. Drizzle the sesame oil over the ingredients in the bag. Double fold the bag to seal.

Ginger-Shrimp and Broccoli

3 Slide the bag onto the grill or leave it in the pan and place it in the oven. Grill for 15 to 20 minutes in a covered grill or bake for 25 to 30 minutes, or until the shrimp is firm and pink.

4 Hold the bag with oven mitts and cut it open with a knife. Carefully fold back the top of the bag so that steam can escape. Sprinkle the food with soy sauce before serving.

. . .

Sonoran Shrimp Packets

PREP TIME
15 minutes

COOK TIME
14 minutes

MAKES
4 servings

One 10-ounce package frozen whole kernel corn, thawed

1 pound medium raw shrimp, peeled and deveined

1 cup chunky salsa

4 teaspoons fresh lime juice

1 teaspoon roasted garlic oil or olive oil

1 teaspoon chicken bouillon granules

1 teaspoon chili powder

2 cups uncooked instant brown rice

1 Preheat the oven to 450°F or prepare a charcoal or gas grill so that the coals are medium-hot.

2 Lay four 12-by-18-inch sheets of heavy duty aluminum foil on the countertop. Spoon a quarter of the corn in the center of each sheet. Top with shrimp and salsa and drizzle with lime juice and oil.

3 Bring up the sides of the foil. Double fold the top and ends to seal the packets, leaving room for heat circulation inside. Repeat to make 4 packets. If using the oven, put the packets on a cookie sheet.

4 Put the cookie sheet in the oven or slide the packets onto the grill rack. Bake for 14 to 18 minutes or grill for 12 to 16 minutes in a covered grill, or until the shrimp are firm and pink.

5 Meanwhile, in a saucepan, combine the chicken bouillon granules, chili powder, and rice. Following the instructions on the package, add water and cook the rice. Serve the shrimp with the hot rice.

. . .

Shrimp Creole Packets

3 cups cooked rice

One 14$\frac{1}{2}$-ounce can garlic and onion diced tomatoes

1 medium green bell pepper, chopped

$\frac{1}{2}$ cup sliced celery

$\frac{1}{2}$ cup chopped onion

1 tablespoon Creole seasoning

2 to 3 teaspoons packed brown sugar

$\frac{1}{2}$ teaspoon dried oregano

1 pound medium raw shrimp, peeled and deveined

PREP TIME
10 minutes

COOK TIME
14 minutes

MAKES
4 servings

Shrimp Creole Packets

1 Preheat the oven to 450°F or prepare a charcoal or gas grill so that the coals are medium-hot.

2 Put the rice in a large mixing bowl. Add the tomatoes, green pepper, celery, onion, Creole seasoning, brown sugar, and oregano, and stir gently to mix. Stir in shrimp.

3 Lay four 12-by-18-inch sheets of non-stick aluminum foil on the countertop, non-stick (dull) side facing up. Spoon a quarter of the mixture in the center of each sheet.

4 Bring up the sides of the foil. Double fold the top and ends to seal the packets, leaving room for heat circulation inside. Repeat to make 4 packets. If using the oven, put the packets on a cookie sheet.

5 Put the cookie sheet in the oven or slide the packets onto the grill rack. Bake for 14 to 16 minutes or grill for 8 to 10 minutes in a covered grill, or until the shrimp are firm and pink.

...

Caribbean Shrimp Packets

One 15¼-ounce can pineapple chunks in juice, drained

1½ pounds medium raw shrimp, peeled and deveined

1 medium red bell pepper, chopped

1 medium jalapeño pepper, seeded and finely chopped

1 tablespoon grated fresh ginger

1 tablespoon seafood seasoning

½ cup butter or margarine, cut in pieces

¼ cup packed brown sugar

1½ tablespoons lemon juice

Hot cooked rice

PREP TIME
10 minutes

COOK TIME
12 minutes

MAKES
4 servings

1 Preheat the oven to 450°F or prepare a charcoal or gas grill so that the coals are medium-hot.

2 Lay four 12-by-18-inch sheets of heavy duty aluminum foil on the countertop. Spoon a quarter of the pineapple chunks in the center of each sheet. Arrange the shrimp on top of the pineapple.

3 Mix together the peppers, ginger, and seasoning. Sprinkle over the shrimp. Top with butter and brown sugar, and then drizzle with lemon juice.

4 Bring up the sides of the foil. Double fold the top and ends to seal the packets, leaving room for heat circulation inside. Repeat to make 4 packets. If using the oven, put the packets on a cookie sheet.

5 Put the cookie sheet in the oven or slide the packets onto the grill rack. Bake for 12 to 14 minutes or grill for 8 to 10 minutes in a covered grill, or until the shrimp are firm and pink. Serve with rice.

Caribbean Shrimp Packets

Shrimp with Confetti Rice Packets

PREP TIME
15 minutes

COOK TIME
15 minutes

MAKES
4 servings

1 pound medium raw shrimp, peeled and deveined

1 1/2 cups uncooked instant rice

3/4 cup water

1/2 cup shredded carrots

1/3 cup teriyaki marinade

1/4 cup sliced green onions

2 teaspoons sesame oil

1/2 teaspoon garlic powder

2 tablespoons sliced almonds (optional)

1 Preheat the oven to 450°F or prepare a charcoal or gas grill so that the coals are medium-hot.

2 Mix together the shrimp, rice, water, carrots, marinade, onions, oil, and garlic powder. Stir to combine well.

3 Lay four 12-by-18-inch sheets of heavy duty aluminum foil on the countertop. Spoon a quarter of the shrimp mixture in the center of each sheet.

4 Bring up the sides of the foil. Double fold the top and ends to seal the packets, leaving room for heat circulation inside. Repeat to make 4 packets. If using the oven, put the packets on a cookie sheet.

5 Put the cookie sheet in the oven or slide the packets onto the grill rack. Bake for 15 to 18 minutes or grill for 8 to 10 minutes in a covered grill, or until the shrimp are firm and pink. Sprinkle with almonds and additional teriyaki marinade before serving, if desired.

> **REYNOLDS KITCHENS TIP**
>
> *Combine precut vegetables and bottled sauces with fish for whole meals in a packet. For best flavor, sprinkle seasonings directly on the fish. Top with vegetables and season again to taste.*

Shrimp and Scallop Dinner

PREP TIME
15 minutes

GRILL TIME
15 minutes

MAKES
5 to 6 servings

1 pound medium raw shrimp, peeled and deveined

1/2 pound sea scallops

1 1/2 cups uncooked instant rice

3/4 cup chicken broth

1/4 cup butter or margarine, melted

2 tablespoons Worcestershire sauce

1 teaspoon hot sauce

1/2 teaspoon cayenne pepper

1/2 teaspoon salt

1/2 teaspoon black pepper

1/4 teaspoon dried oregano

3 cloves garlic

1 lemon, quartered

1 Prepare a charcoal or gas grill or preheat the oven to 450°F. The coals should be medium-hot. Put a large extra heavy duty foil bag in a 1-inch-deep pan. Spray inside the bag with cooking spray.

2 In a large bowl, mix together all the ingredients except the lemon quarters. Spoon into the bag and spread in an even layer. Top with the lemon quarters. Double fold the bag to seal.

Shrimp and Scallop Dinner

3 Slide the bag onto the grill or leave it in the pan and place it in the oven. Grill for 15 to 20 minutes in a covered grill or bake for 25 to 30 minutes or until the shrimp are firm and pink and the scallops are opaque.

4 Hold the bag with oven mitts and cut it open with a knife. Carefully fold back the top of the bag so that steam can escape.

REYNOLDS KITCHENS TIP

When selecting sea scallops, look for those that are creamy white or tinged with pink. Avoid any that are bright white, which indicates they have been soaked in a solution to extend their shelflife. While safe, the soaking liquid dilutes the flavor of the scallops and adds water weight.

. . .

Scallops with Peanut Sauce

PREP TIME	10 minutes
GRILL TIME	15 minutes
MAKES	5 to 6 servings

2^1/$_2$ cups coarsely shredded carrots

1^1/$_2$ to 2 pounds sea scallops

^{2}/$_3$ cup teriyaki sauce

^{1}/$_3$ cup smooth peanut butter

1^1/$_2$ teaspoons cornstarch

1 teaspoon ground coriander

^{1}/$_4$ teaspoon crushed red pepper flakes

2^1/$_2$ cups fresh snow peas or sugar snap peas

Hot cooked whole wheat or regular spaghetti

Sliced green onions

Chopped roasted peanuts (optional)

1 Prepare a charcoal or gas grill or preheat the oven to 450°F. The coals should be medium-hot. Put a large extra heavy duty foil bag in a 1-inch-deep pan.

2 Arrange the carrots in the bag in an even layer and top with the scallops.

3 In a small bowl, whisk together the teriyaki sauce, peanut butter, cornstarch,

coriander, and red pepper flakes until smooth. Spoon evenly over the scallops. Arrange the snow peas on top in an even layer. Double fold the bag to seal.

4 Slide the bag onto the grill or leave it in the pan and place it in the oven. Grill for 15 to 17 minutes in a covered grill or bake for 25 to 27 minutes, or until the scallops are opaque all the way through.

5 Hold the bag with oven mitts and cut it open with a knife. Carefully fold back the top of the bag so that steam can escape. Spoon the scallops, vegetables, and sauce over the spaghetti, and garnish with green onions and peanuts, if desired.

Scallops with Peanut Sauce

Honey-Glazed Salmon

PREP TIME

10 minutes

COOK TIME

20 minutes

MAKES

4 servings

1/4 cup honey

2 tablespoons Dijon mustard

1 tablespoon melted butter

1 teaspoon Worcestershire sauce

Salt and pepper to taste

Four 4- to 6-ounce salmon fillets

1 pound fresh asparagus spears, ends trimmed

1/2 cup chopped walnuts

1 Preheat the oven to 400°F. Line a 9-by-13-by-2-inch baking pan with non-stick aluminum foil, non-stick (dull) side facing up.

2 In a small bowl, stir together the honey, mustard, butter, and Worcestershire sauce. Season to taste with salt and pepper.

3 Put the salmon fillets in the center of the pan and arrange the asparagus around the salmon. Sprinkle with the walnuts and drizzle with the honey-mustard sauce.

4 Bake for 20 to 22 minutes, or until salmon flakes when tested with a fork.

> **REYNOLDS KITCHENS TIP**
>
> *Even salmon coated with a honey-mustard sauce won't stick to non-stick aluminum foil.*

Ginger-Sesame Salmon Packets

Ginger-Sesame Salmon Packets

PREP TIME
10 minutes

COOK TIME
16 minutes

MAKES
4 servings

4 thin slices onion, separated in rings

2 medium carrots, cut in julienne strips or shredded

Four 4- to 6-ounce salmon fillets

2 teaspoons grated fresh ginger

2 tablespoons seasoned rice vinegar

1 teaspoon sesame oil

Salt and pepper

Fresh spinach leaves

1 Preheat the oven to 450°F or prepare a charcoal or gas grill so that the coals are medium-hot.

2 Lay four 12-by-18-inch sheets of heavy duty aluminum foil on the countertop. Put the onion rings and carrots in the center of each. Top with salmon and sprinkle with the ginger. Drizzle the salmon with vinegar and oil and season to taste with salt and pepper.

3 Bring up the sides of the foil. Double fold the top and ends to seal the packets, leaving room for heat circulation inside. Repeat to make 4 packets. If using the oven, put the packets on a cookie sheet.

4 Put the cookie sheet in the oven or slide the packets onto the grill rack. Bake for 16 to 20 minutes or grill for 14 to 18 minutes in a covered grill, or until the salmon flakes when tested with a fork. Serve the salmon and vegetables on a bed of spinach leaves. Sprinkle with additional seasoned rice vinegar, if desired.

> **REYNOLDS KITCHENS TIP**
>
> *Cooking foods wrapped in foil is a quick, low-fat method for sealing moisture and flavor in delicate foods, such as fish. Little or no added fat is necessary.*

Salmon with Rainbow Peppers

PREP TIME
10 minutes

GRILL TIME
15 minutes

MAKES
6 servings

Six 4- to 6-ounce salmon fillets

1 medium red bell pepper, cut in strips

1 medium yellow bell pepper, cut in strips

1 medium green bell pepper, cut in strips

1½ teaspoons garlic salt

1½ teaspoons dried thyme

1   Prepare a charcoal or gas grill or preheat the oven to 450°F. The coals should be medium-hot. Put a large extra heavy duty foil bag in a 1-inch-deep pan. Spray the inside of the bag with cooking spray.

2   Arrange the salmon and peppers in the bag in an even layer. Sprinkle with the garlic salt and thyme. Double fold the bag to seal.

3   Slide the bag onto the grill or leave it in the pan and place it in the oven. Grill for 15 to 20 minutes in a covered grill or bake for 35 to 40 minutes, or until the salmon flakes when tested with a fork.

4   Hold the bag with oven mitts and cut it open with a knife. Carefully fold back the top of the bag so that steam can escape.

> **REYNOLDS KITCHENS TIP**
>
> *When you slice bell peppers, be sure to remove the seeds and membranes before cutting into strips.*

Salmon with Rainbow Peppers

Savory Salmon Provençal

PREP TIME
10 minutes

GRILL TIME
14 minutes

MAKES
5 servings

1 red onion, sliced

Six 4- to 6-ounce salmon fillets

2 cloves garlic, minced

$1/2$ teaspoon salt

$1/4$ teaspoon black pepper

$1 1/2$ teaspoons Herbes de Provence or dried salad herbs

2 cups coarsely chopped plum tomatoes (approximately 1-inch chunks)

One 6-ounce jar marinated artichoke hearts

$1/3$ cup pitted Kalamata olives, halved

1 Prepare a charcoal or gas grill or preheat the oven to 450°F. The coals should be medium-hot. Put a large extra heavy duty foil bag in a 1-inch-deep pan.

2 Put the onion slices in the bag. Put the salmon fillets, skin-side down, on top of the onions. Sprinkle with garlic, salt, pepper, and ¾ teaspoon of Herbes de Provence. Layer the tomatoes, artichoke hearts, and olives over the salmon. Sprinkle with the remaining herbs. Double fold the bag to seal.

3 Slide the bag onto the grill or leave it in the pan and place it in the oven. Grill for 14 to 16 minutes in a covered grill or bake for 25 to 30 minutes, or until the salmon flakes when tested with a fork.

4 Hold the bag with oven mitts and cut it open with a knife. Carefully fold back the top of the bag so that steam can escape.

REYNOLDS KITCHENS TIP

It's a good idea to cook salmon—or any fish—within 24 hours of purchase. Remove the fish from the store wrapping and rewrap in plastic wrap. To keep it as cold as possible, store the fish in the rear of the refrigerator. If you will have to store it for more than six or eight hours, lay the wrapped fish on a bed of crushed ice in the refrigerator, which keeps it very cold without freezing.

Salmon with Asparagus and Sun-Dried Tomatoes

PREP TIME

8 minutes

COOK TIME

18 minutes

MAKES

2 servings

½ pound fresh asparagus, ends trimmed

Two 4- to 6-ounce salmon fillets

2 teaspoons dried thyme

¼ teaspoon salt

¼ cup oil-packed sun-dried tomatoes, drained and sliced

2 tablespoons balsamic vinaigrette

¼ cup crumbled feta cheese (optional)

1 Preheat the oven to 450°F or prepare a charcoal or gas grill so that the coals are medium-hot.

2 Lay four 12-by-18-inch sheets of non-stick aluminum foil on the countertop, non-stick (dull) side facing up. Divide the asparagus spears among the sheets and top with the salmon. Sprinkle with thyme and salt, and top with sun-dried tomatoes. Drizzle with vinaigrette.

3 Bring up the sides of the foil. Double fold the top and ends to seal the packets, leaving room for heat circulation inside. Repeat to make 2 packets. If using the oven, put the packets on a cookie sheet.

4 Put the cookie sheet in the oven or slide the packets onto the grill rack. Bake for 18 to 20 minutes or grill for 12 to 14 minutes in a covered grill, or until the salmon flakes when tested with a fork. Serve the salmon sprinkled with feta cheese, if desired.

> **REYNOLDS KITCHENS TIP**
>
> *Keep grilled foods hot until serving time by wrapping them in aluminum foil. There will be fewer dishes to wash after the meal.*

Ranch Salmon with Vegetables

PREP TIME
8 minutes

COOK TIME
15 minutes

MAKES
2 servings

Two 4- to 6-ounce salmon fillets

4 teaspoons Monterey-style spice blend or your favorite garlic spice blend

4 tablespoons ranch dressing

3 cups mixed broccoli florets, baby carrots, and cauliflower florets, or mixed broccoli florets, baby carrots, and sugar snap peas

1   Preheat the oven to 450°F or prepare a charcoal or gas grill so that the coals are medium-hot.

2   Lay two 12-by-18-inch sheets of heavy duty aluminum foil on the countertop. Center a salmon fillet on each sheet. Sprinkle with spice blend and top each fillet with 2 tablespoons of ranch dressing. Arrange the mixed vegetables around the salmon. Sprinkle the vegetables with more spice blend, if desired.

3   Bring up the sides of the foil. Double fold the top and ends to seal the packets, leaving room for heat circulation inside. Repeat to make 2 packets. If using the oven, put the packets on a cookie sheet.

4   Put the cookie sheet in the oven or slide the packets onto the grill rack. Bake for 15 to 18 minutes or grill for 9 to 11 minutes in a covered grill, or until the fish flakes when tested with a fork.

> **REYNOLDS KITCHENS TIP**
>
> *Packet cooking lets you customize your meals to suit the individual tastes in your family. If someone doesn't like broccoli or cauliflower, just leave that ingredient out of their packet.*

. . .

Microwave Orange Roughy

PREP TIME
5 minutes

COOK TIME
13 minutes

MAKES
4 servings

1 tablespoon flour

Four 6-ounce frozen orange roughy or red snapper fillets

1 large tomato, chopped

$1/4$ cup chopped fresh basil or 1 teaspoon dried basil

$1/4$ cup sliced green onion

2 cloves garlic, minced

$1/3$ cup freshly grated Parmesan cheese

1 Add the flour to a large oven bag, shake the bag to distribute the flour, and put the bag in a 9-by-13-by-2-inch microwave-safe baking dish.

2 Put the orange roughy in the bag. Sprinkle with tomato, basil, green onion, and garlic. Close the oven bag with the provided nylon tie and cut six ½-inch slits in the top.

3 Microwave on high power for 13 to 14 minutes or until fish flakes when tested with a fork. Turn the dish halfway through cooking time. Let the fish stand in the oven bag for 1 minute. Sprinkle with Parmesan cheese and let stand 1 minute longer before serving.

> **REYNOLDS KITCHENS TIP**
>
> *If using fresh orange roughy fillets, microwave on high power for 5 to 6 minutes.*

. . .

Oriental Red Snapper

One 1½- to 2-pound whole red snapper or sea bass, cleaned and ready to cook

6 large mushrooms, sliced

6 slices fresh ginger

6 green onions, sliced

1 teaspoon dark sesame oil

Soy sauce (optional)

PREP TIME
10 minutes

GRILL TIME
7 to 8 minutes

MAKES
4 servings

1 Prepare a charcoal or gas grill or preheat the oven to 450°F. The coals should be medium-hot. Put a large extra heavy duty foil bag in a 1-inch-deep pan. Spray the inside of the bag with cooking spray.

2 Cut 3 slits on each side of the fish. Tuck a slice of mushroom and of ginger in each slit. Put the fish in the bag and sprinkle with the remaining mushrooms and green onions. Drizzle with sesame oil. Double fold the bag to seal.

> **REYNOLDS KITCHENS TIP**
>
> *Extra heavy duty foil bags are the no-mess way to make great-tasting dinners on the grill or in the oven. Just put your food in these premade foil bags, seal, and cook on the grill or in the oven.*

3 Slide the bag onto the grill or leave it in the pan and place it in the oven. Grill for 7 to 8 minutes per inch.

in a covered grill or bake for 10 to 15 minutes per inch, or until the fish flakes when tested with a fork.

4 Hold the bag with oven mitts and cut it open with a knife. Carefully fold back the top of the bag so that steam can escape. Serve with soy sauce, if desired.

Oriental Red Snapper

Lemon-Pepper Tilapia

PREP TIME
10 minutes

GRILL TIME
12 minutes

MAKES
4 servings

Four 6-ounce tilapia fish fillets, each $1/2$- to $3/4$-inch thick

2 teaspoons lemon pepper seasoning

2 medium yellow squash, sliced

I cup grape or cherry tomatoes

$1/4$ cup sliced green onions

2 tablespoons butter, cut in pieces

$1/2$ cup shredded Parmesan cheese

1 Prepare a charcoal or gas grill or preheat the oven to 450°F. The coals should be medium-hot. Put a large extra heavy duty foil bag in a 1-inch-deep pan.

2 Put the fish fillets in the bag in an even layer. Sprinkle with 1 teaspoon of lemon pepper seasoning. Top with the squash, tomatoes, and onions. Sprinkle with the remaining seasoning and top with butter. Double fold the bag to seal.

3 Slide the bag onto the grill or leave it in the pan and place it in the oven. Grill for 12 to 14 minutes in a covered grill or bake for 22 to 26 minutes, or until the fish flakes when tested with a fork.

4 Hold the bag with oven mitts and cut it open with a knife. Carefully fold back the top of the bag so that steam can escape. Sprinkle with Parmesan cheese before serving.

> **REYNOLDS KITCHENS TIP**
>
> *To ensure that your meal cooks within the recommended cooking times, always preheat the oven to 450°F before cooking. Preheating takes at least 20 minutes. Extra heavy duty foil bags are made of extra heavy aluminum foil so they can take the heat.*

. . .

Tuscan Halibut Packets

PREP TIME
10 minutes

COOK TIME
16 minutes

MAKES
4 servings

Two 15-ounce cans Great Northern or cannellini beans, rinsed and drained

2 medium tomatoes, chopped

$1 1/2$ teaspoons dried basil

Four 4- to 6-ounce halibut steaks

4 teaspoons olive oil

4 teaspoons lemon juice

2 teaspoons lemon pepper

4 lemon slices

1 Preheat the oven to 450°F or prepare a charcoal or gas grill so that the coals are medium-hot.

2 In a mixing bowl, stir together the beans, tomatoes, and ½ teaspoon of the basil.

3 Lay four 12-by-18-inch sheets of heavy duty aluminum foil on the countertop. Spoon a quarter of the bean mixture in the center of each sheet. Top with the halibut steaks and drizzle with olive oil and lemon juice. Sprinkle with the remaining basil and the lemon pepper. Top each with a lemon slice.

4 Bring up the sides of the foil. Double fold the top and ends to seal the packets, leaving room for heat circulation inside. Repeat to make 4 packets. If using the oven, put the packets on a cookie sheet.

5 Put the cookie sheet in the oven or slide the packets onto the grill rack. Bake for 16 to 20 minutes or grill for 14 to 18 minutes in a covered grill, or until the fish flakes when tested with a fork.

Tuscan Halibut Packets

Swordfish with Corn and Salsa

PREP TIME
10 minutes

COOK TIME
18 minutes

MAKES
2 servings

Two 5-ounce swordfish or tuna steaks

2 cloves garlic, minced

One 8^3/$_4$-ounce can whole kernel corn, drained

^{1}/$_2$ cup medium or hot salsa

^{1}/$_4$ teaspoon salt

1 medium green bell pepper, cut in thin strips

1 Preheat the oven to 450°F or prepare a charcoal or gas grill so that the coals are medium-hot.

2 Lay two 12-by-18-inch sheets of non-stick aluminum foil on the countertop, non-stick (dull) side facing up. Lay a swordfish steak in the center of each sheet. Top with garlic.

3 In a small bowl, stir together the corn, salsa, and salt, and then spoon it evenly on top of the fish steaks. Top with pepper strips.

4 Bring up the sides of the foil. Double fold the top and ends to seal the packets, leaving room for heat circulation inside. Repeat to make 2 packets. If using the oven, put the packets on a cookie sheet.

5 Put the cookie sheet in the oven or slide the packets onto the grill rack. Bake for 18 to 20 minutes or grill for 8 to 10 minutes in a covered grill, or until the swordfish flakes when tested with a fork.

> **REYNOLDS KITCHENS TIP**
>
> *Foil packets can be placed directly on the grill but need a cookie sheet for support when baking.*

...

Cajun Catfish with Potato Wedges

PREP TIME
18 minutes

GRILL TIME
8 minutes

MAKES
4 servings

4 medium red potatoes, each cut into 8 wedges

Olive oil

Cajun seasoning

Four 4- to 6-ounce catfish fillets

1 medium green bell pepper, cut into rings

Juice of ^{1}/$_2$ lemon

1 Put the potato wedges in a microwave-safe dish and microwave on high power for 10 minutes or until tender. Brush the cut sides of the potatoes with oil and sprinkle with Cajun seasoning.

2 Brush the fish with oil and sprinkle with Cajun seasoning.

3 Prepare a charcoal or gas grill so that the coals are medium-hot. Make holes for drainage in a sheet of non-stick aluminum foil and lay it on the grill rack with the non-stick (dull) side facing up. Arrange the fish and vegetables on the foil.

4 Grill 8 to 10 minutes in a covered grill or until the fish flakes when tested with a fork. Remove the fish and vegetables from the foil sheet with tongs or a spatula and serve immediately. Let the juices cool before handling and discarding the foil. Squeeze the lemon juice over the fish and serve.

> **REYNOLDS KITCHENS TIP**
>
> *Laying a sheet of non-stick aluminum foil on the grill rack allows you to grill fish directly over the hot coals without it sticking or slipping through the rack. Be sure to make holes in the foil for drainage and heat conduction.*

· · ·

Fish Steaks with Herbed Vegetables

		PREP TIME
2 pounds halibut or swordfish steaks, each ¾- to 1-inch thick	**1 medium green bell pepper, finely chopped**	12 minutes
2 teaspoons dried thyme	**1 small onion, finely chopped**	**GRILL TIME**
Salt and pepper	**¼ cup grated Parmesan cheese**	12 minutes
2 medium carrots, shredded	**1 tablespoon olive oil**	**MAKES**
		5 to 6 servings

1 Prepare a charcoal or gas grill or preheat the oven to 450°F. The coals should be medium-hot. Put a large extra heavy duty foil bag in a 1-inch-deep pan. Spray the inside of the bag with cooking spray.

2 Put the fish steaks in the bag in an even layer. Sprinkle with half the thyme and the salt and pepper.

3 In a mixing bowl, stir together the carrots, bell pepper, onion, cheese, olive oil, and

remaining teaspoon of dried thyme. Spoon evenly over the fish. Double fold the bag to seal.

4 Slide the bag onto the grill or leave it in the pan and place it in the oven. Grill for 12 to 14 minutes in a covered grill or bake for 25 to 30 minutes, or until the fish flakes when tested with a fork.

5 Hold the bag with oven mitts and cut it open with a knife. Carefully fold back the top of the bag so that steam can escape.

Fish Steaks with Herbed Vegetables

Fish with Lemon-Dill Butter Sauce

PREP TIME
8 minutes

COOK TIME
15 minutes

MAKES
4 servings

1 tablespoon flour

$^1/_4$ cup water

2 tablespoons lemon juice

1 clove garlic, minced

$^1/_2$ teaspoon dried dill

1 pound mild fish fillets, such as cod, haddock, or flounder, each about $^1/_2$-inch thick

1 tablespoon butter, cut in pieces

1 Preheat the oven to 350°F. Add the flour to a large oven bag, shake the bag to distribute the flour, and put in a 9-by-13-by-2-inch baking pan.

2 Add the water, lemon juice, garlic, and dill to the bag. Squeeze the bag to blend the ingredients. Put the fish fillets in the bag and turn to coat with the sauce.

3 Arrange the fish so that they are in an even layer. Top with butter. Close the bag, securing it with the provided nylon tie. Cut six ½-inch slits in the top of the bag.

4 Bake for 15 to 20 minutes, or until the fish flakes when tested with a fork.

. . .

Lemon Fish with Rice Pilaf Packets

PREP TIME
15 minutes

COOK TIME
12 minutes

MAKES
4 servings

Two 4.2-ounce packages rice and sauce pilaf

Grated peel and juice of 1 lemon

Four 4- to 6-ounce pollock, cod, or flounder fillets

Butter-flavored cooking spray

$1^1/_2$ teaspoons lemon and herb seasoning or lemon pepper

$^1/_2$ medium red bell pepper, chopped

$^1/_4$ cup almonds, toasted

1 Preheat the oven to 450°F or prepare a charcoal or gas grill so that the coals are medium-hot.

2 Prepare the pilaf mixes according to the package instructions. Fluff the pilaf with a fork, let it cool slightly, and then stir in the lemon peel and juice.

3 Lay four 12-by-18-inch sheets of heavy duty aluminum foil on the countertop. Put a fish fillet in the center of each sheet. Spray the fish with the cooking spray and

sprinkle with lemon and herb seasoning. Spoon the pilaf beside the fish and top with red bell pepper.

4 Bring up the sides of the foil. Double fold the top and ends to seal the packets, leaving room for heat circulation inside. Repeat to make 4 packets. If using the oven, put the packets on a cookie sheet.

5 Put the cookie sheet in the oven or slide the packets onto the grill rack. Bake for 12 to 14 minutes or grill for 10 to 12 minutes in a covered grill, or until the fish flakes when tested with a fork. Sprinkle with almonds before serving.

REYNOLDS KITCHENS TIP

Toasting nuts before adding them to a recipe makes them crispy and intensifies their flavor—which means you may be able to use less without any loss of flavor.

To toast, line a shallow baking pan with aluminum foil. Spread shelled nuts in a single layer in the pan and toast in a preheated 350°F oven for 8 to 10 minutes, stirring occasionally, or until the nuts are fragrant and light brown. Watch closely so that they don't burn. Different kinds of nuts may brown at slightly different rates.

Slide the nuts onto a fresh sheet of foil or a plate to halt the cooking. Let them cool completely before using. Toasted nuts can be stored, wrapped tightly, in a cool, dry place for up to 2 weeks.

Lemon Fish with Rice Pilaf Packets

Parmesan-Baked Fish Packets

Four 4- to 6-ounce orange roughy, cod, or sole fillets

$1/4$ cup mayonnaise

$1/4$ cup grated Parmesan cheese

Cayenne pepper

2 medium zucchini, sliced

$1/2$ medium red bell pepper, cut in strips

PREP TIME
8 minutes

COOK TIME
18 minutes

MAKES
4 servings

1 Preheat the oven to 450°F or prepare a charcoal or gas grill so that the coals are medium-hot.

2 Lay four 12-by-18-inch sheets of non-stick aluminum foil on the countertop, non-stick (dull) side facing up. Put a fish fillet in the center of each sheet. Spread each fillet with mayonnaise and then sprinkle with cheese and cayenne pepper to taste. Top with the vegetables.

3 Bring up the sides of the foil. Double fold the top and ends to seal the packets, leaving room for heat circulation inside. Repeat to make 4 packets. If using the oven, put the packets on a cookie sheet.

4 Put the cookie sheet in the oven or slide the packets onto the grill rack. Bake for 18 to 22 minutes or grill for 10 to 12 minutes in a covered grill, or until the fish flakes when tested with a fork.

Parmesan-Baked Fish Packets

Herbed Fish and Vegetable Packets

Four 4- to 6-ounce pollock, haddock, or orange roughy fillets

¹/₂ teaspoon dried thyme

¹/₂ teaspoon dried marjoram

4 teaspoons lemon juice

One 16-ounce package frozen broccoli, carrots, and cauliflower

¹/₄ cup chopped green onions

Salt and pepper

2 tablespoons butter or margarine, cut in pieces

PREP TIME
8 minutes

COOK TIME
18 minutes

MAKES
4 servings

1 Preheat the oven to 450°F or prepare a charcoal or gas grill so that the coals are medium-hot.

2 Lay four 12-by-18-inch sheets of heavy duty aluminum foil on the countertop. Put a fish fillet in the center of each sheet. Sprinkle the fish with thyme, marjoram, and lemon juice. Spoon the frozen vegetables next to the fish. Sprinkle the green onions over the fish and vegetables, and season with salt and pepper. Top with butter.

3 Bring up the sides of the foil. Double fold the top and ends to seal the packets, leaving room for heat circulation inside. Repeat to make 4 packets. If using the oven, put the packets on a cookie sheet.

4 Put the cookie sheet in the oven or slide the packets onto the grill rack. Bake for 18 to 22 minutes or grill for 16 to 20 minutes in a covered grill, or until the fish flakes when tested with a fork.

> **REYNOLDS KITCHENS TIP**
>
> *Most mild white-fleshed fish work well cooked in packets. Choose your favorite, but most importantly, select the freshest fish available or high-quality frozen fish. Fresh fish is firm and moist with no fishy smell.*

Herbed Fish and Vegetable Packets

Hawaiian Fish Packets

PREP TIME

8 minutes

COOK TIME

12 minutes

MAKES

4 servings

Four 4- to 6-ounce mild fish fillets, such as cod, flounder, or haddock

One 15¼-ounce can pineapple chunks, drained, reserve juice

1 medium green bell pepper, cut in strips

3 tablespoons teriyaki sauce

1 tablespoon packed brown sugar

¼ teaspoon ground ginger

1 Preheat the oven to 450°F or prepare a charcoal or gas grill so that the coals are medium-hot.

2 Lay four 12-by-18-inch sheets of non-stick aluminum foil on the countertop, non-stick (dull) side facing up. Put a fish fillet in the center of each sheet. Top with the pineapple and green pepper.

3 In a small bowl, stir together 1 tablespoon of the reserved pineapple juice, teriyaki sauce, brown sugar, and ginger. Spoon over the fish, pineapple, and pepper.

4 Bring up the sides of the foil. Double fold the top and ends to seal the packets, leaving room for heat circulation inside. Repeat to make 4 packets. If using the oven, put the packets on a cookie sheet.

5 Put the cookie sheet in the oven or slide the packets onto the grill rack. Bake for 12 to 14 minutes or grill for 8 to 10 minutes in a covered grill, or until the fish flakes when tested with a fork.

> **REYNOLDS KITCHENS TIP**
>
> *Fish and vegetables are easy to remove from non-stick foil because they don't stick. And, there's no cleanup!*

Dilled Fish and Garden Vegetable Packets

PREP TIME
15 minutes

COOK TIME
15 minutes

MAKES
4 servings

1 lemon, thinly sliced

Four 4- to 6-ounce halibut, pollock, or cod fillets

Salt and pepper

$^1/_2$ small zucchini, cut in thin strips

$^1/_2$ small yellow squash, cut in thin strips

1 medium carrot, cut in thin strips

1 medium onion, cut in thin wedges

1 teaspoon dried dill

Dilled Fish and Garden Vegetable Packets

1   Preheat the oven to 450°F or prepare a charcoal or gas grill so that the coals are medium-hot.

2   Lay four 12-by-18-inch sheets of non-stick aluminum foil on the countertop, non-stick (dull) side facing up. Center several lemon slices on each sheet. Lay the fish on top of the lemon slices and sprinkle with salt and pepper. Top with zucchini, squash, carrot, and onion. Sprinkle the fish and vegetables with the dill.

3   Bring up the sides of the foil. Double fold the top and ends to seal the packets, leaving room for heat circulation inside. Repeat to make 4 packets. If using the oven, put the packets on a cookie sheet.

4   Put the cookie sheet in the oven or slide the packets onto the grill rack. Bake for 15 to 18 minutes or grill for 8 to 10 minutes in a covered grill, or until the fish flakes when tested with a fork.

Center ingredients on a sheet (12 x 18 inches) of Reynolds Wrap Heavy Duty Aluminum Foil.

Bring up foil sides. Double fold top and ends to seal packet, leaving room for heat circulation inside. Repeat to make four packets.

Bake on a cookie sheet, in preheated 450°F oven, or grill on medium-high in covered grill.

After cooking, open end of foil packet first to allow steam to escape. Then open top of foil packet.

Poultry and Meat

We get more calls about pot roast than any other dish, which shows how important comfort food is to our consumer. If I plan ahead, I put all the ingredients for a pot roast in an oven bag, leave it in the refrigerator, and my daughter can pop it in the oven when she gets home from school. By the time I arrive from work, the house smells great!
—Pat

It's really easy to roast a whole chicken at home. I like to add herbs for seasoning, and I always line the pan with foil to simplify cleanup!
—Betty

WITHOUT QUESTION, OUR CONSUMERS LOVE chicken and beef. Although Americans still buy more beef than chicken, most of us cook a lot of both.

A hands-down favorite in the Reynolds Kitchens is skinless, boneless chicken breast halves. It's no wonder they are the best-selling cut of chicken. Boneless chicken breasts are so versatile. They cook quickly and do especially well in oven bags and foil packets. After discovering how well chicken turned out when cooked in packets, one of our young marketing managers told us that he didn't realize chicken breasts didn't have to be tough and dry!

When it comes to beef, sirloin, tenderloin, briskets, round roasts, and steak are the most popular cuts we work with, although nationwide, more ground beef is sold than all other beef.

Poultry

Have you noticed the popularity of the small rotisserie-cooked chickens? You can buy them in fast-food restaurants, supermarket delis, and even club stores. But you can easily prepare them at home by either quick roasting in a foil-lined pan or in an oven bag. If you're lucky enough to have leftovers, the cold chicken can be used for sandwiches, salads, soups, and casseroles.

For a unique flavor, try inserting herbs and other seasonings directly under the skin of the chicken. It's easy and the flavor permeates the meat. Even if you remove the skin before serving, the goodness of the herb has cooked into the meat.

We also develop a lot of recipes for chicken parts: bone-in legs, thighs, and chicken breasts. A good example is our Crispy Baked Chicken, one of our most popular recipes. The coated breaded chicken is a classic, and because we bake it on Reynolds Wrap Release Non-Stick Aluminum Foil, all of the bread crumbs and Parmesan cheese stay on the chicken, not in the pan. We use a skinless, boneless chicken breast version of this recipe to test the performance of various production runs of our non-stick foil. We've made literally hundreds of chicken breasts this way, and we've never had the coating stick to the non-stick foil.

A popular way of cooking a turkey is with an oven bag. That's because the cooking time is shorter. The bird is moist and tender, and turns an appetizing golden brown color. Best of all, there's very little cleanup.

We have recipes on these pages, too, for those cooks who prefer our tried-and-true foil tent method for roasting a turkey. This is a good way to hold in the heat during the first part of roasting and prevent the bird from browning too much. When the foil is removed, the skin turns crisp with a deep golden brown color.

In addition to use with whole turkeys, oven bags are also great for turkey breasts. The oven bags hold in moisture so the turkey breast is always moist and tender. And, the oven bag is large enough for cooking two breasts at once, so you can employ one of our favorite tricks: cook once, eat twice! More and more home cooks are cooking turkey breasts rather than whole turkeys. They're good any time of year for a meal and a few days' worth of leftovers for sandwiches, casseroles, and salads.

Meat

The number one meat question answered by the Reynolds Consumer Response team is how long to cook a pot roast. Good old comfort food never goes out of style. In this chapter, we've included two of our best pot

roast recipes, Today's Beef Roast and Homestyle Pot Roast. The meat and vegetables cook together to achieve the ultimate in a comfort meal and in the oven bag, there's no pan to scrub.

Reynolds products make cooking beef so easy. You can roast large cuts in oven bags, grill steaks directly on foil-lined grill racks (with drainage holes punched in the foil to promote fast cooking), broil smaller cuts on foil-lined broiler pans, or wrap the meat in individual foil packets for cooking in the oven or on the grill.

If you like ribs, Betty says you can't beat cooking ribs in foil. And coming from North Carolina, where good ribs and pork barbecue are a way of life, she knows what she's talking about!

Wrapping the ribs for grilling eliminates the need for parboiling and all the accompanying mess. Pat recalls an informal rib cook-off at a neighbor's house, where she volunteered for end-of-the day cleanup duty. The greasy mess left behind on the stove (by someone *else*, she emphasizes), not to mention the pans themselves, confirmed her loyalty to the Reynolds method of foil wrapping.

Pork tenderloin, loin roast, and chops are perfect for large oven bags. A whole ham is another idea that turns out great in a turkey size oven bag.

Words of Wisdom

While it's a good idea to cook poultry and meat as soon as possible after purchase, if you can't, freeze it. Nothing will be lost in flavor, texture, or nutrients, and you'll have food on hand for meals several weeks or months in the future.

Keep track of what's in your freezer, and be sure to date the food. Wrap it well in non-stick aluminum foil, pressing it to fit the contours of the meat to eliminate air pockets and freezer burn.

Let the food thaw in the refrigerator rather than at room temperature. It takes longer but is far safer. Once the poultry or meat is thawed, proceed with the recipe as directed.

Orange-Basil Roasted Chicken

PREP TIME
10 minutes

COOK TIME
1¼ hours

MAKES
9 to 12 servings

1 tablespoon flour

One 5- to 7-pound roasting chicken

8 large fresh basil leaves

1 large orange, thinly sliced

1 medium onion, sliced

Vegetable oil

1 teaspoon freshly ground black pepper

1 Preheat the oven to 350°F. Add the flour to a large oven bag, shake the bag to distribute the flour, and put in a 9-by-13-by-2-inch baking pan.

2 Rinse the chicken and pat dry. Loosen the skin over the breast meat by slipping your fingers or a dull kitchen knife under the skin. (Do not detach the skin completely from the chicken.) Slide the basil leaves and 4 of the orange slices under the skin.

3 Divide onion slices and remaining orange slices and place some in the cavity of the chicken and the rest in the bottom of the bag. Tuck the wings under the chicken and tie the legs together, if desired. Brush the chicken with vegetable oil and sprinkle with pepper. Put the chicken in the bag on top of the onion and orange slices.

4 Close the bag with the provided nylon tie and cut six ½-inch slits in the top.

5 Roast for 1¼ to 1½ hours or until the chicken is tender, the juices run clear, and an instant-read or meat thermometer registers 180°F for the thigh. For easy slicing, let the chicken stand for 10 minutes.

REYNOLDS KITCHENS TIP

Placing herbs or other seasonings under the skin of the breast meat on a whole chicken is a common practice, but one with which you may not be familiar. It's very easy to do. As soon as you try it, you'll start to enjoy the wonderful flavor benefits as the herbs perfume the chicken as it cooks.

Shortcut Salsa Chicken

PREP TIME
10 minutes

COOK TIME
25 minutes

MAKES
4 servings

2 tablespoons flour

One 16-ounce jar chunky salsa

4 skinless, boneless chicken breast halves

1 medium green bell pepper, cut in rings

Flour tortillas or tortilla chips

1 Preheat the oven to 350°F. Add the flour to a large oven bag, shake the bag to distribute the flour, and put in a 9-by-13-by-2-inch baking pan.

2 Add the salsa to the bag and squeeze the bag so the salsa and flour blend.

3 Rinse the chicken and pat dry. Add to the bag and turn the bag to coat the breasts with the salsa. Arrange the chicken in an even layer and then top with the pepper rings.

4 Close the bag with the provided nylon tie and cut six $\frac{1}{2}$-inch slits in the top.

5 Bake for 25 to 30 minutes, or until the chicken is tender, the juices run clear, and an instant-read or meat thermometer registers 170°F. Serve with flour tortillas or tortilla chips.

> **REYNOLDS KITCHENS TIP**
>
> *To make Shortcut Italian Chicken, substitute a 14-ounce jar of pasta sauce for the salsa and serve the chicken with hot, cooked spaghetti instead of tortillas.*

· · ·

Honey-Dijon Chicken

PREP TIME
10 minutes

COOK TIME
30 minutes

MAKES
4 servings

1 tablespoon flour

One 10$\frac{3}{4}$-ounce can cream of mushroom soup, undiluted

One 4$\frac{1}{2}$-ounce jar sliced mushrooms, drained

2 tablespoons Dijon mustard

1 tablespoon honey

$\frac{1}{8}$ teaspoon paprika, plus more for sprinkling

$\frac{1}{8}$ teaspoon garlic powder

4 skinless, boneless chicken breast halves

Hot cooked noodles or rice

1 Preheat the oven to 350°F. Add the flour to a large oven bag, shake the bag to distribute the flour, and put in a 9-by-13-by-2-inch baking pan.

2   Add the soup, mushrooms, mustard, honey, paprika, and garlic powder to the bag, and squeeze the bag to blend the ingredients.

3   Rinse the chicken and pat dry. Sprinkle with a little more paprika and arrange the chicken in an even layer in the bag.

4   Close the bag with the provided nylon tie and cut six ½-inch slits in the top.

5   Bake for 30 to 35 minutes, or until the chicken is tender, the juices run clear, and an instant-read or meat thermometer registers 170°F. Serve with hot noodles or rice.

. . .

Easy-Stuffed Chicken

1 tablespoon flour

1 medium onion, sliced

1 stalk celery, sliced

One 5- to 7-pound whole roasting chicken

One 6-ounce package stuffing mix for chicken (the package may weigh a little more or less than 6 ounces)

Vegetable oil

Paprika

Salt and pepper

PREP TIME
15 minutes
COOK TIME
1¾ hours
MAKES
6 to 9 servings

1   Preheat the oven to 350°F. Add the flour to a large oven bag, shake the bag to distribute the flour, and put in a 9-by-13-by-2-inch baking pan.

2   Put the onion and celery in the oven bag. Rinse the chicken and pat it dry.

3   Prepare stuffing mix according to the package directions. Loosely pack the stuffing in the chicken cavity and brush the chicken with oil. Sprinkle with paprika, salt, and pepper, and put the chicken in the bag on top of the vegetables.

4   Close the bag with the provided nylon tie and cut six ½-inch slits in the top.

5   Roast for 1¾ to 2 hours or until the chicken is tender, the juices run clear, and an instant-read or meat thermometer registers 170°F for the breast and 180°F for the thigh. For easy slicing, let the chicken stand for 10 minutes.

Pesto Chicken

2 tablespoons flour

$1/2$ cup canned chicken broth

$1/2$ cup pesto

$1/2$ teaspoon lemon pepper

One 5- to 7-pound whole roasting chicken

3 medium red potatoes, cut in quarters

1 red bell pepper, seeded and cut in 8 pieces

PREP TIME
15 minutes

COOK TIME
1¼ hours

MAKES
6 to 9 servings

1 Preheat the oven to 350°F. Add the flour to a large oven bag, shake the bag to distribute the flour, and put in a 9-by-13-by-2-inch baking pan.

2 Pour the chicken broth into the bag and add 2 tablespoons of the pesto and the lemon pepper. Squeeze the bag to blend the flour with the other ingredients.

3 Rinse the chicken and pat it dry. Loosen the skin over the breast meat by slipping your fingers or a dull kitchen knife under the skin. (Do not detach the skin completely from the chicken.) Spread the rest of the pesto over the breast meat under the skin. Put the chicken in the bag. Arrange the vegetables in an even layer around the chicken.

4 Close the bag with the provided nylon tie and cut six ½-inch slits in the top.

5 Roast for 1¼ to 1½ hours or until the chicken is tender, the juices run clear, and an instant-read or meat thermometer registers 170°F for the breast and 180°F for the thigh. For easy slicing, let the chicken stand for 10 minutes.

> **REYNOLDS KITCHENS TIP**
>
> *While the chicken stands for 10 minutes, the juices have time to set so that the meat is easier to carve.*

. . .

Crispy Baked Chicken

2½ to 3 pounds chicken, cut into 6 pieces (legs, thighs, breasts, or any combination)

2 eggs, beaten

2 tablespoons milk

$1/2$ cup grated Parmesan cheese

$1/3$ cup bread crumbs

1 teaspoon dried Italian seasoning

$1/4$ teaspoon pepper

PREP TIME
10 minutes

COOK TIME
35 minutes

MAKES
4 to 6 servings

1 Preheat the oven to 400°F. Line a 9-by-13-by-2-inch baking pan with non-stick aluminum foil, non-stick (dull) side facing up.

2 Rinse the chicken pieces and pat them dry.

3 In a shallow bowl, whisk together the eggs and milk with a fork.

4 Combine the Parmesan cheese, bread crumbs, Italian seasoning, and pepper on a sheet of wax paper.

5 Dip each chicken piece in the beaten eggs and then roll it in the crumb mixture. Turn the chicken to coat evenly. Lay the chicken in the foil-lined pan.

6 Bake for 35 to 40 minutes, or until the chicken is tender, the juices run clear, and an instant-read or meat thermometer registers 170°F for the breast and 180°F for the leg or thigh.

REYNOLDS KITCHENS TIP

When coated chicken is baked on non-stick aluminum foil, the coating stays on the chicken—not on the foil.

Crispy Baked Chicken

Roasted Herbed Chicken

One 2½- to 3-pound broiler-
fryer chicken

1 tablespoon vegetable or
olive oil

2 teaspoons dried basil

1 teaspoon seasoned salt

½ teaspoon paprika

PREP TIME
10 minutes

COOK TIME
55 minutes

MAKES
4 to 5 servings

1 Preheat the oven to 450°F. Center a sheet of heavy duty aluminum foil in a 9-by-13-by-2-inch baking pan, leaving generous foil overhangs at each end. You need enough foil to cover the chicken.

2 Rinse the chicken and pat dry. Put it in the pan and brush with vegetable oil.

3 Combine the basil, seasoned salt, and paprika on a sheet of wax paper. Sprinkle and rub the seasoning evenly into the chicken. Pull the foil up and over the chicken, overlapping and folding the ends to seal loosely.

4 Bake for 20 minutes. Open the foil and turn it back to expose the chicken. Bake for 35 to 40 minutes longer or until the chicken is tender, the juices run clear, and an instant-read or meat thermometer registers 180°F for the thigh. Let the chicken stand for about 10 minutes before slicing.

> **REYNOLDS KITCHENS TIP**
>
> *The foil traps the heat during the first 20 minutes of roasting. This gives the small chicken a head start so it cooks evenly. When the foil is turned back to expose the bird, the skin has plenty of time to brown.*

Citrus-Herb Chicken

PREP TIME

10 minutes

COOK TIME

35 minutes

MAKES

6 to 9 servings

6 to 9 chicken pieces

2 tablespoons lemon, lime, or orange juice

I teaspoon garlic salt

I teaspoon dried oregano, crushed

$^1/_2$ teaspoon chili powder

$^1/_8$ teaspoon pepper

I   Preheat the oven to 425°F. Line a baking pan with an 18-by-12-inch sheet of heavy duty aluminum foil.

2   Remove the skin from the chicken, if desired. Rinse the chicken and pat dry. Lay the chicken in an even layer in the foil-lined pan. Drizzle with juice.

3   Combine the garlic salt, oregano, chili powder, and pepper on a sheet of wax paper. Sprinkle and rub seasoning mixture over chicken, turning the pieces to coat evenly.

4   Bake for 35 to 40 minutes, or until the chicken is tender, the juices run clear, and an instant-read or meat thermometer registers 170°F for the breast and 180°F for the leg or thigh. Spoon the pan juices over the chicken before serving.

REYNOLDS KITCHENS TIP

To line a pan with foil easily, turn the baking pan upside down and press a sheet of heavy duty aluminum foil around it. Remove the foil. Flip the pan over and drop the formed foil liner inside. Crimp the edges of foil to the rim of the pan.

Crunchy Baked Chicken

PREP TIME
15 minutes

COOK TIME
35 minutes

MAKES
4 to 6 servings

2$\frac{1}{2}$ to 3 pounds chicken, cut into 6 pieces (legs, thighs, breasts, or any combination), skin removed

$\frac{1}{4}$ cup vegetable oil

1 teaspoon salt

$\frac{1}{2}$ teaspoon garlic powder

$\frac{1}{2}$ teaspoon chili powder

$\frac{1}{8}$ teaspoon black pepper

$\frac{1}{8}$ teaspoon cayenne pepper

One 5$\frac{1}{2}$-ounce bag ridged barbecue potato chips, finely crushed

1 Preheat the oven to 400°F. Line a 10½-by-15½-by-1-inch baking pan with non-stick aluminum foil, non-stick (dull) side facing up.

2 Rinse the chicken and pat it dry.

3 In a large bowl, stir together the oil, salt, garlic powder, chili powder, black pepper, and cayenne pepper. Add the chicken and stir to coat.

4 Spread the crushed chips on a sheet of wax paper. Lift the chicken from the bowl, letting the seasoned oil drip back into the bowl, and roll the chicken in the chips to coat evenly. Press additional crumbs onto the chicken if necessary. Lay in a single layer in the foil-lined pan.

5 Bake for 35 to 40 minutes, or until the chicken is tender, the juices run clear, and an instant-read or meat thermometer registers 170°F for breasts and 180°F for legs and thighs.

> **REYNOLDS KITCHENS TIP**
>
> *Spread crushed potato chips—or other dry crumb coating—on a sheet of wax paper and then roll chicken pieces in it. The wax paper is large enough for easy rolling and cleanup is easy. Gather the leftover chips in the paper and toss the whole thing!*

Barbecue Chicken

5 to 6 chicken pieces (legs, thighs, breasts, or any combination)

⅔ cup barbecue sauce

PREP TIME
10 minutes

COOK TIME
40 minutes

MAKES
4 to 6 servings

1 Preheat the oven to 450°F. Line a 9-by-13-by-2-inch baking pan with non-stick aluminum foil, non-stick (dull) side facing up.

2 Rinse the chicken and pat dry. Coat both sides of the chicken pieces with about half of the barbecue sauce. Lay the chicken in the foil-lined pan. Reserve the rest of the barbecue sauce for basting.

3 Bake for 40 to 45 minutes, brushing the top of the chicken with barbecue sauce every 15 minutes, until the chicken is tender, the juices run clear, and an instant-read or meat thermometer registers 170°F for the breast and 180°F for the leg or thigh.

REYNOLDS KITCHENS TIP

Oven-barbecued chicken won't stick and bake on when you line the pan with non-stick foil.

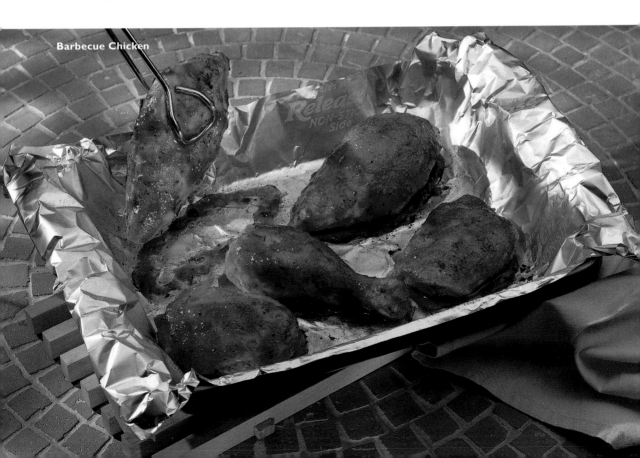

Barbecue Chicken

Chicken Baked-Your-Way

3 to 3½ pounds chicken, cut
into 6 to 8 pieces (breasts, legs,
thighs or any combination)

Seasoning Rub, see below

PREP TIME
15 minutes
COOK TIME
35 minutes
MAKES
4 to 8 servings

1 Preheat the oven to 400°F. Line a 9-by-13-by-2-inch pan with aluminum foil.

2 Remove the skin from the chicken pieces, if desired. Rinse the chicken and pat dry. Lay the chicken in the foil-lined pan.

3 Sprinkle and rub the seasoning rub of your choice over the chicken, turning to coat the pieces evenly.

4 Bake for 35 to 40 minutes or until the chicken is tender, the juices run clear, and an instant-read or meat thermometer registers 170°F for the breast or 180°F for the thighs and legs.

REYNOLDS KITCHENS TIP

Seasoning rubs are an easy way to add versatility to your meals and season your chicken the way you like it. Choose one of the following to turn any chicken meal into something special.

BARBECUE SEASONING RUB: Combine ¾ teaspoon salt and ¾ teaspoon sugar with ½ teaspoon of grated lemon peel, ½ teaspoon garlic powder, ½ teaspoon onion powder, ½ teaspoon chili powder, ½ teaspoon paprika, ⅛ teaspoon cayenne pepper, and ⅛ teaspoon black pepper.

ASIAN SEASONING RUB: Combine ¼ cup packed brown sugar with 2 tablespoons soy sauce, ½ teaspoon garlic powder, and ¼ teaspoon cayenne pepper.

HERB SEASONING RUB: Combine 3 teaspoons dried basil leaves and 1½ teaspoons seasoned salt with 1 teaspoon garlic powder and ¼ teaspoon pepper.

SOUTHWESTERN SEASONING RUB: Combine 1 teaspoon chili powder, 1 teaspoon ground cumin, and 1 teaspoon garlic salt with ½ teaspoon dried oregano leaves and ½ teaspoon black pepper.

CAJUN SEASONING RUB: Combine 1½ teaspoons garlic powder with 1 teaspoon salt, ¾ teaspoon dried basil, ¾ teaspoon dried thyme, ¾ teaspoon cayenne pepper, ½ teaspoon onion powder, and ¼ teaspoon black pepper.

CARIBBEAN SEASONING RUB: Combine 1 tablespoon vegetable oil with 2 teaspoons ground allspice, 1 teaspoon dried thyme, 1 teaspoon salt, 1 teaspoon paprika, and 1 teaspoon cayenne pepper.

Sweet-and-Sour Chicken

PREP TIME
10 minutes

COOK TIME
30 minutes

MAKES
4 servings

2 tablespoons flour

$1/4$ cup packed brown sugar

$1/4$ cup vinegar

2 tablespoons soy sauce

4 skinless, boneless chicken breast halves

One 20-ounce can pineapple chunks in juice, drained

1 medium green bell pepper, cut in rings or strips

Hot cooked rice

1 Preheat the oven to 350°F. Add the flour to a large oven bag, shake the bag to distribute the flour, and put in a 9-by-13-by-2-inch baking pan.

2 Add sugar, vinegar, and soy sauce to the bag. Squeeze the bag to blend the ingredients with the flour. Rinse the chicken and pat dry. Add the pineapple, bell pepper, and chicken, and turn to coat the chicken with sauce. Arrange the chicken in an even layer in the bag.

3 Close the bag with the provided nylon tie and cut six $1/2$-inch slits in the top.

4 Bake for 30 to 35 minutes, or until the chicken is tender, the juices run clear, and an instant-read or meat thermometer registers 170°F. Serve over hot rice.

REYNOLDS KITCHENS TIP

This recipe is great in the microwave. Put the ingredients in the bag and lay the bag in a 9-by-13-by-2-inch microwave-safe dish. Arrange the chicken with meaty portions toward the outside. Close and tie the bag as directed above and microwave on high power for 5 minutes. Rotate the dish and microwave on high power for 5 to 7 minutes longer, or until an instant-read meat thermometer registers 170°F. Let the chicken stand in the oven bag 5 minutes before serving.

Chicken Cacciatore

2 tablespoons flour

One 1-ounce envelope onion soup mix

One 14$\frac{1}{2}$-ounce can whole tomatoes, undrained

One 8-ounce can tomato sauce

One 4$\frac{1}{2}$-ounce jar sliced mushrooms, drained

2 teaspoons dried oregano

$\frac{1}{2}$ teaspoon garlic powder

6 skinless chicken pieces

Hot cooked spaghetti

PREP TIME
10 minutes

COOK TIME
50 minutes

MAKES
4 servings

1 Preheat the oven to 350°F. Add the flour to a large oven bag, shake the bag to distribute the flour, and put in a 9-by-13-by-2-inch baking pan.

2 Add the soup mix, tomatoes, tomato sauce, mushrooms, oregano, and garlic powder to the bag, and squeeze the bag to blend the ingredients.

3 Rinse the chicken and pat dry. Add the chicken to the bag and turn the bag to coat the chicken with sauce. Arrange the ingredients in an even layer in the bag.

4 Close the bag with the provided nylon tie and cut six ½-inch slits in the top.

5 Bake for about 50 minutes or until the chicken is tender, the juices run clear, and an instant-read or meat thermometer registers 170°F for the breast or 180°F for the thighs and legs. Serve over hot spaghetti.

REYNOLDS KITCHENS TIP

Put the oven bag in a baking pan before putting the food in the bag. Once the chicken and other ingredients are in the bag, gently turn the bag to coat the food with the sauce and seasonings.

Chicken Thighs with Vegetable Stuffing

PREP TIME

10 minutes

COOK TIME

35 minutes

MAKES

3 to 4 servings

1 tablespoon flour

$^1/_2$ cup shredded carrots

$^1/_2$ cup coarsely chopped broccoli

$^1/_2$ cup herb-seasoned stuffing mix

1 egg, beaten

6 chicken thighs

2 tablespoons grated Parmesan cheese

$^1/_2$ teaspoon paprika

1　Preheat the oven to 375°F. Add the flour to a large oven bag, shake the bag to distribute the flour, and put in a 9-by-13-by-2-inch baking pan.

2　In a mixing bowl, combine the carrots, broccoli, stuffing mix, and egg. Set aside.

3　Rinse the chicken thighs and pat dry. Loosen the skin over the thigh meat by slipping your fingers or a dull kitchen knife under the skin. Leave one side attached. Put the thighs on a sheet of wax paper.

4　Spoon about ¼ cup of the vegetable-stuffing mixture evenly under the skin of each thigh. Stretch the skin over the stuffing to hold it in place.

5　Combine the Parmesan and paprika on a sheet of wax paper. Sprinkle over the chicken. Transfer the chicken to the oven bag and arrange in an even layer.

6　Close the bag with the provided nylon tie and cut six ½-inch slits in the top.

7　Bake for 35 to 40 minutes, or until the chicken is tender, the juices run clear, and an instant-read or meat thermometer registers 180°F.

> **REYNOLDS KITCHENS TIP**
>
> *As much as possible, arrange food in an even layer in the oven bag. This promotes even cooking. It's easy and mess-free to do this by turning and pushing gently on the food from the outside of the bag.*

Quick-and-Easy Parmesan Chicken

2 tablespoons flour

One 14-ounce jar spaghetti sauce

4 skinless, boneless chicken breast halves

1 cup shredded mozzarella cheese

1/4 cup grated Parmesan cheese

One 8-ounce package spaghetti, cooked, drained

PREP TIME
10 minutes

COOK TIME
25 minutes

MAKES
4 servings

1 Preheat the oven to 350°F. Add the flour to a large oven bag, shake the bag to distribute the flour, and put in a 9-by-13-by-2-inch baking pan.

2 Add the spaghetti sauce to the bag and squeeze the bag to blend the sauce with the flour.

3 Rinse the chicken and pat dry. Add to the bag and turn the bag to coat the chicken with sauce. Arrange the chicken in an even layer in the bag.

4 Close the bag with the provided nylon tie and cut six 1/2-inch slits in the top.

5 Bake for 25 to 30 minutes, or until the chicken is tender, the juices run clear, and an instant-read or meat thermometer registers 170°F. Carefully cut the bag open and sprinkle the chicken with both cheeses. Let the chicken stand until the cheese melts. Serve over the spaghetti.

REYNOLDS KITCHENS TIP

The oven bag ties are found in the box, tucked inside the recipe-cooking chart brochure enclosed in every package. After securing the bag with the tie, cut six slits in the top of the bag to allow steam to escape.

Pizzeria Chicken Packets

Four 4- to 6-ounce skinless, boneless chicken breast halves

1 cup pizza or spaghetti sauce

1 cup shredded mozzarella cheese

20 thin slices pepperoni

1 medium green bell pepper, seeded and chopped

1 small onion, chopped

Grated Parmesan cheese (optional)

PREP TIME
10 minutes

COOK TIME
20 minutes

MAKES
4 servings

1 Preheat the oven to 450°F or prepare a charcoal or gas grill so that the coals are medium-hot.

2 Lay four 12-by-18-inch sheets of non-stick aluminum foil on a countertop, non-stick (dull) side facing up. Rinse the chicken and pat dry. Put a chicken breast in the center of each sheet and spoon pizza sauce over each one. Sprinkle with cheese and then top with pepperoni, bell pepper, and onion.

3 Bring up the sides of the foil. Double fold the top and ends to seal the packets, leaving room for heat circulation inside. Repeat to make 4 packets. If using the oven, put the packets on a cookie sheet.

4 Put the cookie sheet in the oven or slide the packets onto the grill rack. Bake for 20 to 24 minutes or grill for 12 to 14 minutes in a covered grill, or until the chicken is tender, the juices run clear, and an instant-read or meat thermometer registers 170°F. Sprinkle with grated Parmesan cheese before serving, if desired.

Pizzeria Chicken Packets

Foil Tent–Roasted Turkey

One 8- to 24-pound turkey, thawed

Your favorite stuffing (optional)

Vegetable oil or butter

PREP TIME
10 minutes

COOK TIME
2½ to 5 hours

MAKES
10 to 30 servings

1 Preheat the oven to 325°F. Line a 2-inch or deeper roasting pan with heavy duty aluminum foil and set aside.

2 Remove the neck and giblets from the turkey's cavity and discard or reserve for another use. Rinse the turkey and pat it dry. Put the turkey in the foil-lined roasting pan.

3 If desired, loosely stuff the turkey with the stuffing of your choice. Brush the turkey with oil and insert a meat thermometer into the thickest part of the inner thigh without touching the bone.

4 Make a foil tent by putting a large sheet of folded foil over the turkey, leaving about one inch between the top of the turkey and the foil tent for heat circulation. Crimp the foil along the long sides of the pan.

5 Roast for 2½ to 3 hours for an 8- to 12-pound turkey; 3 to 3½ hours for a 12- to 16-pound turkey; 3½ to 4 hours for a 16- to 20-pound turkey; and 4 to 5 hours for a 20- to 24-pound turkey. The turkey is done when the meat is tender, juices run clear, and the meat thermometer registers 180°F. Add 30 minutes to the total roasting time for stuffed turkeys.

6 To brown the turkey, remove the foil tent after 1 hour of roasting. When the turkey is done, tent it with foil and let it stand for 15 minutes for easy slicing.

REYNOLDS KITCHENS TIP

Tenting a turkey with a large sheet of aluminum foil ensures even cooking within the recommended time period. Removing the tent after an hour of roasting encourages good browning. And, tenting the bird during its standing period helps hold in the heat.

The best guide for determining when a turkey is done is to rely on an instant-read or meat thermometer. For a whole turkey, insert the thermometer into the thickest part of the inner thigh so that it does not touch the bone.

If you don't have a thermometer, press the thickest part of the drumstick with protected fingers. The turkey is done if the meat feels soft and the drumstick twists easily in the socket. Or, insert a long-tined fork into the thickest part of the thigh to see if the juices run clear, which indicates the turkey is done.

110 **Pat and Betty's No-Fuss Cooking**

Foil Wrapped–Roasted Turkey

One 8- to 24-pound turkey, thawed

Your favorite stuffing (optional)

Vegetable oil or butter

PREP TIME
10 minutes

COOK TIME
1½ to 3¾ hours

MAKES
10 to 30 servings

1 Preheat the oven to 450°F.

2 Remove the neck and giblets from the turkey's cavity and discard or reserve for another use. Rinse the turkey and pat dry. If desired, loosely stuff the turkey with the stuffing of your choice. Brush with oil.

3 Tear off a sheet of heavy duty aluminum foil 2½ times longer than the turkey. Center the turkey lengthwise on the foil. Close the foil loosely by overlapping the ends. Turn up short sides of foil to hold in juices. Do not seal the foil so that it's airtight.

4 Transfer the foil-wrapped turkey to a 2-inch or deeper roasting pan. Insert a meat thermometer through the foil into the thickest part of the inner thigh, without touching the bone.

5 Roast for 1½ to 2¼ hours for an 8- to 12-pound turkey; 2¼ to 2¾ hours for a 12- to 16-pound turkey; 2¾ to 3¼ hours for a 16- to 20-pound turkey; and 3¼ to 3¾ hours for a 20- to 24-pound turkey. The turkey is done when the meat is tender, juices run clear, and the meat thermometer registers 180°F. Add 30 minutes to the total roasting time for stuffed turkeys.

6 To brown the turkey, open and turn back the foil during the final 30 minutes of roasting. When the turkey is done, tent it with foil and let it stand for 15 minutes for easy slicing.

> ## REYNOLDS KITCHENS TIP
>
> *For generous servings of turkey plus leftovers, allow one pound per person. We recommend wrapping a turkey in foil for a moist and tender bird. It reduces the roasting time, and results in a golden brown turkey with some variation in color. The skin will not be as crisp as it is when roasted under a foil tent in a more traditional method.*

Herbed Turkey Breast

PREP TIME
10 minutes

GRILL TIME
1 hour

MAKES
6 to 9 servings

¼ cup water

1 tablespoon flour

1½ teaspoons dried rosemary

1½ teaspoons dried thyme

1½ teaspoons dried tarragon

One 5- to 7-pound bone-in turkey breast, thawed

Seasoned salt and pepper

1 Prepare a charcoal or gas grill so that the coals are medium-hot or preheat the oven to 450°F. Spray the inside of a large extra heavy duty foil bag with cooking spray. If cooking in the oven, put the bag in a 1-inch-deep pan.

2 In a small bowl, mix together the water and flour, and pour this into the bag.

3 Combine the rosemary, thyme, and tarragon on a sheet of wax paper. Rinse the turkey and pat it dry. Rub herbs into the turkey breast, turning it to coat evenly. Sprinkle with salt and pepper, and then put the turkey breast in the foil bag. Double fold the bag to seal.

4 Slide the bag onto the grill rack or put the baking pan in the oven. Grill for 1 to 1½ hours or bake for 1½ to 1¾ hours. The turkey is done when the meat is tender, the juices run clear, and an instant-read or meat thermometer registers 170°F.

5 Hold the bag with oven mitts and cut it open with a knife. Carefully fold back the top of the bag so that steam can escape. Let the turkey breast stand in the bag for about 15 minutes before slicing.

REYNOLDS KITCHENS TIP

Thaw turkey in the refrigerator. Do not let it thaw at room temperature on the kitchen counter—you want to keep the turkey cold during thawing. Plan ahead, since it can take days for a frozen turkey to thaw. Put the turkey in its original wrapping on a tray and refrigerate. For whole turkeys, allow 24 hours for every four to five pounds. For a turkey breast, figure on one to two days; turkey parts need 24 hours in the fridge.

Two-at-Once Roasted Turkey Breast

PREP TIME
10 minutes

COOK TIME
1½ hours

MAKES
10 to 20 servings

1 tablespoon flour

4 stalks celery, sliced

2 medium onions, cut in eighths

Two 4- to 8-pound bone-in turkey breasts, thawed

Vegetable oil

Seasoned salt

Black pepper

1 Preheat the oven to 350°F. Add the flour to a turkey size oven bag, shake the bag to distribute the flour, and put in a 2-inch-deep roasting pan.

2 Put the celery and onions in the bag.

3 Rinse the turkey breasts and pat them dry. Brush with oil and sprinkle with seasoned salt and pepper. Put the turkey breasts in the bag on top of the vegetables.

4 Close the bag with the provided nylon tie and cut six ½-inch slits in the top.

5 Bake for 1½ to 2 hours, or until the meat is tender, the juices run clear, and an instant-read or meat thermometer registers 170°F. Let the turkey breasts stand in the bag for about 15 minutes before slicing.

> **REYNOLDS KITCHENS TIP**
>
> *Roasting two turkey breasts at once epitomizes our philosophy of "cooking once, eating twice." Eat one for dinner and save the other for sandwiches and casseroles later in the week. Choose breasts that are close to the same size. For roasting time, use the time recommended for the larger turkey breast and add 15 minutes.*

Oven Bag–Roasted Turkey

1 tablespoon flour

2 stalks celery, sliced

1 medium onion, sliced

One 12- to 24-pound turkey, thawed

Your favorite stuffing (optional)

Vegetable oil or butter

PREP TIME
10 minutes

COOK TIME
2 to 3½ hours

MAKES
15 to 30 servings

| Preheat the oven to 350°F. Add the flour to a turkey size oven bag, shake the bag to distribute the flour, and put in a 2-inch or deeper roasting pan. Spray the inside

Oven Bag–Roasted Turkey

of the oven bag with cooking spray to prevent sticking, if desired.

2 Add the celery and onion to the bag.

3 Remove the neck and giblets from the turkey's cavity and discard or reserve for another use. Rinse the turkey and pat dry. If desired, loosely stuff the turkey with the stuffing of your choice and then brush with oil. Put the turkey on top of the vegetables.

4 Close the bag with the provided nylon tie and cut six ½-inch slits in the top.

5 Roast for 2 to 2½ hours for a 12- to 16-pound turkey; 2½ to 3 hours for a 16- to 20-pound turkey; and 3 to 3½ hours for a 20- to 24-pound turkey. The turkey is done when the meat is tender, juices run clear, and an instant-read or meat thermometer registers 180°F for the thigh. Add 30 minutes to the total roasting time for stuffed turkeys.

6 When the turkey is done, let it stand in the bag for 15 minutes for easy slicing. If the turkey sticks when you try to take it from the bag, gently loosen the bag from the turkey.

REYNOLDS KITCHENS TIP

Roasting a turkey in a turkey size oven bag is so easy and much faster than open pan roasting. The oven bag holds in moist heat so your turkey will be tender and juicy, even without basting. And best of all, there is no messy pan to scrub.

While we recommend thawing a frozen turkey in the refrigerator, thawing it in cold water is also an acceptable method. Submerge the turkey or turkey parts, still in the original wrapping, in a sink or large tub of cold water. Change the water as often as needed to keep it cold. This is very important! For a whole turkey, allow about 30 minutes to the pound; for a turkey breast, allow 4 to 8 hours to thaw; for turkey parts, allow 2 to 2½ hours.

Do not thaw a turkey at room temperature on the countertop. For safety, it's important to keep it cold during defrosting. We recommend the refrigerator method (page 112) or the cold water method (above).

Turkey Breast and Gravy

PREP TIME
5 minutes

COOK TIME
1¼ hours

MAKES
5 to 10 servings

1 tablespoon flour

Two ⅞-ounce packets turkey gravy mix

¾ cup water

One 4- to 8-pound bone-in turkey breast, thawed

Salt and pepper

2 medium onions, quartered

1 Preheat the oven to 350°F. Add the flour to a large oven bag, shake the bag to distribute the flour, and put in a 9-by-13-by-2-inch baking pan.

2 Add the gravy mix and water to the bag and squeeze the bag to blend the flour and gravy.

3 Rinse the turkey breast and pat dry. Sprinkle with salt and pepper and put in the bag. Arrange the onion quarters around the turkey.

4 Close the bag with the provided nylon tie and cut six ½-inch slits in the top.

5 Bake for 1¼ to 2 hours or until the meat is tender, the juices run clear, and an instant-read or meat thermometer registers 170°F. Let the turkey breast stand in the bag for about 10 minutes before slicing. Stir the gravy before serving.

> **REYNOLDS KITCHENS TIP**
>
> *Leftover turkey can be refrigerated for later use. Once it's cooled, slice the meat and wrap it, in sandwich-size portions, in aluminum foil or pop-up foil sheets.*

• • •

Florentine Turkey Meat Loaf

PREP TIME
14 minutes

COOK TIME
45 minutes

MAKES
6 to 8 servings

1¼ pounds ground turkey

1 cup spaghetti sauce

½ cup Italian-seasoned bread crumbs

½ cup finely chopped onion

2 eggs, slightly beaten, or 1 egg and 2 egg whites

2 tablespoons grated Parmesan cheese

½ teaspoon fennel seed, crushed (optional)

One 10-ounce package frozen chopped spinach, thawed and well drained

1 cup low-fat shredded mozzarella cheese

1 Preheat the oven to 350°F. Line an 8- or 9-inch loaf pan with non-stick aluminum foil, non-stick (dull) side facing up.

2 In a mixing bowl, combine the turkey with ¼ cup of the spaghetti sauce, the bread crumbs, onion, eggs, Parmesan cheese, and fennel seed, if using. Use a large spoon or your hands to mix the ingredients well.

3 Press half the turkey into the foil-lined pan. With the back of a spoon, press a 1-inch-deep indentation down the center, leaving a 1-inch wide border on all sides.

4 In another bowl, toss together the spinach and ¾ cup of the mozzarella cheese. Spoon the spinach mixture into the indentation. Press the remaining turkey mixture evenly over the top, pressing gently to seal the edges along the sides of the pan.

5 Bake for 45 to 50 minutes. Spoon the remaining spaghetti sauce over the meat loaf and sprinkle with the rest of the mozzarella cheese, if desired. Bake for about 15 minutes longer or until the meat is cooked through, the sauce is bubbling, and the cheese melts. Let stand for 10 minutes before serving.

> **REYNOLDS KITCHENS TIP**
>
> *Baking turkey meat loaf in a pan lined with non-stick aluminum foil means the meat loaf slices will lift easily from the pan. Be sure to let the meat loaf stand for at least 10 minutes before slicing so it holds together.*

Florentine Turkey Meat Loaf

Moroccan-Style Turkey Breast

1 tablespoon flour

2 teaspoons garlic salt

1 1/2 teaspoons ground cumin

1 teaspoon ground cinnamon

1/2 teaspoon cayenne pepper

One 4- to 8-pound bone-in turkey breast

2 tablespoons lemon juice

Hot cooked couscous or rice

PREP TIME
15 minutes

COOK TIME
1 1/4 hours

MAKES
4 to 8 servings

1 Preheat the oven to 350°F. Add the flour to a large oven bag, shake the bag to distribute the flour, and put in a 9-by-13-by-2-inch baking pan.

2 Combine the garlic salt, cumin, cinnamon, and cayenne pepper on a sheet of wax paper.

3 Rinse the turkey breast and pat it dry. Loosen the skin over the breast meat by slipping your fingers or a dull kitchen knife under the skin. (Do not detach the skin completely from the turkey.) Sprinkle half of the spice mixture directly on the meat under the skin. Turn the breast over and sprinkle the remaining spices in the turkey's cavity. Put the turkey in the oven bag, skin-side up. Drizzle lemon juice over the turkey breast.

4 Close the bag with the provided nylon tie and cut six 1/2-inch slits in the top.

5 Bake for 1 1/4 to 2 hours, or until the meat is tender, the juices run clear, and an instant-read or meat thermometer registers 170°F.

6 Let the turkey breast stand in the bag for about 15 minutes before slicing. Strain the juices and serve them, spooned over the hot couscous or rice, alongside the turkey.

Today's Beef Roast

PREP TIME
10 minutes

COOK TIME
1½ hours

MAKES
7 to 8 servings

¼ cup flour

One 14¼-ounce can Italian-style stewed tomatoes, undrained

One 1-ounce envelope onion soup mix

¼ teaspoon pepper

One 3- to 3½-pound boneless beef rump or round tip roast

4 medium potatoes, quartered

4 medium carrots, cut into 2-inch pieces

1 Preheat the oven to 325°F. Add the flour to a large oven bag, shake the bag to distribute the flour, and put in a 9-by-13-by-2-inch baking pan.

2 Add the tomatoes, soup mix, and pepper to the bag and squeeze to blend them with the flour. Add the roast to the bag and turn the bag to coat the meat with the sauce. Arrange the potatoes and carrots around the roast.

3 Close the bag with the provided nylon tie and cut six ½-inch slits in the top.

4 Bake for 1½ to 2 hours, or until the meat is tender and an instant-read meat thermometer registers 160°F for rump roast and 145°F for round tip roast. Stir the gravy before serving.

> **REYNOLDS KITCHENS TIP**
>
> *Place the baking pan on the center rack in the oven to provide ample room for the bag to expand during cooking without touching the oven walls or racks.*

· · ·

London Broil au Jus

PREP TIME
10 minutes

COOK TIME
55 minutes

MAKES
12 to 14 servings

1 tablespoon flour

½ cup water

One 3- to 3½-pound beef London broil (top round steak), about 1½ inches thick

1 teaspoon dried thyme

½ teaspoon salt

¼ teaspoon black pepper

1 Preheat the oven to 325°F. Add the flour to a large oven bag, shake the bag to distribute the flour, and put in a 9-by-13-by-2-inch baking pan.

2 Add the water to the bag and squeeze the bag to blend it with the flour. Sprinkle

the beef with thyme, salt, and pepper, and rub the seasonings into the meat. Put the roast in the bag and turn the bag to coat the meat.

3 Close the bag with the provided nylon tie and cut six ½-inch slits in the top.

4 Bake for 55 to 60 minutes or until an instant-read or meat thermometer registers 145°F.

5 Carefully open the bag and transfer the beef to a cutting board or serving platter. Slice the meat on the diagonal across the grain. Stir the juices in the bag and spoon them over the sliced beef.

REYNOLDS KITCHENS TIP

After removing the meat from the bag, let any remaining juices in the bag cool. Gather the bag, lift it from the baking pan, and toss it. Easy!

. . .

Homestyle Pot Roast

¼ cup flour

⅔ cup water

One 1-ounce envelope onion soup mix

One 3- to 3½-pound boneless beef chuck pot roast

6 to 8 small whole red potatoes

1 medium onion, cut in quarters

One 16-ounce package peeled fresh baby carrots

Chopped parsley (optional)

PREP TIME
15 minutes

COOK TIME
2½ to 3 hours

MAKES
7 to 8 servings

1 Preheat the oven to 325°F. Add the flour to a large oven bag, shake the bag to distribute the flour, and put in a 9-by-13-by-2-inch baking pan.

2 Add the water and soup mix to the bag and squeeze the bag to blend them with the flour. Put the roast in the bag and turn the bag to coat the meat with the sauce. Arrange the potatoes, onion, and carrots around the roast.

3 Close the bag with the provided nylon tie and cut six ½-inch slits in the top.

REYNOLDS KITCHENS TIP

Squeeze the oven bag to blend the flour and other ingredients together. This makes the sauce smoother and prevents the flour from clumping at the bottom of the bag.

4 Bake for 2½ to 3 hours, or until the beef is tender.

5 Open the bag carefully and transfer the meat and vegetables to a serving platter. Stir the gravy and spoon it over the meat and vegetables. Sprinkle the meat and vegetables with parsley before serving, if desired.

Homestyle Pot Roast

Orange-Teriyaki Beef Roast

PREP TIME
15 minutes

CHILL TIME
1½ hours

COOK TIME
35 minutes

MAKES
8 servings

2 tablespoons flour

½ cup orange juice

½ cup teriyaki sauce

¼ cup packed brown sugar

3 cloves garlic, minced

1 teaspoon grated orange peel

½ teaspoon crushed red pepper flakes

One 2-pound beef top round roast, about 1-inch thick

Hot cooked rice (optional)

¼ cup sliced green onions

1 Add the flour to a large oven bag, shake the bag to distribute the flour, and put in a 9-by-13-by-2-inch baking pan.

2 Add the orange juice, teriyaki sauce, brown sugar, garlic, orange peel, and crushed red pepper to the oven bag, and squeeze the bag to blend them with the flour. Put the roast in the bag and turn the bag to coat the meat with the sauce.

Orange-Teriyaki Beef Roast

3 Close the bag with the provided nylon tie. Put the bag, still in the pan, in the refrigerator to marinate for 1½ to 2 hours.

4 Preheat the oven to 325°F.

5 Cut six ½-inch slits in the top of the bag. Bake for 35 to 45 minutes or until an instant-read or meat thermometer registers 145°F.

6 Open the bag carefully. Transfer the meat to a serving platter and slice thinly. Stir the sauce and serve it spooned over rice, if desired. Serve the meat topped with chopped green onions.

REYNOLDS KITCHENS TIP

Tuck the ends and corners of the oven bag inside the baking pan so that the bag does not hang over the baking pan.

. . .

Easy Corned Beef Brisket

| PREP TIME |
| 15 minutes |
| COOK TIME |
| 2½ to 3 hours |
| MAKES |
| 7 to 9 servings |

1 tablespoon flour

One 2½- to 3-pound corned beef brisket

1 medium carrot, sliced

1 stalk celery, sliced

1 medium onion, sliced

1 small orange, sliced

1 cup water

1 tablespoon pickling spice

1 Preheat the oven to 325°F. Add the flour to a large oven bag, shake the bag to distribute the flour, and put in a 9-by-13-by-2-inch baking pan.

2 Rinse the brisket under cool running water to remove any surface salt and then put the brisket in the oven bag. Arrange the carrot, celery, onion, and orange slices around the brisket. Pour the water over the brisket and sprinkle with pickling spice.

3 Close the bag with the provided nylon tie and cut six ½-inch slits in the top.

4 Bake for 2½ to 3 hours, or until the brisket is tender. Let stand in the bag for 5 minutes.

5 Open the bag carefully and transfer the brisket to a cutting board or serving platter before slicing on the diagonal across the grain. Discard any vegetables and drippings.

REYNOLDS KITCHENS TIP

The brisket is cut from behind the lower foreshank and nearly always is cut into flat half briskets. If cured, brisket is called corned beef. Whether cured or not, brisket requires slow, moist cooking—ideal for an oven bag.

Creole Eye of Round Roast

3 tablespoons flour

One 14½-ounce can diced tomatoes with onions and garlic

2 to 3 teaspoons Creole seasoning

One 2- to 2½-pound beef eye of round roast

2 stalks celery, cut in ½-inch slices

1 medium green bell pepper, cut in strips

Hot cooked rice (optional)

PREP TIME
10 minutes

COOK TIME
1 hour

MAKES
8 to 10 servings

1 Preheat the oven to 325°F. Add the flour to a large oven bag, shake the bag to distribute the flour, and put in a 9-by-13-by-2-inch baking pan.

2 Add the tomatoes and Creole seasoning to the oven bag and squeeze the bag to blend them with the flour. Put the roast, celery, and bell pepper in the bag and turn

Creole Eye of Round Roast

the bag to coat the meat with the sauce. Arrange the ingredients in an even layer in the oven bag.

3 Close the bag with the provided nylon tie and cut six ½-inch slits in the top.

4 Bake for 1 to 1¼ hours, or until an instant-read or meat thermometer registers 145°F.

5 Open the bag carefully and transfer the meat and vegetables to a serving platter. Stir the sauce and serve it spooned over the rice, if desired. Slice the beef thinly and serve.

...

Fiesta Eye of Round Roast

¼ cup flour

One 16-ounce jar chunky salsa

1 clove garlic, crushed

One 3- to 3½-pound boneless beef eye of round roast

7 medium carrots, diagonally sliced

4 medium red potatoes, cut in quarters

1 green or yellow bell pepper, cut in strips

1 medium onion, cut in thin wedges

PREP TIME
15 minutes
COOK TIME
2 to 2½ hours
MAKES
12 to 14 servings

1 Preheat the oven to 325°F. Add the flour to a large oven bag, shake the bag to distribute the flour, and put in a 9-by-13-by-2-inch baking pan.

2 Add the salsa and garlic to the oven bag and squeeze the bag to blend them with the flour. Put the roast in the bag and turn the bag to coat the roast with the salsa. Arrange the carrots, potatoes, bell pepper, and onion around the roast.

3 Close the bag with the provided nylon tie and cut six ½-inch slits in the top.

4 Bake for 2 to 2½ hours, or until the meat is tender and an instant-read or meat thermometer registers 145°F. Let the roast stand in the oven bag for 5 minutes for easy slicing.

5 Open the bag carefully and transfer the meat and vegetables to a serving platter before slicing.

REYNOLDS KITCHENS TIP

If you prefer to use a conventional meat thermometer, insert it through one of the slits in the top of the oven bag and into the meat before you put the baking pan in the oven.

Easy Beef Stroganoff

3 tablespoons flour

One 10¾-ounce can cream of mushroom soup, undiluted

One 4-ounce can sliced mushrooms, undrained

1 small onion, thinly sliced

¼ cup light sour cream

1½ pounds boneless beef sirloin steak, cut in thin strips

Hot cooked noodles

PREP TIME
10 minutes

COOK TIME
40 minutes

MAKES
4 servings

1 Preheat the oven to 350°F. Add the flour to a large oven bag, shake the bag to distribute the flour, and put in a 9-by-13-by-2-inch baking pan.

2 Add the soup, mushrooms, onion, and sour cream to the oven bag and squeeze to blend with the flour. Put the meat in the bag and turn the bag to coat the meat with the sauce. Arrange the ingredients in an even layer in the oven bag.

3 Close the bag with the provided nylon tie and cut six ½-inch slits in the top.

4 Bake for 40 to 45 minutes, or until the meat is tender.

5 Open the bag carefully. Stir well and serve spooned over hot noodles.

> **REYNOLDS KITCHENS TIP**
>
> *When ready to open the bag, use kitchen shears and cut open the top of the bag. Don't cut too far toward the end of the bag or the sauce will run out.*

. . .

Asian Beef with Snow Peas

½ cup soy sauce

3 tablespoons water

2 tablespoons packed brown sugar

1½ tablespoons sesame oil or vegetable oil

2 teaspoons grated fresh ginger

2 teaspoons minced garlic

One 1¼-pound boneless beef sirloin steak, about 1½ inches thick

½ pound snow peas or sugar snap peas

2 tablespoons water

1 tablespoon sesame seeds

Hot cooked rice

PREP TIME
20 minutes

COOK TIME
10 minutes

MAKES
4 servings

1 In a small glass baking dish, whisk together the soy sauce, water, brown sugar, 1 tablespoon of the oil, the ginger, and the garlic. Lay the steak in the dish and turn to coat with the marinade.

2 Cover the dish with plastic wrap and refrigerate for at least 2 hours and up to 12 hours.

3 Preheat the broiler.

4 Remove the steak from the marinade and let the marinade drip back into the dish. Discard the marinade.

5 Broil the steak for 5 to 7 minutes on each side for medium-rare meat. Slice thinly and arrange over the hot rice.

6 Meanwhile, put the snow peas and water in a 2-quart microwave-safe dish. Cover with plastic wrap and turn back one corner to vent. Microwave on high power for 5 minutes, stirring once after 3 minutes.

7 Toss the snow peas with the remaining ½ tablespoon of oil and the sesame seeds. Serve these spooned over the steak and rice.

> **REYNOLDS KITCHENS TIP**
>
> *To make cleanup a snap, line the broiler pan with non-stick aluminum foil with the non-stick (dull) side facing up. Cut slits in foil at the broiler rack openings for good heat circulation.*

...

Spicy Pepper Steak

PREP TIME
15 minutes
GRILL TIME
25 minutes
MAKES
6 to 8 servings

1½ cups sliced celery

1 medium red bell pepper, cut in strips

½ cup chopped onion

One 1- to 1.2-ounce envelope brown gravy mix or peppercorn sauce mix

1 tablespoon flour

½ cup water

1½ to 2 pounds beef flank steak, cut in 5 to 6 pieces

Seasoned salt

1½ to 2 teaspoons freshly ground black pepper

1 Prepare a charcoal or gas grill so that the coals are medium-hot, or preheat the oven to 450°F. Put a large extra heavy duty foil bag in a 1-inch-deep pan.

2 Arrange the celery, red bell pepper, and onion in the bag in an even layer.

3 In a small bowl, stir the gravy mix, flour, and water until smooth. Pour over the vegetables in the bag. Sprinkle the steak pieces with seasoned salt and then press black pepper into the top and sides of each piece. Put the steak pieces on top of the vegetables in an even layer. Double fold the bag to seal.

4 Slide the bag onto the grill or leave it in the pan and place it in the oven. Grill for 25 to 27 minutes in a covered grill or bake for 55 to 60 minutes.

5 Hold the bag with oven mitts and cut it open with a knife. Carefully fold back the top of the bag so that steam can escape. Stir the vegetables and serve them spooned over the steak pieces.

REYNOLDS
KITCHENS TIP

For best results, make sure the coals are medium-hot before sliding the foil bag onto the grill rack. This means the charcoal or briquettes should be covered with a thin layer of gray ash and glow deep red below the ash.

Spicy Pepper Steak

Chimichurri Steak Strips

PREP TIME
30 minutes

GRILL TIME
4 minutes

MAKES
4 servings

CHIMICHURRI SAUCE

1 cup fresh parsley

3 cloves garlic

1/4 cup olive oil

1 tablespoon red wine vinegar

1 tablespoon fresh lemon juice

1/2 teaspoon dried oregano

1/4 teaspoon crushed red pepper flakes

1/4 teaspoon salt

1/4 teaspoon freshly ground black pepper

STEAK STRIPS

1 pound boneless beef sirloin steak, cut diagonally in 1/4-inch-wide strips

2 teaspoons olive oil

1 teaspoon steak-seasoning spice blend

1 To make the chimichurri sauce, put the parsley, garlic, oil, vinegar, lemon juice, oregano, crushed red pepper flakes, salt, and pepper in a blender or food processor. Blend until smooth.

2 Lay the steak strips in a shallow glass dish. Add the oil and spice blend and turn the steak several times to coat. Cover with plastic wrap and set aside while preparing the grill or preheating the oven. (Do not leave the meat at room temperature for more than 20 minutes; if you must wait before cooking, refrigerate the steak.) Lift the meat from the marinade and let any liquid still clinging to the meat drip back into the dish. Discard the marinade.

3 Prepare a charcoal or gas grill so that the coals are medium-hot. Punch holes in a large sheet of non-stick aluminum foil and lay it on the grill rack, non-stick (dull) side facing up.

4 Arrange the steak strips on the foil and grill uncovered for 4 to 8 minutes, turning once, or until the steak reaches the desired degree of doneness. Remove the steak from the grill and let the juices cool before discarding the foil.

5 Serve the steak with chimichurri sauce.

> **REYNOLDS KITCHENS TIP**
>
> *Save dishes by placing raw meat on foil when carrying it to the grill. Put the cooked meat on a different sheet of foil to bring it to the table.*

Tex-Mex Meat Loaf Packets

1 pound extra lean ground beef

1/4 cup finely crushed tortilla chips

1/4 cup finely chopped onion

2 teaspoons chili powder

2 teaspoons Worcestershire sauce

1/2 teaspoon garlic salt

3/4 cup barbecue sauce

One 10-ounce package frozen whole kernel corn or one 15 1/4-ounce can whole kernel corn, drained

PREP TIME
15 minutes

COOK TIME
18 minutes

MAKES
4 servings

1 Preheat the oven to 450°F or prepare a charcoal or gas grill so that the coals are medium-hot.

2 Lay four 12-by-18-inch sheets of non-stick aluminum foil on the countertop, non-stick (dull) side facing up.

3 In a mixing bowl, combine the beef, tortilla chips, onion, chili powder, Worcestershire sauce, garlic salt, and 1/4 cup of the barbecue sauce. Use a large spoon or your

Tex-Mex Meat Loaf Packets

hands to mix the ingredients well. Form into 4 meat loaves and flatten each one slightly.

4 Put a meat loaf in the center of each sheet of foil. Top with corn and then spoon the remaining barbecue sauce over the corn and meat loaves.

5 Bring up the sides of the foil. Double fold the top and ends to seal the packets, leaving room for heat circulation inside. Repeat to make 4 packets. If using the oven, put the packets on a cookie sheet.

6 Put the cookie sheet in the oven or slide the packets onto the grill rack. Bake for 18 to 20 minutes or grill for 12 to 14 minutes in a covered grill or until an instant-read or meat thermometer registers 160°F when inserted in the center of a loaf.

...

Pork Tenderloin with Honey-Mustard Sauce

PREP TIME
15 minutes

COOK TIME
40 minutes

MAKES
5 to 6 servings

1 tablespoon flour	Dried basil
1/3 cup orange juice	Seasoned salt
2 tablespoons honey	4 medium carrots, sliced
2 tablespoons Dijon mustard	2 medium apples, cored and sliced in eighths
Two 3/4-pound pork tenderloins	

1 Preheat the oven to 350°F. Add the flour to a large oven bag, shake the bag to distribute the flour, and put in a 9-by-13-by-2-inch baking pan.

2 Add the orange juice, honey, and mustard to the bag, and squeeze the bag to blend the ingredients.

3 Sprinkle the tenderloin with the basil and seasoned salt. Put in the bag, tucking

the narrow end of each tenderloin under for even cooking. Arrange the carrot and apple slices around the tenderloins.

4 Close the bag with the provided nylon tie and cut six ½-inch slits in the top.

5 Bake for 40 to 45 minutes, or until an instant-read or meat thermometer registers 160°F.

6 Open the bag carefully. Transfer the tenderloin to a serving platter before slicing. Stir the sauce and spoon it over the sliced tenderloin.

Pork Tenderloin with Honey-Mustard Sauce

Pork Tenderloin Sauté

CHILL TIME
30 minutes

COOK TIME
8 minutes

MAKES
2 to 3 servings

1/4 cup olive oil

2 tablespoons soy sauce

2 tablespoons orange juice

1/4 teaspoon garlic powder

1/4 teaspoon dried rosemary

1/4 teaspoon freshly ground black pepper

One 3/4-pound pork tenderloin, sliced 3/4-inch thick

1 In a glass or ceramic bowl large enough to hold the pork, stir together the olive oil, soy sauce, orange juice, garlic powder, rosemary, and pepper. Add the pork and toss to coat with the marinade.

2 Cover the bowl with plastic wrap and refrigerate at least 30 minutes and up to 2 hours.

3 Spray a skillet with cooking spray. Remove pork from marinade, drain well, and put the pork in the skillet. Discard the marinade.

4 Sauté the pork for 8 to 10 minutes, over medium-high heat, turning several times, until browned, tender, and cooked through.

> **REYNOLDS KITCHENS TIP**
>
> *Stretched tightly over the top of a bowl, plastic wrap can help prevent messy spills.*

...

Pork Chops with Apple Stuffing

PREP TIME
15 minutes

COOK TIME
35 minutes

MAKES
4 servings

1 tablespoon flour

1 cup apple juice

1/2 teaspoon ground cinnamon

2 Golden Delicious apples, cored and sliced

2 cups stuffing mix for chicken

1/4 cup raisins

2 tablespoons butter or margarine, melted

Four 1/2-inch-thick pork loin chops, fat trimmed

1 Preheat the oven to 350°F. Add the flour to a large oven bag, shake the bag to distribute the flour, and put in a 9-by-13-by-2-inch baking pan.

2 Add 1/4 cup of the apple juice and the cinnamon to the bag and squeeze the bag to

blend with the flour. Add the apple slices and turn the bag to coat the apples with the juice. Push the apple slices to the outer edge of the bag.

3 In a mixing bowl, stir together the stuffing mix, the raisins, butter, and the remaining ¾ cup of apple juice. Let stand for about 1 minute to give the stuffing time to absorb the juice.

4 Arrange the pork chops in a single layer in the center of the bag. Mound the stuffing mixture evenly over the pork chops.

5 Close the bag with the provided nylon tie and cut six ½-inch slits in the top.

6 Bake for 35 to 40 minutes, or until the pork chops are cooked through and tender and the stuffing is browned and an instant-read or meat thermometer registers 160°F when inserted in the meatiest part of a pork chop.

REYNOLDS KITCHENS TIP

Oven bags give you the convenience of a seasoning bag but let you customize your meal with the seasonings you and your family like.

. . .

Spice-Rubbed Pork Tenderloin

PREP TIME
10 minutes

COOK TIME
20 minutes

MAKES
4 servings

1 tablespoon olive oil

1 teaspoon dried basil, crushed

½ teaspoon dried rosemary, crushed

⅛ teaspoon salt

One 12- to 16-ounce pork tenderloin

3 cloves garlic

One 2-by-1-inch piece lemon peel

1 Preheat the oven to 425°F. Line a shallow baking pan with an 18-by-20-inch sheet of heavy duty aluminum foil.

2 In a small bowl, mix together the olive oil, basil, rosemary, and salt.

3 Place the pork in the foil-lined pan. Rub the herb mixture over the tenderloin, turning to coat it evenly.

4 Cut each clove of garlic lengthwise into quarters. Cut the lemon peel crosswise

into twelve 1-inch long strips. Cut 12 small slits in top of roast and insert a garlic sliver and lemon strip in each one.

5   Roast for 20 to 30 minutes or until an instant-read or meat thermometer registers 160°F when inserted in the thickest part of the meat. Slice before serving.

REYNOLDS KITCHENS TIP

Be sure to cook pork to the recommended temperature. You want to cook it thoroughly but not overcook it so it's dry.

· · ·

Asian-Style Peach-Glazed Ribs

PREP TIME
15 minutes
GRILL TIME
1 hour
MAKES
4 servings

RIBS

3 pounds baby-back pork ribs

1/2 cup water

SEASONING RUB

1 tablespoon packed brown sugar

1 teaspoon 5-spice powder or ground ginger

1 teaspoon celery salt

1/2 teaspoon paprika

1/4 teaspoon ground red pepper

GLAZE

2/3 cup peach preserves

2 teaspoons fresh lemon juice

1 teaspoon soy sauce

1   Prepare a charcoal or gas grill so that the coals are medium-hot.

2   Cut each rack of ribs into thirds. Divide the ribs between two 18-by-24-inch sheets of heavy duty aluminum foil.

3   To make the rub, stir together brown sugar, 5-spice powder, celery salt, paprika, and ground red pepper. Sprinkle over the ribs and rub into the meat, turning to coat the ribs evenly.

4   Bring up the sides of the foil. Double fold the top and one end. Pour 1/4 cup of the water into the packet and then seal. Leave room for heat circulation inside. Repeat to make 2 packets.

5   Slide the packets onto the grill rack.

6   Grill for 45 minutes to 1 hour in a covered grill. Unwrap the foil carefully, lift the ribs from the packets with tongs, and put the ribs directly on grill.

7 Meanwhile, make the glaze by combining the preserves, lemon juice, and soy sauce. Brush the ribs generously with the glaze and continue to grill, uncovered, for 10 to 15 minutes, turning every 5 minutes to ensure even cooking.

. . .

Baby-Back Barbecue Ribs

3 pounds baby-back pork ribs

1 tablespoon packed brown sugar

1 tablespoon paprika

2 teaspoons garlic powder

1 1/2 teaspoons pepper

1/2 cup water

1 1/2 cups barbecue sauce

PREP TIME
5 minutes
GRILL TIME
1 hour
MAKES
5 servings

1 Prepare a charcoal or gas grill so that the coals are medium-hot, or preheat the oven to 400°F.

2 Divide the ribs between two 12-by-30-inch sheets of heavy duty aluminum foil.

3 In a small bowl, stir together the brown sugar, paprika, garlic powder, and pepper. Sprinkle over the ribs and rub into the meat, turning the ribs over to coat evenly.

4 Bring up the sides of the foil. Double fold the top and one end. Pour 1/4 cup of the water into the packet and then seal. Leave room for heat circulation inside. Repeat to make 2 packets.

5 Slide the packets onto the grill rack, or put the cookie sheet in the oven.

6 Grill for 45 minutes to 1 hour in a covered grill or bake for 45 minutes to 1 hour. Unwrap the foil carefully, lift the

ribs from the packets with tongs, and put the ribs directly on the grill or on a broiler pan.

7 Brush the ribs generously with barbecue sauce. Grill or broil 4 to 5 inches from the broiler for 10 to 15 minutes, brushing with the remaining barbecue sauce and turning every 5 minutes to ensure even cooking.

Baby-Back Barbecue Ribs

Southwestern Spareribs

PREP TIME

10 minutes

COOK TIME

1½ hours

MAKES

4 servings

¼ cup flour

1½ cups barbecue sauce

1 medium onion, cut in wedges

2 teaspoons chili powder

1 teaspoon dry mustard

¼ teaspoon garlic powder

¼ teaspoon cayenne pepper

3 pounds pork spareribs

1 Preheat the oven to 325°F. Add the flour to a large oven bag, shake the bag to distribute the flour, and put in a 9-by-13-by-2-inch baking pan.

2 Add the barbecue sauce, onion, chili powder, dry mustard, garlic powder, and cayenne pepper, and squeeze the bag to blend with the flour. Put the ribs in the bag and turn the bag to coat the ribs with sauce. Arrange the ribs in an even layer in the bag.

3 Close the bag with the provided nylon tie and cut six ½-inch slits in the top.

4 Bake for 1½ hours or until the ribs are tender.

. . .

Chili-Lime Pork

PREP TIME

20 minutes

COOK TIME

1¼ hours

MAKES

8 servings

1 tablespoon flour

3 tablespoons honey

2 tablespoons chili powder

2 teaspoons grated lime peel

One 2½-pound boneless top loin pork roast

3 medium sweet potatoes, peeled and cut in quarters

1 Preheat the oven to 325°F. Add the flour to a large oven bag, shake the bag to distribute the flour, and put in a 9-by-13-by-2-inch baking pan.

2 In a small bowl, stir together the honey, chili powder, and lime peel. Pat the surface of the pork dry. Spread half the chili powder mixture over the bottom of the roast. Put the pork in the bag and spread the remaining chili powder mixture over the top of the roast. Arrange the sweet potatoes around the pork in an even layer.

3 Close the bag with the provided nylon tie and cut six ½-inch slits in the top.

4 Bake for 1¼ hours or until an instant-read or meat thermometer registers 160°F.

5 Carefully open the bag and transfer the pork to a serving platter. Stir the juices and spoon them over the pork.

Chili-Lime Pork

Pineapple-Glazed Ham

2 tablespoons flour

One 15¼-ounce can sliced pineapple, drained, juice reserved

½ cup packed brown sugar

1 tablespoon lemon juice

⅛ teaspoon ground cinnamon

One 10- to 12-pound fully cooked bone-in ham

Whole cloves (optional)

PREP TIME
20 minutes

COOK TIME
2 to 2½ hours

MAKES
30 to 36 servings

1 Preheat the oven to 325°F. Add the flour to a turkey size oven bag, shake the bag to distribute the flour, and put in a 2-inch or deeper roasting pan.

2 Add the reserved pineapple juice, brown sugar, lemon juice, and cinnamon to the bag. Squeeze the bag to blend the ingredients. Put the pineapple slices in the bag and arrange in an even layer around the sides of the bag.

3 Lightly score the surface of the ham in a diamond pattern. Insert the cloves, if desired, in the center of the diamonds. Put the ham in the bag in the center of the pineapple slices.

4 Close the bag with the provided nylon tie and cut six ½-inch slits in the top.

5 Bake for 2 to 2½ hours or until the ham is heated all the way through and an instant-read or meat thermometer registers 140°F.

6 Carefully open the bag and transfer the ham to a serving platter. Stir the glaze and pineapple and spoon over the ham.

REYNOLDS KITCHENS TIP

Serve any leftovers from the ham for another meal or two. Add cooked ham to stir-fried vegetables or pasta. Make sandwiches with sliced ham, lettuce, and tomatoes. Refrigerate leftover cooked ham no longer than 3 to 5 days.

Ham with Peach Sauce Packets

PREP TIME
10 minutes

COOK TIME
15 minutes

MAKES
4 servings

One 1- to 1½-pound center-cut ham slice, cut in 4 pieces

One 15-ounce can peach slices in juice, drained

⅓ cup maple-flavored syrup

¼ cup Dijon mustard

1 tablespoon butter or margarine, melted

1 Preheat the oven to 450°F or prepare a charcoal or gas grill so that the coals are medium-hot.

2 Lay four 12-by-18-inch sheets of heavy duty aluminum foil on the countertop. Center a piece of ham on each sheet and arrange the peach slices on top of the ham.

3 In a small bowl, stir together the syrup, mustard, and butter until smooth. Spoon over the ham and peaches.

4 Bring up the sides of the foil. Double fold the top and ends to seal the packets, leaving room for heat circulation inside. Repeat to make 4 packets. If using the oven, put the packets on a cookie sheet.

5 Put the cookie sheet in the oven or slide the packets onto the grill rack. Bake for 15 to 18 minutes or grill for 8 to 10 minutes in a covered grill, until the ham is heated through and the sauce is hot.

Holiday Cooking

Herb-Roasted Holiday Turkey

Sausage and Sage Corn Bread Dressing

Turkey Gravy

Orange-Glazed Cornish Hens

Standing Rib Roast and Three-Potato Bake

Peppered Eye of Round Roast

Beef Brisket with Fruited Carrots

Boneless Roast Leg of Lamb

Fennel Pork Roast and Red Potatoes

Country Ham

Ham with Apple-Raisin Sauce

Herbed Green Beans with Roasted Peppers

Cranberry-Apple Sweet Potato Packet

Sweet Potato Casserole

"Non-Sticky" Buns

Carrot-Raisin Muffins

Cinnamon-Pecan Coffee Cake

My mother recently told me about a delicious turkey a friend had roasted in an oven bag. She had seasoned it with herbs and citrus for a holiday celebration. Of course, this sounded like the way I cook—I open the cabinet and start sprinkling herbs on the food. It's how I was taught when I was growing up.

—Betty

When my husband and I moved into our first house in Florida years ago, our real estate agent gave us a turkey. I had never roasted one and it was a miserable failure—raw in the middle. I didn't know about oven bags then!

—Pat

WE BOTH CELEBRATE THE HOLIDAYS with our families and dear friends, but we also celebrate it with our consumers. For the few weeks leading up to Thanksgiving, the Reynolds Turkey Tips Line, a toll-free telephone advice line, rings off the hook. It's not that much quieter in the time between Thanksgiving and Christmas. Our consumers are excited about cooking these yearly feasts, but understandably, they have questions and a good amount of anxiety.

Thanksgiving

People put so much pressure on themselves at Thanksgiving. Everyone wants a Norman Rockwell picture-perfect holiday meal. We believe that with a little planning, you can have a wonderful meal, but it doesn't have to be stressful!

We urge people to make sure they know how to cook turkey safely. Some people ask if they can partially cook the bird and then transport it miles away, to finish cooking there. This is unwise in terms of food safety, and so we suggest transporting side dishes and desserts and let whoever is hosting the meal roast the turkey.

Cooked turkey needs some resting time before it's carved. Make use of this time to cook the side dishes. Don't forget the microwave as a good place for heating vegetables, potatoes, and gravy. Utilize the grill, too! Vegetable packets can be made in advance and popped on the grill at just the right moment.

We're happy to hold our consumers' hands during this stressful time—we often are the voices at the other end of the phone, but if we don't personally answer, one of six or seven other people will. The holiday phone line is a major event around here. We are fully staffed with experts who are all ready to help.

A big turkey is daunting, but in reality, it's about the easiest thing to cook. No one has to worry about a dry old bird if they use a turkey size oven bag! Most of the queries that come into the tips line are about roasting turkey in the bag. The question we get the most often is: Will the turkey brown in the oven bag? It sure will, if brushed first with oil, butter, or margarine. We're also asked if there will be enough juices for gravy. There will be more juices, all collected at the bottom of the bag, because so little evaporates during roasting.

Some people are roasting really big birds these days, ones weighing up to 25 or 30 pounds. We suggest you make sure your oven can hold a turkey that size and that you have the right size roasting pan. If most of your family likes white meat, you might consider roasting two turkey breasts in an oven bag.

Food safety is a big concern of our holiday callers. Stuffing is a particular concern since many have heard that it might be a breeding ground for bacteria. To stuff the bird, we advise packing the stuffing loosely in the turkey and cooking the rest in a casserole dish. Pat always puts a little stuffing in the cavity of her own turkey because she likes the flavor it gives the meat and then makes a casserole of the remaining stuffing. We recommend that home cooks use an instant-read thermometer to test whether the stuffing is hot enough. Push the tip of the thermometer into the middle of the stuffing; it should register 165°F. It's also important to remove all the stuffing before storing the turkey—don't leave it in the cavity overnight even if everything is cooked.

December Holidays

Betty remembers Christmas in North Carolina as a girl, when there was a variety of different meats—turkey, ham, and homemade chicken and dumplings—as well as collard greens, candied yams, and green beans. Pat recalls her Minnesota Christmases, when the table was fully extended and angled across the room to accommodate a large family as well as the Christmas ham, cheese potatoes, and fruit salad with marshmallows.

Turkey is certainly the main event at Thanksgiving, but at Christmas, we hear from those who are planning to serve standing rib roast beef, ham, or brisket. For good measure, we've included a lovely recipe for leg of lamb and another for pork roast. These are great during the holidays—or anytime for that matter.

It's not unusual for home cooks to stumble when they think beyond the main course. What to serve as side dishes, particularly during those holidays that are not as tradition-bound as Thanksgiving, is a question we frequently receive. We like to think that all of our recipes are wonderful, but occasionally a recipe really resonates with our consumers. One such hit is a recipe that Pat developed several years ago, Cranberry-Apple Sweet Potato Packet. It combines all the best things—traditional flavors, colorful ingredients, and a super-simple technique. The Herbed Green Beans with Roasted Peppers rounds out the meal.

We can't forget about breakfast, which is why we've included "Non-Sticky" Buns and Cinnamon-Pecan Coffee Cake in this chapter. Both are memorable for special winter breakfasts, and with our Reynolds Wrap Release Non-Stick Aluminum Foil, the sticky buns stick only to your fingers!

Words of Wisdom

Since so many of our consumers use turkey size oven bags, it's important to understand why the package directions instruct you to add flour to the bag. You may not want flour in your recipe, but in this case, it's crucial. The flour blends with the fats and juices so that they emulsify rather than separate during roasting. Following package directions will guarantee good results.

Herb-Roasted Holiday Turkey

PREP TIME
15 minutes

COOK TIME
2 to 3½ hours

MAKES
15 to 30 servings

1 tablespoon flour

2 stalks celery, sliced

1 medium onion, sliced

One 12- to 24-pound turkey, thawed

Vegetable oil or butter

1 tablespoon dried sage

1 teaspoon dried thyme

1 teaspoon dried rosemary

1 teaspoon seasoned salt

1 Preheat the oven to 350°F. Add the flour to a turkey size oven bag, shake the bag to distribute the flour, and put in a 2-inch or deeper roasting pan. Spray the inside of the oven bag with cooking spray to prevent sticking, if desired.

2 Put the celery and onion slices in the bag.

3 Remove the neck and giblets from the turkey. Rinse the turkey and pat dry. Brush with vegetable oil.

4 In a small bowl, combine the sage, thyme, rosemary, and seasoned salt. Sprinkle on the turkey, rubbing it gently into the skin. Turn the turkey over to coat it evenly with seasoning. Put the turkey in the bag on top of the vegetables.

5 Close the bag with the provided nylon tie and cut six ½-inch slits in the top.

6 Roast for 2 to 2½ hours for a 12- to 16-pound turkey; 2½ to 3 hours for a 16- to 20-pound turkey; and 3 to 3½ hours for a 20- to 24-pound turkey. The turkey is done when the meat is tender, juices run clear, and an instant-read or meat thermometer registers 180°F for the thigh.

7 When the turkey is done, let it stand in the bag for 15 minutes for easy slicing. If the turkey sticks when you try to take it from the bag, gently loosen the bag from the turkey.

> **REYNOLDS KITCHENS TIP**
>
> *For the best holiday turkey, use a turkey size oven bag. Its self-basting method of roasting means the turkey cooks up tender and juicy with no messy cleanup.*
>
> *The oven bag method can be used for turkeys up to 24 pounds, and is faster than the foil tent method. The turkey will brown, although not as deeply as with the foil tent or foil-wrapped methods, but will be very tender and juicy, and cleanup is easy. This is the method that will give you the moistest turkey.*

Sausage and Sage Corn Bread Dressing

PREP TIME
25 minutes

COOK TIME
40 minutes

MAKES
10 to 12
servings

3 cups cubed dry bread or stuffing cubes

3 cups cubed corn bread

6 tablespoons butter or margarine, melted

1 cup chopped onion

1 cup chopped celery

1 cup chopped red or yellow bell pepper

1 pound sausage, crumbled

2 $\frac{1}{2}$ cups chicken broth

2 eggs, beaten

1 tablespoon dried sage

1 tablespoon poultry seasoning

$\frac{1}{2}$ teaspoon seasoned salt

1 Preheat the oven to 375°F. Line a 9-by-13-by-2-inch baking pan with non-stick aluminum foil, non-stick (dull) side facing up.

2 In a large bowl, combine the bread and corn bread.

3 In a large skillet, heat 2 tablespoons of the melted butter. Add the onion, celery, and red pepper and cook over medium heat, stirring, for 4 to 5 minutes, until the onion softens. Add the crumbled sausage and cook, stirring frequently, until the sausage browns and is cooked through.

4 Add the sausage and vegetable mixture to the bowl and stir with the bread. Add the broth, eggs, remaining 4 tablespoons of butter, sage, poultry seasoning, and seasoned salt. Mix well and spread in the foil-lined pan.

5 Bake for 40 to 45 minutes or until heated through and the top of the dressing is lightly browned.

> **REYNOLDS KITCHENS TIP**
>
> *Before baking, set aside 1½ to 2 cups of the Sausage and Sage Corn Bread Dressing and use it to stuff the turkey loosely, if desired. If you do, reduce the cooking time for the dressing by about 5 minutes, to 35 to 40 minutes.*
>
> *When you don't have a large bowl (or it's being used for another culinary purpose), use an oven bag to mix the ingredients for stuffing. Prepare all the dry ingredients the day before and store them in a turkey size oven bag. When ready to stuff the turkey or cook the stuffing in a separate pan, add the cooked ingredients, such as vegetables and sausage, to the bag, tie with the provided nylon tie, and toss the food in the bag to mix.*

Turkey Gravy

PREP TIME
15 minutes

COOK TIME
6 minutes

MAKES
2 cups

Pan drippings from roasted turkey

¹⁄₄ cup flour

¹⁄₄ to ¹⁄₂ teaspoon salt

¹⁄₄ teaspoon poultry seasoning

1 Pour the pan drippings into a large glass measuring cup. Skim the fat from the surface of the drippings. Discard all but 3 to 4 tablespoons of fat.

2 Put the reserved fat in a medium saucepan. Add the flour, salt, and poultry seasoning, and stir to mix well. Cook over medium-high heat, stirring constantly, for about 1 minute or until smooth and bubbling.

3 If necessary, add water to the reserved turkey drippings to measure 2¹⁄₂ cups. Gradually stir the drippings into the flour mixture. Bring to a boil and cook, stirring frequently, for 5 to 7 minutes, or until the gravy is hot, smooth, and thick. Adjust the seasoning before serving.

REYNOLDS KITCHENS TIP

Fat rises to the top of pan drippings, so after you pour the pan drippings into the measuring cup, wait for a few minutes and then use a spoon to skim the fat that collects on top. Some cooks use a paper towel to blot fat, and others pour the drippings into a fat separator, which makes it easy to pour the fat-free drippings into another container. A fat separator resembles a pitcher with a long spout that originates near the bottom of the pitcher.

. . .

Orange-Glazed Cornish Hens

PREP TIME
10 minutes

COOK TIME
1 hour

MAKES
4 servings

3 tablespoons flour

Four 1¹⁄₂-pound Cornish hens

1 cup orange marmalade

2 tablespoons soy sauce

1¹⁄₂ teaspoons ground ginger

1 Preheat the oven to 350°F. Add 1 tablespoon of the flour to a large oven bag, shake the bag to distribute the flour, and put in a 9-by-13-by-2-inch baking pan.

2 Rinse the hens and pat them dry. Put them in the bag.

3 In a small bowl, stir together the remaining 2 tablespoons of flour, marmalade, soy sauce, and ginger until smooth. Spoon the sauce over the hens.

4 Close the bag with the provided nylon tie and cut six ½-inch slits in the top.

5 Bake for 1 to 1½ hours or until the hens are tender, the juices run clear, and an instant-read or meat thermometer registers 180°F. Let the hens sit in the bag for 5 minutes before serving with the sauce from the bag, if desired.

REYNOLDS
KITCHENS TIP

*Cornish hens are usually
sold frozen and in pairs.
Thaw them completely
before cooking.*

. . .

Standing Rib Roast and Three-Potato Bake

PREP TIME
15 minutes

COOK TIME
2 hours

MAKES
10 to 12
servings

2 tablespoons flour

1½ teaspoons beef bouillon granules

1½ teaspoons dried rosemary, crushed

1 teaspoon lemon pepper

2 large cloves garlic, minced

One 5- to 6-pound bone-in beef rib roast

2 medium sweet potatoes, peeled and halved

2 small russet potatoes, peeled and halved

2 small Yukon Gold potatoes, peeled and halved

Salt and pepper

1 Preheat the oven to 325°F. Add the flour to a large oven bag, shake the bag to distribute the flour, and put in a 9-by-13-by-2-inch baking pan.

2 In a small bowl, mix together the bouillon granules, rosemary, lemon pepper, and garlic. Rub into the beef, gently working the spices into all sides of the meat. Put the meat, fat side up, in the bag. Arrange the potatoes around the roast in an even layer.

3 Close the bag with the provided nylon tie and cut six ½-inch slits in the top.

4 Roast for 2 to 2½ hours, or until an instant-read or meat thermometer registers 145°F for medium-rare.

5 Open the bag carefully and transfer the meat and potatoes to a serving platter. Season the pan juices with salt and pepper, if desired. Serve with the pan juices spooned over the beef and potatoes.

. . .

Peppered Eye of Round Roast

	PREP TIME
	5 minutes
	COOK TIME
	1¼ to 2 hours
	MAKES
	12 to 20 servings

One 3- to 5-pound beef eye of round roast

1 to 2 tablespoons olive oil

4 teaspoons dried thyme

4 teaspoons coarsely ground black pepper

1 teaspoon garlic salt

Salt and pepper

1 Preheat the oven to 325°F. Line a 9-by-13-by-2-inch baking pan with non-stick aluminum foil, non-stick (dull) side facing up.

2 Brush the roast with olive oil.

3 In a small bowl, mix together the thyme, pepper, and garlic salt. Rub into the beef, gently working the spices into all sides of the meat. Put the meat in the pan. Cover tightly with a sheet of non-stick aluminum foil, non-stick (dull) side facing down.

4 Roast for 45 minutes. Remove the foil cover and continue roasting for 30 minutes to 1¼ hours, or until an instant-read or meat thermometer registers 145°F for medium-rare or 160°F for medium.

5 Let the roast stand for 10 minutes before slicing into thin slices. Stir the pan juices and season with salt and pepper, if desired. Serve with the pan juices spooned over the beef.

Beef Brisket with Fruited Carrots

PREP TIME
10 minutes

COOK TIME
2½ hours

MAKES
9 to 10
servings

3 tablespoons flour

½ cup water

2 tablespoons packed brown sugar

1 tablespoon apple cider vinegar

1 teaspoon kosher salt

½ teaspoon pepper

1 pound carrots, cut in ½-inch slices

2 medium onions, cut in ½-inch wedges

One 8-ounce package mixed dried fruit, cut in 1-inch pieces

One 3- to 3½-pound boneless beef brisket

1 Preheat the oven to 325°F. Add the flour to a large oven bag, shake the bag to distribute the flour, and put in a 9-by-13-by-2-inch baking pan.

2 Add the water, brown sugar, vinegar, salt, and pepper to the bag, and squeeze the bag to blend ingredients with the flour. Arrange the carrots, onions, and dried fruit in an even layer in the bag. Put the brisket on top of the vegetables and fruit.

Beef Brisket with Fruited Carrots

3 Close the bag with the provided nylon tie and cut six ½-inch slits in the top.

4 Bake for 2½ to 3 hours or until the brisket is tender. Let the meat stand in the bag for 5 minutes before removing it to a cutting board and slicing it thinly diagonally across the grain. Season the sauce with salt and pepper, if desired, and serve spooned over the brisket with the vegetables and fruit.

. . .

Boneless Roast Leg of Lamb

1 tablespoon flour	**2 teaspoons dried thyme**
One 4- to 5-pound boneless leg of lamb	**1 teaspoon dried rosemary**
	1 teaspoon salt
1 tablespoon olive or vegetable oil	**½ teaspoon pepper**
4 cloves garlic, minced	

PREP TIME
10 minutes
COOK TIME
1¾ hours
MAKES
16 to 20 servings

1 Preheat the oven to 325°F. Add the flour to a large oven bag, shake the bag to distribute the flour, and put in a 2-inch or deeper roasting pan.

2 Trim all but a thin layer of fat from the lamb. Rub all sides of the meat with oil.

3 In a small bowl, mix together the garlic, thyme, rosemary, salt, and pepper. Rub on the lamb, gently working the spices into the meat. Put the lamb in the bag.

4 Close the bag with the provided nylon tie and cut six ½-inch slits in the top.

5 Roast for 1½ to 2 hours or until an instant-read or meat thermometer registers 150°F for medium-rare or 160°F for medium. Let the lamb stand in the bag for 15 minutes before slicing.

Fennel Pork Roast and Red Potatoes

PREP TIME
15 minutes

GRILL TIME
50 minutes

MAKES
7 to 9 servings

2 tablespoons water

1 tablespoon flour

$1/4$ cup fresh parsley, chopped

2 teaspoons fennel seeds

$1^1/2$ teaspoons seasoned salt

1 teaspoon coarsely ground black pepper

1 teaspoon onion powder

2 tablespoons olive oil

One 2- to $2^1/2$-pound boneless pork loin roast

6 medium red potatoes, cut in wedges

1   Prepare a charcoal or gas grill for indirect grilling or preheat the oven to 450°F. The coals should be medium-hot. Put a large extra heavy duty foil bag in a 1-inch-deep pan.

2   In a small bowl, stir together the water and flour until smooth. Pour over one side of the bottom of the bag.

3   In another bowl, combine the parsley, fennel, seasoned salt, pepper, onion powder, and oil. Rub this into the top and sides of the roast. Put the roast in the bag on top of the flour mixture. Arrange the potatoes on the opposite side of the bag and drizzle with more olive oil, if desired. Double fold the bag to seal and leave it in the pan to transport it to and from the grill or oven.

4   Slide the bag onto the grill or leave it in the pan and place it in the oven. Grill for 50 to 55 minutes in a covered grill or bake for 70 to 75 minutes, or until an instant-read or meat thermometer registers 155°F. Let the meat stand in the bag for 10 minutes.

5   Hold the bag with oven mitts and cut it open with a knife. Carefully fold back the top of the bag so that steam can escape.

> **REYNOLDS KITCHENS TIP**
>
> *For indirect heat, the coals or ignited gas burners are on one side of grill. Set the foil bag on the side of the grill away from the heat. This results in slower, more gentle cooking.*

Country Ham

One 12- to 15-pound country ham

1 tablespoon flour

4 cups water

1 cup fresh bread crumbs

1 cup packed brown sugar

PREP TIME
24 hours

COOK TIME
3½ hours

MAKES
36 to 45 servings

1 Soak the ham in cold water to cover by several inches for 24 hours, at room temperature or in the refrigerator. This removes much of the saltiness. Drain.

2 Preheat the oven to 325°F. Add the flour to a turkey size oven bag, shake the bag to distribute the flour, and put in a 2-inch or deeper roasting pan.

3 Scrub the ham with warm water and a stiff brush. Rinse well. Put the ham in the bag and add the 4 cups of water.

4 Close the bag with the provided nylon tie and cut six ½-inch slits in the top.

5 Bake for 3½ to 4½ hours or until an instant-read or meat thermometer registers 160°F. Let the ham stand in the bag for 15 minutes. Slit the bag down the center and carefully remove the ham. Discard the bag and the drippings.

6 Increase the oven temperature to 400°F.

7 Meanwhile, in a small bowl, combine the bread crumbs and sugar.

8 Line the roasting pan with heavy duty aluminum foil. Return the ham to the pan and trim the skin and fat from ham, leaving a thin layer of fat. Rub the bread crumb mixture over the ham.

9 Bake the coated ham for 5 to 10 minutes longer or until the topping is golden brown. To serve, slice very thin.

> **REYNOLDS KITCHENS TIP**
>
> *A country ham is dry-cured, salted, smoked, and aged for 3 to 12 months. It needs long soaking before it's roasted to remove some of its saltiness. Country ham is served in very thin slices, as it is very rich. One of the best-known types of country ham is Smithfield.*

Ham with Apple-Raisin Sauce

1 tablespoon flour

2 medium apples, peeled and chopped

1 cup apple juice

1/2 cup raisins

1/4 cup packed brown sugar

1/2 teaspoon ground cinnamon

One 4- to 6-pound boneless, fully-cooked ham

Whole cloves (optional)

PREP TIME

15 minutes

COOK TIME

1 1/4 hours

MAKES

16 to 24 servings

1 Preheat the oven to 325°F. Add the flour to a large oven bag, shake the bag to distribute the flour, and put in a 9-by-13-by-2-inch baking pan.

2 Add the apples, apple juice, raisins, brown sugar, and cinnamon to the bag, and squeeze the bag to blend the ingredients.

3 Using a sharp knife, lightly score the ham in a diamond pattern. Insert the cloves in the diamonds, if desired. Put the ham in the bag.

4 Close the bag with the provided nylon tie and cut six 1/2-inch slits in the top.

5 Bake for 1 1/4 to 1 3/4 hours, or until an instant-read or meat thermometer registers 140°F. Stir the sauce before serving.

> **REYNOLDS KITCHENS TIP**
>
> *For warm and hearty dinners that require little time or effort, oven bags are great choices. Sauces and gravies cook in the oven bag. There is no need for mixing bowls, because the sauce is mixed right in the bag.*

Ham with Apple-Raisin Sauce

Herbed Green Beans with Roasted Peppers

PREP TIME

14 minutes

COOK TIME

30 minutes

MAKES

8 to 10 servings

2 pounds whole green beans, trimmed, or two 16-ounce packages frozen whole green beans

One 7-ounce jar roasted red peppers, drained and cut in strips

1/4 cup French fried onions, crushed

2 teaspoons dried basil

3/4 teaspoon salt

1/8 teaspoon pepper

2 tablespoons water

1 tablespoon melted butter or olive oil

1 Preheat the oven to 450°F or prepare a charcoal or gas grill so that the coals are medium-hot.

2 Lay an 18-by-24-inch sheet of heavy duty aluminum foil on the countertop. Put the green beans in the center of the sheet and top with peppers, onions, basil, salt, and pepper. Sprinkle with water and butter or olive oil.

3 Bring up foil sides. Double fold top and ends to form one large foil packet, leaving room for heat circulation inside. Transfer to a cookie sheet.

4 Bake on the cookie sheet or slide the packet onto the grill. Bake for 30 to 35 minutes or grill for 15 to 20 minutes in a covered grill, or until the beans are tender. Serve sprinkled with more French fried onions, if desired.

> **REYNOLDS KITCHENS TIP**
>
> *If using frozen green beans, increase baking time to 35 to 40 minutes and grilling time to 20 to 25 minutes.*

Cranberry-Apple Sweet Potato Packet

PREP TIME
15 minutes

COOK TIME
25 minutes

MAKES
6 to 8 servings

$1\frac{1}{2}$ pounds sweet potatoes (about 4 medium potatoes), peeled and cut into $\frac{1}{4}$-inch-thick slices

2 Granny Smith or Golden Delicious apples, cored and sliced into thin rings

$\frac{1}{2}$ cup dried cranberries or raisins

$\frac{1}{2}$ cup packed brown sugar

3 tablespoons butter or margarine, melted

$\frac{1}{2}$ teaspoon ground cinnamon

1 Preheat the oven to 450°F or prepare a charcoal or gas grill so that the coals are medium-hot.

2 Lay an 18-by-24-inch sheet of heavy duty aluminum foil on the countertop. Put the sweet potatoes, apples, and cranberries in the center of the foil sheet. Sprinkle with brown sugar.

3 In a small dish, mix together the butter and cinnamon, and drizzle over the brown sugar.

4 Bring up foil sides. Double fold top and ends to form one large foil packet, leaving room for heat circulation inside. Transfer to a cookie sheet.

5 Bake on the cookie sheet or slide the packet onto the grill. Bake for 25 to 30 minutes or grill for 20 to 25 minutes in a covered grill, or until the sweet potatoes are tender.

> **REYNOLDS KITCHENS TIP**
>
> *Packet cooking holds in moisture and all the nutrients so vegetables cook to crisp-tender perfection.*

Sweet Potato Casserole

PREP TIME
15 minutes

COOK TIME
40 minutes

MAKES
12 to 16
servings

4 cups cooked, mashed, fresh sweet potatoes (about 2 pounds potatoes)

3/4 cup packed brown sugar

1/2 cup milk

3 eggs, beaten

1/4 cup butter or margarine, melted

1 teaspoon vanilla extract

1 teaspoon grated orange peel

1/2 teaspoon ground nutmeg

1/4 cup flaked sweetened coconut

1/4 cup pecan halves or pieces

1/4 cup dried sweetened cranberries

1 Preheat the oven to 350°F for at least 20 minutes and arrange an oven rack so that it is in the center of the oven. Put a 1½-quart disposable plastic cookware pan on a cookie sheet, so that the pan does not hang over the sides.

2 In a large bowl, blend the sweet potatoes with the brown sugar, milk, eggs, butter, vanilla, orange peel, and nutmeg. Pour into the disposable cookware.

3 Sprinkle the coconut and pecans over the center of the sweet potatoes, leaving a border around the outside edges.

4 Bake on the cookie sheet for 40 to 45 minutes, or until the sweet potatoes are set. Use the cookie sheet to remove the pan from the oven and let it stand on the sheet for at least 2 minutes before lifting it by the handles. Garnish with dried cranberries and serve.

> **REYNOLDS KITCHENS TIP**
>
> *Be sure to keep the disposable plastic cookware pan on a cookie sheet to support it as you put it in and pull it out of the oven.*

...

"Non-Sticky" Buns

PREP TIME
8 minutes

COOK TIME
25 minutes

MAKES
10 servings

1/2 cup packed brown sugar

3 tablespoons butter or margarine, melted

2 tablespoons light corn syrup

1/2 cup coarsely chopped pecans

Two 1-pound (approximately) cans refrigerated big cinnamon rolls

1 Preheat the oven to 350°F. Line a 9-by-13-by-2-inch baking pan with non-stick aluminum foil, non-stick (dull) side facing up.

2 In a small bowl, stir together the brown sugar, butter, and corn syrup. Pour into the pan and sprinkle evenly with pecans. Put the cinnamon rolls on top of the syrup.

3 Bake for 25 to 29 minutes, or until the rolls are golden brown. Let the rolls stand in the pan for 5 minutes and then invert onto a platter. Remove the foil and serve warm.

> **REYNOLDS KITCHENS TIP**
>
> *To reheat rolls, muffins, coffee cake, and other breads, wrap them in aluminum foil and reheat in a medium (350°F) oven until hot. They will be as fresh and light as when first baked.*

"Non-Sticky" Buns

Carrot-Raisin Muffins

PREP TIME
15 minutes

COOK TIME
20 minutes

MAKES
12 muffins

2 cups flour

2 teaspoons ground cinnamon

1 teaspoon ground nutmeg

1 teaspoon baking powder

1/2 teaspoon salt

3/4 cup packed brown sugar

2 eggs, beaten

1/2 cup vegetable oil

1/2 cup milk

2 cups shredded carrots

1/2 cup raisins

1 Preheat the oven to 400°F. Place 12 foil baking cups in a muffin pan or on a cookie sheet.

2 In a large bowl, whisk the flour with the cinnamon, nutmeg, baking powder, and salt. Add the brown sugar, eggs, vegetable oil, and milk. Stir with a wooden spoon just until the dry ingredients are moistened. Stir in the carrots and raisins.

3 Spoon the batter into the baking cups, filling each one about 3/4 full.

4 Bake for 20 to 25 minutes or until a toothpick inserted in the center comes out clean. Cool for 5 minutes in the pan before removing and cooling completely on a wire rack.

> **REYNOLDS KITCHENS TIP**
>
> *Holiday decorated baking cups add a festive touch to breakfast or snack muffins.*

• • •

Cinnamon-Pecan Coffee Cake

PREP TIME
15 minutes

COOK TIME
35 minutes

MAKES
12 servings

COFFEE CAKE

2 cups flour

1 1/4 cups sugar

1 1/2 teaspoons baking powder

1/2 teaspoon baking soda

1/2 teaspoon ground cinnamon

1/4 teaspoon salt

3/4 cup butter or margarine, softened

1 cup sour cream

1/4 cup milk

2 eggs

1 teaspoon vanilla extract

TOPPING

1 1/2 cups chopped pecans

1/4 cup sugar

2 teaspoons ground cinnamon

1 Preheat the oven to 350°F. Line a 9-by-13-by-2-inch baking dish with parchment paper.

2 In a large bowl, mix the flour with the sugar, baking powder, baking soda, cinnamon, and salt. Using fingers, a fork, or a pastry blender, work the butter into the
   flour until the mixture resembles coarse crumbs.

3 In the bowl of an electric mixer, stir together the sour cream, milk, eggs, and
   vanilla. Add to the dry ingredients. Turn on the mixer and beat at medium speed
   until smooth and fluffy.

4 Spoon half the batter into the prepared pan.

5 Meanwhile, combine the topping ingredients. Sprinkle half of
   the topping over the batter. Spread the remaining batter over
   the topping. Sprinkle with the remaining topping.

6 Bake for 35 to 40 minutes or until a wooden toothpick inserted
   into the center comes out clean. Let the coffee cake cool in the
   pan set on a wire rack.

Cinnamon-Pecan Coffee Cake

Casseroles, Packet Meals, and One-Dish Dinners

Spinach Lasagna

Parmesan Tuna Casserole

Curried Chicken

Fiesta Chicken

Everyday Favorite Chicken

Creamy Chicken and Vegetables

Chicken Tetrazzini

Chicken Pot Pie

Chicken and Broccoli Casserole

Chicken and Garden Vegetables

Easy Chicken Fajitas

Southwestern Chicken-and-Corn Dinner

All-American Chicken and Vegetable Dinner

Chicken en Papillote

Chicken Divan

Far East–Spiced Chicken

Greek Chicken and Vegetables

Mexican Chicken Dinner

Roasted Chicken and Vegetables

Easy Chicken and Rice

Chicken with Pine Nut Couscous

Baked Fiesta Enchiladas

Sausage and Black Bean Dinner

Layered Tortilla Casserole

Ribeye Roast and Roasted Garlic Vegetables

Hearty Beef Stew

Baked Spaghetti

Satay-Style Beef

Pepper Steak Packets

Oriental Pork Tenderloin Packets

Easy Pork Chop Packets

I grew up eating casseroles, although we called them "hotdishes"—saying it as though it were one word. Maybe that's unique to Minnesota!
—Pat

We never ate casseroles when I was growing up, except macaroni and cheese. Today, I really like packet meals, partly because I am the dishwasher in the house.
—Betty

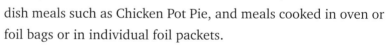

ONE-DISH MEALS ARE THE TRUE convenience food. Meat and vegetables go in one baking dish, one packet, or one bag, so they're easy to make, easy to cook, and easy to clean up. Plus, almost anything goes when it comes to these meals, from tuna to sausages to pork chops!

Even cooks who "don't want to cook" have little difficulty managing these one-dish wonders. Many can be cooked ahead of time and frozen, which is a great convenience. Cooking is easy: Put them in the oven or on the grill and go about your life. No hovering required. Of course, we never suggest you leave home, but you can relax, monitor homework, or complete another task while they cook. Leftovers are delicious (a number of these dishes fall into the "taste better on the second day" category) and are easy to heat up. We believe the following recipes are about as family-friendly, homey, and easy as can be. They truly epitomize our culinary philosophy!

So many of our recipes fall into this category because we cook so many dishes in oven or foil bags, foil packets, and Reynolds Pot Lux Disposable Cookware. We confess that selecting the recipes for this chapter was a challenge because of the wealth of choices. In the end, we chose a mixture of classic casseroles, such as the Parmesan Tuna Casserole, traditional one-

dish meals such as Chicken Pot Pie, and meals cooked in oven or foil bags or in individual foil packets.

Casseroles

A casserole is a savory baked dish with ingredients that are prepped ahead of time so that pieces are already bite-sized. Many are soft and creamy, which is why they're sometimes crowned with a crunchy topping such as crushed crackers or potato chips.

Casseroles are ideal for church suppers, potluck dinners, and helping out friends or neighbors with the birth of a baby or death in the family.

Pot Lux cookware comes in so handy for casseroles as diverse as the Parmesan Tuna Casserole, Chicken Tetrazzini, and the Baked Fiesta Enchiladas. The cookware withstands oven heat up to 400°F, and when it's time to store the leftovers, the lid snaps into place to make it easy. For planning ahead, they're convenient, too, because you can freeze the cooked and cooled casserole right in them. Be sure to follow package directions for preheating the oven and placing the pans on a cookie sheet for baking.

Our favorite tip to share from the Reynolds Kitchens is how we line pans with aluminum foil for easy cleanup. Flip the pan over and shape the foil over the back. Take the foil off and when you turn the pan upright, the foil fits snugly inside. Use this tip for making Spinach Lasagna, Layered Tortilla

Casserole, and Baked Spaghetti. We've heard that Italian and Mexican foods are popular all over the world, and these are some of the most delicious family favorites going.

Packet Meals

When you wrap food in aluminum foil and then oven bake or grill it, you have ultimate control over this very easy preparation. No tending, no stirring, no fussing. The ingredients cook evenly and their flavors mingle, and when you open the packets, the flavor and aroma burst out to impress your family and friends.

We tear off 18-inch long sheets of heavy duty aluminum foil to make individual packets. The food is wrapped in such a way that there's plenty of room for air circulation so the food bubbles happily away during cooking but is completely contained. Each packet can be customized for family members—if someone doesn't like garlic, leave it out.

Most of our packet meals, such as the Satay-Style Beef, Pepper Steak Packets, and Greek Chicken and Vegetables, give you a choice of grilling or cooking the food in the oven. Either way works fine, and the food cooks quickly.

We particularly like this method of grilling because it's so easy to wrap the food in the foil packets and then carry them to the grill on a tray or in a shallow pan. You could even pack the prepared packets in an ice-packed cooler and grill them once you get to the beach or picnic area. Just remember to keep the food very cold (about 38° to 40°F) and grill it as soon as you can.

Finally, we have one recipe in which the food is cooked in parchment paper, Chicken en Papillote. This old-fashioned and elegant method of cooking is the original. Long before aluminum foil was invented, chefs recognized how moist and tender fragile foods, such as the chicken breasts and mushrooms, were when cooked in an enclosed package of parchment paper. Don't worry. The parchment won't burn, although it may brown lightly.

One-Dish Dinners

For one-dish dinners, we can't recommend the oven bags and foil bags enough. Both are outstanding in the oven, and the foil bag is equally successful on the grill. Both products hold in moisture and flavors, cook evenly, and are so easy to use, you'll wonder how you got along without them. If this sounds like a pitch, we suppose it is. But we believe so strongly in these products, it's hard for us not to rhapsodize!

Try the Ribeye Roast with Roasted Garlic Vegetables, the Easy Chicken Fajitas, or the Hearty Beef Stew, and you'll see what we mean. Simple, straightforward, and tasty meals your family will love. And cleanup doesn't get any easier.

Words of Wisdom

Foil bags save steps. There's no more running back and forth to the kitchen from the grill. The whole meal cooks in a single foil bag, so there's no need to cook side dishes in the kitchen.

When you line pans with foil, leave a little overhang on the sides. This guarantees the foil won't slide down during filling and serving, and makes the dish far easier to clean.

Spinach Lasagna

One 15-ounce container ricotta cheese

Two 10-ounce packages frozen chopped spinach, thawed, squeezed dry

1½ cups grated Parmesan cheese

3 eggs

Two 28-ounce jars pasta sauce

12 lasagna noodles, cooked and drained

One 16-ounce package shredded mozzarella cheese

PREP TIME
20 minutes

COOK TIME
1 hour

MAKES
10 to 12 servings

1 Preheat the oven to 350°F. Line a 9-by-13-by-2-inch baking pan with non-stick aluminum foil, non-stick (dull) side facing up.

2 In a mixing bowl, stir together the ricotta cheese, spinach, 1 cup of the Parmesan cheese, and eggs.

3 Spread 1½ cups of pasta sauce in the foil-lined pan. Arrange 3 noodles over the sauce in a single layer and top with 1½ cups of the cheese mixture. Sprinkle with 1 cup of mozzarella cheese.

4 Repeat the layering process two more times. Lay the final 3 noodles over the mozzarella cheese, spoon the remaining sauce over them, and top with the remaining mozzarella and Parmesan cheese.

5 Cover the pan with non-stick foil, non-stick (dull) side facing down.

6 Bake for 45 minutes. Remove the foil and continue baking for about 15 minutes longer or until the cheese melts and the casserole is hot and bubbling. Let stand for 15 minutes before serving.

REYNOLDS KITCHENS TIP

For easy cleanup, use 2 sheets of non-stick foil to make one large sheet that will completely line a large baking pan. Here's how: Stack 2 foil sheets with the non-stick sides facing each other. Fold the edges on one long side over twice. Open the foil and press the seam flat.

Flip the pan upside down. Lay the foil sheet over the pan with non-stick (dull) side facing toward pan. Press the foil around the pan. Lift the foil from the pan. Flip the pan upright and drop the foil inside. The non-stick (dull) side should be facing up. Crimp the foil's edges to rim of pan.

Parmesan Tuna Casserole

PREP TIME
10 minutes

COOK TIME
30 minutes

MAKES
4 to 5 servings

One 12-ounce can water-packed tuna, drained

One 8-ounce package egg noodles, cooked and drained

One 8-ounce container sour cream

1 cup frozen peas

1 cup milk

One 4-ounce jar diced pimientos, drained

¾ cup grated Parmesan cheese

¾ teaspoon dried thyme

½ teaspoon salt

¼ teaspoon pepper

2 tablespoons crushed fish-shaped cheese crackers

Whole fish-shaped cheese crackers, for garnish (optional)

1 Preheat the oven to 350°F for at least 20 minutes and arrange an oven rack so that it is in the center of the oven. Put an 8-inch square disposable plastic cookware pan on a cookie sheet, so that the pan does not hang over the sides.

2 In a mixing bowl, combine the tuna, cooked noodles, sour cream, peas, milk, pimientos, ½ cup of the Parmesan, thyme, salt, and pepper, and stir well to mix. Spoon into the pan and spread evenly.

3 Mix together the crushed crackers and remaining Parmesan cheese on a sheet of wax paper. Sprinkle over the casserole.

4 Bake, uncovered, on the cookie sheet for 30 to 35 minutes or until the casserole bubbles around the edges and is golden brown. Use the cookie sheet to remove the pan from the oven and let the casserole stand for at least 2 minutes before lifting by the handles. Garnish with whole cheese crackers, if desired.

REYNOLDS KITCHENS TIP

Store leftover tuna casserole in the disposable pan, covered with the provided lid. You can reheat it in the pan, in the oven or in the microwave.

Curried Chicken

PREP TIME
15 minutes

COOK TIME
35 minutes

MAKES
4 servings

2 tablespoons flour

One 14^1/$_2$-ounce can stewed tomatoes

^{1}/$_4$ cup raisins, if desired

2 tablespoons packed brown sugar

1 teaspoon curry powder

^{1}/$_2$ teaspoon salt

1 pound skinless, boneless chicken breast halves, cut in 1-inch pieces

Hot cooked rice

1 Preheat the oven to 350°F. Add the flour to a large oven bag, shake the bag to distribute the flour, and put in a 9-by-13-by-2-inch baking pan.

2 Add the tomatoes, raisins, brown sugar, curry, and salt, and squeeze the bag to blend the ingredients.

3 Rinse the chicken and pat dry. Add to the bag and turn the bag to coat the chicken with sauce. Arrange the ingredients in an even layer in the bag.

4 Close the bag with the provided nylon tie and cut six ^{1}/$_2$-inch slits in the top.

5 Bake for 35 to 40 minutes, or until the chicken is tender, the juices run clear, and an instant-read or meat thermometer registers 170°F. Stir the sauce and spoon it over the chicken and rice.

> **REYNOLDS KITCHENS TIP**
>
> *Always preheat the oven for at least 20 minutes to make sure it is at the correct temperature before cooking. Oven bags should never be put in ovens hotter than 400°F. Some ovens reach higher temperatures than this during the preheating cycle before they stabilize, so it's important that you not put the bag filled with food in the oven during preheating.*

Fiesta Chicken

PREP TIME
15 minutes

COOK TIME
45 minutes

MAKES
4 servings

2 tablespoons flour

One 14^1/$_2$-ounce can diced tomatoes with chili seasonings

2 teaspoons chopped canned or fresh jalapeño pepper

^{1}/$_2$ teaspoon salt

6 chicken pieces, skin removed

One 15-ounce can black beans, drained and rinsed

1 medium yellow bell pepper, cut in 8 pieces

1 Preheat the oven to 350°F. Add the flour to a large oven bag, shake the bag to distribute the flour, and put in a 9-by-13-by-2-inch baking pan.

2 Add the tomatoes, jalapeños, and salt to the bag, and squeeze the bag to blend the ingredients.

3 Rinse the chicken and pat dry. Add to the bag with the black beans and turn the bag to coat the chicken and beans with the sauce. Arrange in an even layer in the bag. Lay the peppers on top of the chicken.

4 Close the bag with the provided nylon tie and cut six ½-inch slits in the top.

5 Bake for 45 to 50 minutes, or until the chicken is tender, the juices run clear, and an instant-read or meat thermometer registers 170°F for the breasts and 180°F for the legs and thighs.

REYNOLDS KITCHENS TIP

It's important to put the oven bag in a pan before putting the food in the bag. Once the chicken and vegetables are added, gently turn the bag to coat all the ingredients with the sauce and seasonings.

Fiesta Chicken

Everyday Favorite Chicken

PREP TIME
14 minutes

COOK TIME
35 minutes

MAKES
4 servings

2 tablespoons flour

One 12-ounce jar chicken gravy

$1/2$ to 1 teaspoon dried basil

4 medium carrots, thinly sliced

2 stalks of celery, thinly sliced

1 small onion, thinly sliced

Four 4- to 6-ounce skinless, boneless chicken breast halves

Rotisserie chicken seasoning

1 Preheat the oven to 350°F. Add the flour to a large oven bag, shake the bag to distribute the flour, and put in a 9-by-13-by-2-inch baking pan.

2 Add the gravy and basil to the bag and squeeze the bag to blend the ingredients. Add the carrots, celery, and onion to the bag, pushing them to the outside edges.

3 Rinse the chicken and pat dry. Rub the chicken with rotisserie chicken seasoning, working it gently into the meat. Put the chicken in the center of the bag.

Everyday Favorite Chicken

4 Close the bag with the provided nylon tie and cut six ½-inch slits in the top.

5 Bake for 35 to 40 minutes, or until the chicken is tender, the juices run clear, and an instant-read or meat thermometer registers 170°F.

6 Transfer the chicken to a serving platter. Stir the gravy and vegetables together before serving.

> **REYNOLDS KITCHENS TIP**
>
> *For other flavorful options for this recipe, try substituting one 10¾-ounce can of cream of mushroom soup for the gravy, seasoned salt and pepper for the rotisserie seasoning, and 1 medium green bell pepper cut in cubes for the celery.*

Creamy Chicken and Vegetables

3 tablespoons flour

One 12-ounce jar chicken gravy

2 teaspoons dried basil

1 teaspoon seasoned salt

⅛ teaspoon pepper

2 cups each frozen green beans and crinkle cut carrots

1 cup frozen whole kernel corn

Four 4- to 6-ounce skinless, boneless chicken breast halves

Hot cooked biscuits, noodles, or rice

PREP TIME
11 minutes
COOK TIME
40 minutes
MAKES
4 servings

1 Preheat the oven to 350°F. Add the flour to a large oven bag, shake the bag to distribute the flour, and put in a 9-by-13-by-2-inch baking pan.

2 Add the gravy, 1 teaspoon of the basil, ½ teaspoon of the seasoned salt, and the pepper, and squeeze the bag to blend the ingredients. Add the green beans and carrots and corn, and turn the bag several times to mix. Arrange the vegetables evenly on both sides of the bag.

3 Rinse the chicken and pat dry. Sprinkle with the remaining basil and seasoned salt. Center the chicken in a single layer in the middle of the vegetables.

> **REYNOLDS KITCHENS TIPS**
>
> ■ *For a quick and easy alternative, substitute one 16-ounce bag of frozen mixed vegetables for the frozen green beans, carrots, and corn.*
>
> ■ *Substitute one 10¾-ounce can condensed cream of chicken or condensed cream of mushroom soup for the jar of gravy. Decrease the amount of flour to 2 tablespoons.*

4 Close the bag with the provided nylon tie and cut six ½-inch slits in the top.

5 Bake for 40 to 45 minutes, or until the chicken is tender, the juices run clear, and an instant-read or meat thermometer registers 170°F. Stir the vegetables and serve the chicken and vegetables with the biscuits, noodles, or rice.

Chicken Tetrazzini

<table>
<tr><td></td><td>PREP TIME</td></tr>
<tr><td></td><td>15 minutes</td></tr>
<tr><td></td><td>COOK TIME</td></tr>
<tr><td></td><td>35 minutes</td></tr>
<tr><td></td><td>MAKES</td></tr>
<tr><td></td><td>6 to 8 servings</td></tr>
</table>

One 10¾-ounce can cream of chicken or mushroom soup, undiluted

1 cup milk

1½ cups grated Parmesan cheese

1 teaspoon onion powder

¼ teaspoon ground nutmeg

¼ teaspoon pepper

8 ounces spaghetti, broken in thirds, cooked and drained

2 cups cubed, cooked chicken

1 cup frozen mixed vegetables, such as broccoli, cauliflower, and carrots

One 4½-ounce jar sliced mushrooms, drained

1 Preheat the oven to 350°F for at least 20 minutes and arrange an oven rack so that it is in the center of the oven. Put a 1½-quart disposable plastic cookware pan on a cookie sheet, so that the pan does not hang over the sides.

2 In a large mixing bowl, stir together the soup, milk, ½ cup of the Parmesan, onion powder, nutmeg, and pepper. Add the cooked spaghetti, chicken, vegetables, and mushrooms, and stir gently to mix. Spread evenly in the pan and sprinkle with the remaining Parmesan.

3 Bake, uncovered, on the cookie sheet for 35 to 40 minutes or until heated through and

REYNOLDS KITCHENS TIPS

▪ *For added color, sprinkle paprika over the top of the casserole before placing it in the oven.*

▪ *Substitute 2 cups of cubed cooked turkey for chicken, if desired.*

▪ *To freeze, let the casserole cool 15 to 20 minutes. Cover with heavy duty aluminum foil and then freeze for up to 1 month.*

▪ *To reheat a frozen casserole, thaw, still covered with foil, in the refrigerator. Preheat the oven to 350°F for at least 20 minutes. Place covered pan on a cookie sheet and reheat for 35 to 40 minutes or until heated through. Remove the foil after the first 20 minutes of heating so the casserole can crisp.*

bubbling around the edges. Use the cookie sheet to remove the pan from the oven and let it stand on the sheet for at least 2 minutes before lifting it by the handles. Let the casserole stand for 5 minutes longer before serving.

Chicken Pot Pie

PREP TIME
12 minutes

COOK TIME
45 minutes

MAKES
6 to 8 servings

4 cups cubed cooked chicken

Two 10¾-ounce cans cream of chicken soup, undiluted

One 16-ounce package frozen mixed vegetables, thawed

½ cup milk

1 teaspoon poultry seasoning

One 10- to 12-ounce can refrigerated buttermilk biscuits

1 Preheat the oven to 350°F for at least 20 minutes and arrange an oven rack so that it is in the center of the oven. Put a 9-by-12½-inch disposable plastic cookware pan on a cookie sheet, so that the pan does not hang over the sides.

2 In a large mixing bowl, combine the chicken, soup, mixed vegetables, milk, and poultry seasoning, and stir well. Spoon into the pan and spread evenly.

3 Bake, uncovered, on the cookie sheet for 30 to 35 minutes or until the casserole begins to bubble around the edges. Use the cookie sheet to remove the pan from the oven. Top the casserole with biscuits, arranging them so that their edges touch.

4 Return to the oven and bake for 15 to 18 minutes longer, or until the biscuits are golden brown. Use the cookie sheet to remove the pan from the oven. Let the casserole stand for at least 2 minutes before lifting it by the handles. Serve hot.

REYNOLDS KITCHENS TIP

Make sure the oven has preheated thoroughly before putting in the disposable cookware pan, supported on a cookie sheet. This takes about 20 minutes. An inexpensive oven thermometer, sold in supermarkets and houseware stores, will help you determine if your oven is accurate.

Chicken and Broccoli Casserole

PREP TIME
20 minutes

COOK TIME
30 minutes

MAKES
10 to 12 servings

2 eggs, lightly beaten

One 10¾-ounce can cream of chicken soup, undiluted

1 cup milk

½ teaspoon pepper

3 cups cubed cooked chicken

Two 14-ounce packages frozen small broccoli florets, thawed and drained

3 cups herb or sage-and-onion-seasoned stuffing

2 cups shredded sharp Cheddar cheese

½ cup finely chopped onion

2 tablespoons butter or margarine, melted

1 Preheat the oven to 350°F. Line a 9-by-13-by-2-inch baking pan with non-stick aluminum foil, non-stick (dull) side facing up.

2 In a mixing bowl, stir together the eggs, soup, milk, and pepper. Add the chicken, broccoli, 2 cups of the stuffing, cheese, and onion. Spoon into the pan and spread into an even layer.

3 In another bowl, crush the remaining cup of stuffing and toss it with the butter. Sprinkle this over the top of the casserole.

4 Bake for 30 to 35 minutes or until the casserole is hot and bubbling and the top is browned.

5 If you desire, sprinkle the top of the casserole with additional cheese arranged in diagonal, decorative rows.

> **REYNOLDS KITCHENS TIP**
>
> *To store the leftover casserole, cover the pan with non-stick aluminum foil, the non-stick (dull) side facing down, on top of the food. This way, the sticky cheese and breaded topping will not stick to the foil.*

Chicken and Garden Vegetables

1 tablespoon flour

2 tablespoons water

1½ teaspoons dried basil

1 teaspoon seasoned salt

¼ teaspoon pepper

Six 4- to 6-ounce skinless, boneless chicken breast halves

2 cups sliced yellow squash

2 cups sliced zucchini

2 medium tomatoes, cut in wedges

⅓ cup shredded Parmesan cheese

PREP TIME
10 minutes

GRILL TIME
20 minutes

MAKES
6 servings

1 Prepare a charcoal or gas grill or preheat the oven to 450°F. The coals should be medium-hot. Put a large extra heavy duty foil bag in a 1-inch-deep pan.

2 In a small bowl, stir together the flour and water until smooth and pour into the bag.

Chicken and Garden Vegetables

3 Combine the basil, seasoned salt, and pepper on a sheet of wax paper.

4 Rinse the chicken and pat dry. Arrange in the bag in an even layer and sprinkle half the seasoning mix over the chicken. Add the squash, zucchini, and tomatoes to the bag, and sprinkle with the remaining seasoning. Double fold the bag to seal.

5 Slide the bag onto the grill or leave it in the pan and place it in the oven. Grill for 20 to 25 minutes in a covered grill or bake for 40 to 45 minutes, or until the chicken is tender, the juices run clear, and an instant-read or meat thermometer registers 170°F.

6 Hold the bag with oven mitts and cut it open with a knife. Carefully fold back the top of the bag so that steam can escape. Sprinkle with cheese before serving.

> **REYNOLDS KITCHENS TIP**
>
> *Save time from start to finish with extra heavy duty foil bags. The food goes right in the foil bag, so prep time is at a minimum. The food cooks evenly over the high heat of the grill and then stays hot as you transport it to a serving platter.*

Easy Chicken Fajitas

| PREP TIME |
| 15 minutes |
| GRILL TIME |
| 15 minutes |
| MAKES |
| 5 to 6 servings |

1 tablespoon flour

1½ pounds chicken tenders or skinless, boneless chicken breast halves, cut in thin strips

1 medium red bell pepper, cut in strips

1 medium green bell pepper, cut in strips

1 medium onion, sliced in rings

2 teaspoons chili powder

1½ teaspoons garlic salt

¼ teaspoon ground cumin

Warm tortillas, salsa, sour cream, shredded Cheddar cheese

1 Prepare a charcoal or gas grill or preheat the oven to 450°F. The coals should be medium-hot. Put a large extra heavy duty foil bag in a 1-inch-deep pan. Sprinkle the flour in the bag.

2 Rinse the chicken and pat dry. Arrange the chicken, bell peppers, and onion in the bag in an even layer.

3 In a small bowl, combine the chili powder, garlic salt, and cumin. Sprinkle the seasoning over the food in the bag. Double fold the bag to seal.

4 Slide the bag onto the grill or leave it in the pan and place it in the oven. Grill for 15 to 18 minutes in a covered grill or bake for 25 to 30 minutes, or until the chicken is tender.

5 Hold the bag with oven mitts and cut it open with a knife. Carefully fold back the top of the bag so that steam can escape. Stir the ingredients.

6 Meanwhile, loosely wrap the tortillas in wax paper and heat in the microwave on high power for 30 seconds to 1 minute.

7 Serve the hot chicken mixture with tortillas, salsa, sour cream, and cheese.

> **REYNOLDS KITCHENS TIP**
>
> *Instead of heating tortillas in the microwave, you can heat them directly on the grill. Wrap them in aluminum foil and set them on the rack for a few minutes. They stay warm and moist in the foil.*

Easy Chicken Fajitas

Southwestern Chicken-and-Corn Dinner

PREP TIME
15 minutes

GRILL TIME
25 minutes

MAKES
5 to 6 servings

1 tablespoon flour

9 bone-in, skinless chicken pieces

4 teaspoons Mexican seasoning blend

3 ears fresh corn, husked and cut in pieces

1 medium green bell pepper, cut into large dice

1 medium red bell pepper, cut into large dice

1 medium onion, cut in eighths

1 Prepare a charcoal or gas grill or preheat the oven to 450°F. The coals should be medium-hot. Put a large extra heavy duty foil bag in a 1-inch-deep pan. Sprinkle the flour in the bag.

2 Rinse the chicken and pat dry. Sprinkle the chicken pieces with half of the Mexican seasoning. Put the chicken, corn, bell peppers, and onion in the bag, and arrange

Southwestern Chicken-and-Corn Dinner

in an even layer. Sprinkle with the remaining season-ing. Double fold the bag to seal.

3 Slide the bag onto the grill or leave it in the pan and place it in the oven. Grill for 25 to 30 minutes in a covered grill or bake for 50 to 55 minutes, or until the chicken is tender, the juices run clear, and an instant-read or meat thermometer registers 170°F for breast meat and 180°F for the other pieces.

4 Hold the bag with oven mitts and cut it open with a knife. Carefully fold back the top of the bag so that steam can escape.

All-American Chicken and Vegetable Dinner

PREP TIME
20 minutes

GRILL TIME
30 minutes

MAKES
5 to 6 servings

1 tablespoon flour

$\frac{1}{4}$ cup water

2 teaspoons grated Parmesan cheese

2 teaspoons garlic salt

1 teaspoon paprika

$\frac{1}{4}$ teaspoon pepper

9 bone-in, skinless chicken pieces

3 ears fresh corn, husked and halved

$\frac{1}{2}$ pound fresh green beans, cut in pieces

1 onion, cut in eighths

1 Prepare a charcoal or gas grill or preheat the oven to 450°F. The coals should be medium-hot. Put a large extra heavy duty foil bag in a 1-inch-deep pan.

2 In a small bowl, stir together the flour and water until smooth, and pour into the bag.

3 In another bowl, mix together the cheese, garlic salt, paprika, and pepper.

4 Rinse the chicken and pat dry. Sprinkle with half the seasoning and then put the chicken in the bag.

5 Sprinkle the remaining seasoning over the corn, beans, and onion. Arrange on top of the chicken. Double fold the bag to seal.

6 Slide the bag onto the grill or leave it in the pan and place it in the oven. Grill for 30 to 35 minutes in a covered grill or bake for 55 to 60 minutes, or until the chicken is tender, the juices run clear, and an instant-read or meat thermometer registers 170°F for the breasts and 180°F for the other pieces.

7 Hold the bag with oven mitts and cut it open with a knife. Carefully fold back the top of the bag so that steam can escape.

Chicken en Papillote

¾ cup dry-packed sun-dried tomatoes

Four 4- to 6-ounce skinless, boneless chicken breast halves

1 teaspoon dried basil or rosemary, crumbled

Salt and pepper

1 medium zucchini, cut in julienne strips

1 cup sliced fresh mushrooms

4 teaspoons butter or margarine

PREP TIME
10 minutes

COOK TIME
20 minutes

MAKES
4 servings

1 Preheat the oven to 400°F.

2 Tear off four 15-inch sheets of parchment paper and fold each one in half. Cut a large heart shape from each sheet, using the folded edge as the center of the heart.

3 Soak sun-dried tomatoes to rehydrate following the package directions. Drain and set aside.

4　Unfold each parchment heart and lay on a countertop. Arrange ¼ of the sun-dried tomatoes on half of each heart near the fold.

5　Rinse the chicken and pat dry. Place one chicken breast half over the tomatoes and sprinkle with basil, salt, and pepper. Top with the zucchini and mushrooms, and put a teaspoon of butter on each.

6　Fold the other half of the heart over the food to enclose it. Starting at the top of each heart, make small overlapping folds to seal the edges together. Twist the last fold at the bottom of the heart several times to make a tight seal. Lay the parchment packages on a large cookie sheet.

7　Bake for 20 to 25 minutes or until the chicken is cooked through and the vegetables are tender.

8　Transfer the parchment packages to dinner plates. Carefully cut an X in top of each package to allow steam to escape. Take care when opening, as the steam is hot.

Chicken en Papillote

Chicken Divan

Four 4- to 6-ounce skinless, boneless chicken breast halves

3 cups frozen broccoli florets

One 10¾-ounce can cream of chicken and broccoli soup, undiluted

1½ cups sliced fresh mushrooms

1 cup shredded Cheddar cheese

Hot cooked rice

PREP TIME

12 minutes

COOK TIME

20 minutes

MAKES

4 servings

1 Preheat the oven to 450°F or prepare a charcoal or gas grill so that the coals are medium-hot.

2 Lay four 12-by-18-inch sheets of heavy duty aluminum foil on the countertop.

3 Rinse the chicken and pat dry. Lay a chicken breast in the center of each foil sheet and arrange the broccoli around them.

4 In a mixing bowl, stir together the soup, mushrooms, and cheese. Spoon over the chicken and broccoli.

Chicken Divan

5 Bring up the sides of the foil. Double fold the top and ends to seal the packets, leaving room for heat circulation inside. Repeat to make 4 packets. If using the oven, put the packets on a cookie sheet.

6 Put the cookie sheet in the oven or slide the packets onto the grill rack. Bake for 20 to 24 minutes or grill for 16 to 18 minutes in a covered grill, or until chicken is tender and juices run clear or meat thermometer reads 170°F. Serve over rice.

Far East–Spiced Chicken

Two 4- to 6-ounce skinless, boneless chicken breast halves	**¼ cup apricot preserves or orange marmalade**
1 teaspoon ground cinnamon	**2 tablespoons orange juice**
½ teaspoon ground coriander	**Garlic salt to taste**
¼ teaspoon ground cumin	**1 cup uncooked rice**
1 medium red bell pepper, cut in strips	**10 dried apricots, chopped**
4 green onions, cut into 1-inch pieces	

PREP TIME
20 minutes

COOK TIME
18 minutes

MAKES
2 servings

1 Preheat the oven to 450°F or prepare a charcoal or gas grill so that the coals are medium-hot.

2 Lay two 12-by-18-inch sheets of non-stick aluminum foil on the countertop, non-stick (dull) side facing up.

3 Combine the cinnamon, coriander, and cumin on a sheet of wax paper.

4 Rinse the chicken and pat dry. Sprinkle the spice mixture over the chicken and gently rub the mixture into the meat to coat evenly. Lay a chicken breast in the center of each foil sheet. Top with bell pepper strips and green onions.

5 In a small bowl, stir together the apricot preserves and orange juice. Drizzle over the chicken and sprinkle with garlic salt.

6 Bring up the sides of the foil. Double fold the top and ends to seal the packets, leaving room for heat circulation inside. Repeat to make 2 packets. If using the oven, put the packets on a cookie sheet.

7 Put the cookie sheet in the oven or slide the packets onto the grill rack. Bake for 18 to 22 minutes or grill for 14 to 18 minutes in a covered grill, or until chicken is tender and juices run clear or meat thermometer reads 170°F.

8 Meanwhile, put the rice and apricots in a saucepan and cook the rice according to the package directions.

9 Serve the chicken and vegetables over the apricot rice.

Far East–Spiced Chicken

Greek Chicken and Vegetables

PREP TIME
8 minutes

COOK TIME
20 minutes

MAKES
4 servings

Four 4- to 6-ounce skinless, boneless chicken breast halves, cut into strips

2 cups fresh or frozen cut green beans or one 15-ounce can cut green beans, drained

One 14$\frac{1}{2}$-ounce can diced tomatoes with garlic and onion

2 teaspoons dried oregano

1 teaspoon salt

$\frac{1}{4}$ teaspoon pepper

4 ounces crumbled feta cheese

1 Preheat the oven to 450°F or prepare a charcoal or gas grill so that the coals are medium-hot.

2 Rinse the chicken and pat dry. Transfer to a mixing bowl and toss with the green beans, tomatoes, oregano, salt, and pepper.

3 Lay four 12-by-18-inch sheets of heavy duty aluminum foil on the countertop. Divide the chicken mixture among the foil sheets.

Greek Chicken and Vegetables

4 Bring up the sides of the foil. Double fold the top and ends to seal the packets, leaving room for heat circulation inside. Repeat to make 4 packets. If using the oven, put the packets on a cookie sheet.

5 Put the cookie sheet in the oven or slide the packets onto the grill rack. Bake for 20 to 24 minutes or grill for 10 to 14 minutes in a covered grill, or until chicken is tender and cooked through. Sprinkle with feta cheese before serving.

REYNOLDS KITCHENS TIP

Canned chopped tomatoes flavored with garlic and onion are easy to find in supermarkets, but if you can't locate them, use another style of canned chopped tomatoes.

Mexican Chicken Dinner

Two 4- to 6-ounce skinless, boneless chicken breast halves

¹/₂ cup chunky salsa

²/₃ cup canned red kidney or black beans, drained (from a 15-ounce can)

¹/₂ cup shredded Mexican blend or Cheddar cheese

Tortilla chips (optional)

PREP TIME
5 minutes

COOK TIME
15 minutes

MAKES
2 servings

1 Preheat the oven to 450°F or prepare a charcoal or gas grill so that the coals are medium-hot.

2 Lay two 12-by-18-inch sheets of heavy duty aluminum foil on the countertop.

3 Rinse the chicken and pat dry. Lay a chicken breast half in the center of each foil sheet and spoon the salsa over the chicken. Top with beans.

4 Bring up the sides of the foil. Double fold the top and ends to seal the packets, leaving room for heat circulation inside. Repeat to make 2 packets. If using the oven, put the packets on a cookie sheet.

5 Put the cookie sheet in the oven or slide the packets onto the grill rack. Bake for 15 to 18 minutes or grill for 11 to 13 minutes in a covered grill, or until chicken is tender and juices run clear. Sprinkle with cheese before serving. Serve with tortilla chips, if desired.

REYNOLDS KITCHENS TIP

Rinse all raw chicken under cool running water and then pat it dry with paper towels.

Roasted Chicken and Vegetables

PREP TIME

20 minutes

COOK TIME

1 hour

MAKES

4 to 5
servings

One $3\frac{1}{2}$- to $4\frac{1}{2}$-pound whole chicken

2 tablespoons olive oil

2 tablespoons lemon juice

3 cloves garlic, minced

2 teaspoons dried Italian seasoning

6 baby portobello mushrooms, halved

2 large zucchini, sliced $\frac{1}{2}$-inch thick

2 large yellow squash, sliced $\frac{1}{2}$-inch thick

1 medium red bell pepper, sliced $\frac{1}{2}$-inch thick

1 medium onion, cut in eighths

Seasoned salt

Black pepper

1 Preheat the oven to 450°F. Line a 9-by-13-by-2-inch baking pan with heavy duty aluminum foil.

2 Rinse the chicken and pat dry. Put in the pan.

3 In a small bowl, stir together the olive oil, lemon juice, garlic, and Italian seasoning until blended. Brush half of the oil mixture on the chicken.

4 Arrange the mushrooms, zucchini, squash, bell pepper, and onion around the chicken. Drizzle the vegetables with the remaining oil mixture and sprinkle the chicken and vegetables with seasoned salt and pepper.

5 Make a foil tent by putting a large sheet of folded foil over the chicken, leaving space between the top of the chicken and foil for heat circulation. Crimp the foil along the long sides of the pan.

6 Bake for 45 minutes. Remove the foil and continue baking for about 15 minutes longer or until the chicken is tender, the juices run clear, or an instant-read or meat thermometer registers 180°F.

> **REYNOLDS KITCHENS TIP**
>
> *Roasting a whole chicken under an aluminum foil tent ensures moist, tender meat and nut-brown, crispy skin. Lining the roasting pan with foil makes cleanup quick and easy.*

Easy Chicken and Rice

PREP TIME
15 minutes

COOK TIME
45 minutes

MAKES
4 servings

2 cups uncooked instant rice

Two 10¾-ounce cans cream of chicken soup, undiluted

½ cup water

1 teaspoon seasoned salt plus more for seasoning

2 medium carrots, sliced

1 medium green bell pepper, cut into large dice

1 small onion, thinly sliced

2½ to 3 pounds skinless chicken pieces, about 6 pieces

Paprika

Seasoned pepper

1 Preheat the oven to 450°F. Line a 9-by-13-by-2-inch baking pan with heavy duty aluminum foil.

2 In a mixing bowl, combine the rice, soup, water, and 1 teaspoon of seasoned salt. Add the carrots, bell pepper, and onion, and toss just to mix. Spoon into the foil-lined pan and spread evenly.

3 Rinse the chicken and pat dry. Lay over the rice in an even layer. Sprinkle with more seasoned salt, paprika, and seasoned pepper.

4 Cover the pan with heavy duty aluminum foil.

5 Bake for 45 to 50 minutes or until the chicken is tender, the juices run clear, and an instant-read or meat thermometer registers 170°F for the breast and 180°F for the other pieces.

6 Remove the chicken pieces from the pan. Stir the rice and serve topped with the chicken.

> **REYNOLDS KITCHENS TIP**
>
> *Aluminum foil is a great cover for casseroles and other dishes, so if you don't have a pan with a cover, don't worry. The foil forms a tight-fitting lid. Use it again when storing leftovers.*

Turn pan upside down and press a sheet of Reynolds Wrap Heavy Duty Aluminum Foil around it.

Remove foil. Flip pan upright and drop foil inside. Crimp edges of foil to rim of pan.

Chicken with Pine Nut Couscous

PREP TIME
12 minutes

COOK TIME
22 minutes

MAKES
2 servings

Two 4- to 6-ounce skinless, boneless chicken breast halves

One 5.6-ounce package pine nut couscous mix

2 tablespoons olive oil

1 medium zucchini, sliced

1 cup cherry tomatoes

1/2 teaspoon dried basil

8 ice cubes

2/3 cup water

1 Preheat the oven to 450°F or prepare a charcoal or gas grill so that the coals are medium-hot.

2 Lay two 12-by-18-inch sheets of non-stick aluminum foil on the countertop, non-stick (dull) side facing up.

3 Rinse the chicken and pat dry. Center a chicken breast on each sheet of foil.

Chicken with Pine Nut Couscous

Arrange couscous around chicken. Sprinkle the chicken and couscous with the spices from the mix and drizzle with olive oil. Top with zucchini and tomatoes and sprinkle with basil. Put the ice cubes over the couscous.

4 Bring up the sides of the foil. Double fold the top and one end of the packet. Pour half the water through the open end of the packet. Double fold remaining end to seal the packet, leaving room for heat circulation inside. Repeat to make 2 packets. If using the oven, put the packets on a cookie sheet.

5 Put the cookie sheet in the oven or slide the packets onto the grill rack. Bake for 22 to 24 minutes or grill for 12 to 14 minutes in a covered grill or until the chicken is tender, the juices run clear, and an instant-read or meat thermometer registers 170°F.

. . .

Baked Fiesta Enchiladas

PREP TIME
25 minutes

COOK TIME
20 minutes

MAKES
6 servings

I medium red bell pepper, chopped

One 8-ounce package sliced fresh mushrooms

$1/2$ cup sliced green onions

I tablespoon butter or vegetable oil

I cup sour cream, plus more for serving

One $10^3/4$-ounce can cream of chicken soup, undiluted

One 8-ounce package shredded sharp Cheddar cheese

One $2^1/2$-ounce jar sliced ripe olives, drained (optional)

2 cups chopped cooked chicken or turkey

Six 8- to 10-inch spinach, tomato, or flour tortillas

One 16-ounce jar salsa

Chopped fresh cilantro (optional)

I Preheat the oven to 350°F for at least 20 minutes and arrange an oven rack so that it is in the center of the oven. Put a 9-by-12½-inch disposable plastic cookware pan on a cookie sheet, so that the pan does not hang over the sides.

2 In a medium saucepan, combine the bell pepper, mushrooms, onions, and butter, and cook over medium-high heat for 7 to 10 minutes, or until the pepper and

mushrooms are tender. Drain and add the sour cream, soup, half of the cheese, and the olives. Add the chicken and stir gently to mix.

3 Lay the tortillas on a wax paper sheet and spoon about ¾ to 1 cup of filling down the center of each. Roll up and place, side by side and seam side down, in the pan. Top with salsa and the remaining cheese.

4 Bake, uncovered, on the cookie sheet for 20 to 25 minutes or until thoroughly heated. Use the cookie sheet to remove the pan from the oven and let the casserole stand for at least 2 minutes before lifting by the handles. Top with additional sour cream and cilantro, if desired.

Baked Fiesta Enchiladas

Sausage and Black Bean Dinner

PREP TIME
10 minutes

GRILL TIME
20 minutes

MAKES
5 to 6 servings

1 tablespoon flour

Two 15-ounce cans black beans, drained and rinsed

Two 10-ounce packages frozen whole kernel corn

One 16-ounce jar chunky salsa

1 pound smoked turkey sausage, sliced

1 cup shredded Colby and Monterey Jack cheese

1 Prepare a charcoal or a gas grill or preheat the oven to 450°F. The coals should be medium-hot. Put a large extra heavy duty foil bag in a 1-inch-deep pan.

2 In a large bowl, stir together the flour, beans, corn, salsa, and sliced sausage. Transfer to the bag and arrange in an even layer. Double fold the bag to seal.

3 Slide the bag onto the grill or leave it in the pan and place it in the oven. Grill for 20 to 25 minutes in a covered grill or bake for 50 to 55 minutes, or until hot.

4 Hold the bag with oven mitts and cut it open with a knife. Carefully fold back the top of the bag so that steam can escape. Sprinkle with cheese before serving.

> **REYNOLDS KITCHENS TIP**
>
> *Turkey sausage is gaining in popularity for its leanness and mild flavor that blends so well with other ingredients. If you prefer another kind of sausage, such as sweet Italian or Mexican chorizo, use it here.*

Sausage and Black Bean Dinner

Layered Tortilla Casserole

Twelve 4-inch corn tortillas, lightly toasted and halved

3 cups coarsely chopped cooked chicken

One 10-ounce package frozen cut-leaf spinach, thawed and well drained

Salt and pepper

5 cups of your favorite tomato sauce

One 8-ounce package shredded Mexican cheese blend

One 15¼-ounce can whole kernel corn, drained

2 poblano chiles, roasted and cut in strips

PREP TIME
25 minutes

COOK TIME
45 minutes

MAKES
8 to 10 servings

Preheat the oven to 350°F. Line a 9-by-13-by-2-inch baking pan with non-stick aluminum foil, non-stick (dull) side facing up.

Layered Tortilla Casserole

2 Arrange about 12 tortilla halves in the bottom of the pan to cover as completely as possible. Top with chicken and spinach, and sprinkle with salt and pepper. Spoon half the sauce and half the cheese over the spinach. Arrange the remaining tortilla halves over the cheese and then top with the corn, chiles, and the remaining sauce and cheese.

3 Cover the pan with non-stick foil, non-stick (dull) side facing down.

4 Bake for 30 minutes. Remove the foil and continue baking for 15 to 20 minutes longer or until the cheese melts and the casserole is hot and bubbling. Let stand for 5 to 10 minutes before cutting into squares for serving.

• • •

Ribeye Roast and Roasted Garlic Vegetables

PREP TIME
15 minutes

COOK TIME
1½ hours

MAKES
9 to 10 servings

1 tablespoon flour

1½ teaspoons dried oregano

¾ teaspoon pepper

½ teaspoon salt

One 3- to 3½-pound boneless beef ribeye roast

1¼ pounds small red potatoes, halved

One 16-ounce package peeled baby carrots

2 medium onions, cut in wedges

1 whole bulb garlic, unpeeled

1 tablespoon butter

1 Preheat the oven to 325°F. Add the flour to a large oven bag, shake the bag to distribute the flour, and put in a 9-by-13-by-2-inch baking pan.

2 Combine the oregano, pepper, and salt on a sheet of wax paper. Rub the spices into the beef, working it gently into the meat.

3 Put the beef in the bag and arrange the potatoes, carrots, and onions around it. Sprinkle with salt and pepper.

4 Cut the top off the garlic bulb and discard the top. Put the bulb in the bag.

5 Close the bag with the provided nylon tie and cut six ½-inch slits in the top.

6 Bake for 1½ to 1¾ hours, or until an instant-read or meat thermometer registers 145°F.

7 Put the vegetables in a serving bowl and transfer the beef to a cutting board.

8 Squeeze the softened garlic pulp into a small bowl. Discard the skin. Add the butter, and mash to mix. Toss with the vegetables and serve with sliced beef.

Ribeye Roast and Roasted Garlic Vegetables

Hearty Beef Stew

2 tablespoons flour

One 12-ounce jar beef gravy

½ teaspoon salt (optional)

½ teaspoon pepper

One 2-pound boneless beef chuck roast, cut in 2-inch chunks

One 16-ounce package peeled baby carrots

1⅓ pounds potatoes (4 medium), peeled and quartered

1 large onion, cut in 1-inch chunks

PREP TIME
20 minutes

COOK TIME
1½ hours

MAKES
4 to 5 servings

1 Preheat the oven to 350°F. Add the flour to a large oven bag, shake the bag to distribute the flour, and put in a 9-by-13-by-2-inch baking pan.

2 Add the gravy, salt, and pepper, and squeeze the bag to blend the ingredients. Add the beef, carrots, potatoes, and onion, and turn the bag to coat the beef and vegetables with the gravy.

3 Close the bag with the provided nylon tie and cut six ½-inch slits in the top.

4 Bake for 1½ to 2 hours, or until the beef and potatoes are tender.

> **REYNOLDS KITCHENS TIP**
>
> *Because the oven bag expands during cooking, make sure it's far enough from the oven walls so that it won't touch them. The center rack of the oven is the best choice for a large oven bag.*

Hearty Beef Stew

Baked Spaghetti

One 8-ounce package spaghetti, cooked and drained

2 tablespoons butter or margarine

1 cup grated Parmesan cheese

One 24-ounce container ricotta cheese or cottage cheese

1 pound ground beef

One 28-ounce jar chunky garden-style pasta sauce

One 8-ounce package shredded mozzarella cheese

PREP TIME
20 minutes

COOK TIME
45 minutes

MAKES
6 servings

1   Preheat the oven to 400°F. Line a 9-by-13-by-2-inch baking pan with non-stick aluminum foil with non-stick (dull) side facing up.

2   In a mixing bowl, toss the hot spaghetti with the butter until the butter melts and

Baked Spaghetti

coats the pasta. Add ½ cup of the Parmesan cheese and toss to coat. Arrange the spaghetti in an even layer in the foil-lined pan.

3 Spread the ricotta cheese over the spaghetti and sprinkle with ¼ cup of the remaining Parmesan cheese.

4 Brown the ground beef in a skillet set over medium-high heat. Drain the fat from the pan. Add the pasta sauce and heat until hot and bubbling. Spoon over the pasta and top with the mozzarella and the remaining Parmesan cheese.

5 Cover with non-stick aluminum foil with the non-stick (dull) side facing down. Bake for 30 minutes. Remove the foil and continue baking for about 15 minutes longer or until the cheese is lightly browned. Let the casserole stand for 10 minutes before serving.

> **REYNOLDS KITCHENS TIP**
>
> *Cheesy casseroles such as this one made with pasta and beef and generous amounts of mozzarella and Parmesan cheeses are so much easier to serve, store, and clean up after when you use non-stick aluminum foil.*

...

Satay-Style Beef

PREP TIME
25 minutes

COOK TIME
14 minutes

MAKES
4 servings

1 pound beef top sirloin steak, ½-inch thick, fat trimmed and sliced into thin strips across the grain

3 cups fresh snow peas

⅓ cup reduced-sodium teriyaki sauce

2½ tablespoons smooth peanut butter

¾ teaspoon cornstarch

Hot cooked angel hair pasta

2 plum tomatoes, chopped

4 green onions, sliced

1 Preheat the oven to 450°F or prepare a charcoal or gas grill so that the coals are medium-hot.

2 Lay four 12-by-18-inch sheets of heavy duty aluminum foil on the countertop. Divide the steak among the foil sheets and top with snow peas.

3 In a small bowl, whisk together the teriyaki sauce, peanut butter, and cornstarch until smooth. Pour over the steak and snow peas.

4 Bring up the sides of the foil. Double fold the top and ends to seal the packets, leaving room for heat circulation inside. Repeat to make 4 packets. If using the oven, put the packets on a cookie sheet.

5 Put the cookie sheet in the oven or slide the packets onto the grill rack. Bake for 14 to 18 minutes or grill for 10 to 14 minutes in a covered grill, or until the beef is tender.

6 Serve over angel hair pasta and sprinkle each serving with tomatoes and green onions.

Satay-Style Beef

Pepper Steak Packets

1 pound boneless beef sirloin steak, $\frac{1}{2}$-inch thick

$\frac{1}{2}$ teaspoon garlic powder

$\frac{1}{4}$ teaspoon black pepper

1 medium green bell pepper, cut in strips

1 medium red bell pepper, cut in strips

$\frac{1}{2}$ cup light teriyaki sauce

Hot cooked rice (optional)

PREP TIME
12 minutes

COOK TIME
12 minutes

MAKES
4 servings

1 Preheat the oven to 450°F or prepare a charcoal or gas grill so that the coals are medium-hot.

2 Rub the steak with the garlic powder and pepper. Slice into thin strips and transfer to a shallow dish. Add the pepper strips and toss with the teriyaki sauce.

Pepper Steak Packets

3 Lay four 12-by-18-inch sheets of heavy duty aluminum foil on the countertop. Divide the steak mixture among the foil sheets.

4 Bring up the sides of the foil. Double fold the top and ends to seal the packets, leaving room for heat circulation inside. Repeat to make 4 packets. If using the oven, put the packets on a cookie sheet.

5 Put the cookie sheet in the oven or slide the packets onto the grill rack. Bake for 12 to 15 minutes or grill for 7 to 9 minutes in a covered grill, or until the beef is tender. Serve over rice, if desired.

> **REYNOLDS KITCHENS TIP**
>
> *When you're in a hurry, keep in mind that meals cooked in foil packets are cooked in less than 20 minutes, either in the oven or on the grill. Some are done in just 15 minutes or less!*

. . .

Oriental Pork Tenderloin Packets

I pound pork tenderloin, sliced	2 green onions, sliced
2 cups broccoli florets	1/4 cup soy sauce
2 cups thinly sliced carrots	4 teaspoons sesame oil
One 8-ounce can sliced water chestnuts, drained	I teaspoon minced fresh ginger
I medium red bell pepper, cut in strips	Hot cooked rice

PREP TIME
15 minutes

COOK TIME
18 minutes

MAKES
4 servings

1 Preheat the oven to 450°F or prepare a charcoal or gas grill so that the coals are medium-hot.

2 Lay four 12-by-18-inch sheets of heavy duty aluminum foil on the countertop. Top each with pork slices, broccoli, carrots, water chestnuts, bell pepper, and onions.

3 In a small bowl, stir together the soy sauce, sesame oil, and ginger. Spoon over the pork and vegetables.

4 Bring up the sides of the foil. Double fold the top and ends to seal the packets, leaving room for heat circulation inside. Repeat to make 4 packets. If using the oven, put the packets on a cookie sheet.

5 Put the cookie sheet in the oven or slide the packets onto the grill rack. Bake for 18 to 22 minutes or grill for 14 to 16 minutes in a covered grill, or until the pork is tender. Serve with rice and more soy sauce, if desired.

Oriental Pork Tenderloin Packets

Easy Pork Chop Packets

PREP TIME
10 minutes

COOK TIME
16 minutes

MAKES
4 servings

1 small onion, thinly sliced

4 boneless pork chops, about $\frac{1}{2}$-inch thick

Salt and pepper

One 10$\frac{3}{4}$-ounce can cream of mushroom soup, undiluted

2 tablespoons soy sauce

1 medium green bell pepper, sliced

Hot cooked rice

I Preheat the oven to 450°F or prepare a charcoal or gas grill so that the coals are medium-hot.

Easy Pork Chop Packets

2 Lay four 12-by-18-inch sheets of heavy duty aluminum foil on the countertop. Top each sheet with one-fourth of the onion slices and a pork chop and sprinkle with salt and pepper.

3 In a mixing bowl, stir together the soup and soy sauce. Spoon over the pork chops. Top with bell pepper slices.

4 Bring up the sides of the foil. Double fold the top and ends to seal the packets, leaving room for heat circulation inside. Repeat to make 4 packets. If using the oven, put the packets on a cookie sheet.

5 Put the cookie sheet in the oven or slide the packets onto the grill rack. Bake for 16 to 18 minutes or grill for 10 to 12 minutes in a covered grill, or until the pork chops are tender. Serve over the rice.

> **REYNOLDS KITCHENS TIP**
>
> *Cooking foods in foil is a quick, low-fat method for sealing in moisture and flavor. This is great for cuts like pork chops, which can be cooked with no added fat so their rich flavor shines through.*

Vegetables and Side Dishes

Italian Vegetable Toss

Teriyaki Roasted Vegetables

Oriental Vegetable Packet

Herbed Vegetable Packet

Lemon-Dill Vegetables

Garden Vegetables

Greek Garden Vegetables

Green Bean Casserole

Asparagus with Mustard Sauce

Herbed Corn on the Cob

Cajun Spiced Corn

Zucchini-Tomato Vegetable Packet

Yellow Squash, Tomato, and Onion Packet

Sesame-Broccoli Packet

Broccoli and Carrots with Oranges

Seasoned Broccoli and Mushrooms

Cauliflower with Fiery Cheese Sauce

Easy Homestyle Vegetables

Honey Carrots

New England Baked Beans

Triple-Cheese Potato Bake

Glazed Sweet Potatoes

Homestyle Fries with Salsa

Packet Potatoes

Southwestern Potato Packet

Roasted Garlic Mashed Potatoes

Creamy Macaroni and Cheese

My grandparents always had a garden when I was a child. Their influence helped me develop a love for fresh vegetables.
—Betty

When I was a kid, my mom's vegetable garden was so enormous, my dad cultivated it with farm equipment.
—Pat

BOTH OF OUR FAMILIES HAD huge gardens when we were growing up. The fresh vegetables tasted so good, our moms didn't have to tell us to eat our vegetables. Today's cooks are in such a hurry to put a meal on the table that often they're doing well just to get the main dish and one side done. Unfortunately, the casualty is often the vegetables. In this chapter, we tackled this problem with some great vegetable combinations and side dishes that are quick to make and taste great.

Vegetables and other side dishes are important for good health and balanced eating. We recommend that everyone follow the national "5 A Day for Better Health Program."

If this chapter had a message it would be, "Eat your veggies!"

Vegetables

It's easy to open a can of beans or cook a package of frozen peas, and while there's nothing inherently wrong with these foods, vegetable sides can be so

much more enticing. Oven-roasted vegetables, such as our Teriyaki Roasted Vegetables, are sweet and rich tasting, and couldn't be easier in a non-stick foil-lined pan.

Our signature vegetable recipes are prepared in foil packets. This is a superior way to cook vegetables. Wrap four to six servings of vegetables with seasonings in a sheet of foil and pop it in the oven to bake or cook it on the grill. The vegetables steam to crisp-tender perfection. Betty's favorite vegetable is yellow squash. So, the Yellow Squash, Tomato, and Onion Packet is her top choice. Probably the simplest vegetable packet you can make is Honey Carrots. They are "quick as a bunny" when you buy the bags of precut and peeled "baby" carrots.

If you like to cook vegetables in the microwave, you are not alone. It's terrific for quick cooking. Cover a microwave-safe dish with wax paper to form a self-venting lid that holds in just the right amount of steam and moisture, as demonstrated in the recipe for Italian Vegetable Toss. Betty keeps a roll of wax paper next to her microwave at home so that she always has a handy lid ready.

Other Sides

Potatoes and pasta round out the sides in this chapter. There are three recipes that are the quintessential potluck or picnic foods—New England

Baked Beans, Triple-Cheese Potato Bake, and Creamy Macaroni and Cheese. Try our famous Creamy Macaroni and Cheese, cooked in a Pot Lux pan, and you'll never go back to the packaged variety.

We cook and serve Glazed Sweet Potatoes in a pan lined with Reynolds Wrap Release Non-Stick Aluminum Foil. Regardless of the copious amounts of brown sugar, butter, and corn syrup, the potatoes never stick, which means you (not the pan!) get all the yummy goodness.

Roasted Garlic Mashed Potatoes were first seen on menus in restaurants. But, with our simple technique, it's easy to make these flavored mashed potatoes at home. The trick is to wrap the garlic heads in foil and roast them for about 25 minutes until soft and mild.

Potato packets are especially good on the grill. Pat's children like the Southwestern Potato Packets, which she grills alongside pork tenderloin for backyard cookouts. The Southwestern Potato Packet is seasoned with chili powder and other Southwestern-inspired ingredients, while our Packet Potatoes are deliciously dressed with nothing more exotic than olive oil, salt, pepper, and an onion.

Words of Wisdom

While these meals do not have to be complicated to be good, nourishing, and wholesome, please don't neglect the side dishes. They are the glue that holds the meal together.

side dishes are

the glue that holds the

meal together

Italian Vegetable Toss

10 medium mushrooms, quartered

2 medium zucchini, sliced

2 medium yellow squash, sliced

1 tablespoon butter or margarine, diced

1 tablespoon fresh basil leaves, snipped

$\frac{1}{4}$ teaspoon cracked black pepper

2 medium tomatoes, cut in 8 wedges

$\frac{1}{4}$ cup shredded Parmesan cheese

PREP TIME
10 minutes

COOK TIME
10 minutes

MAKES
4 servings

1 Put the mushrooms, zucchini, yellow squash, butter, basil, and pepper in a shallow 2-quart microwave-safe casserole. Cover with a sheet of wax paper and microwave on high power for 8 to 10 minutes, or until the squash is crisp-tender. If the microwave does not have a turntable, rotate the bowl halfway through cooking time.

2 Add the tomato wedges and sprinkle the casserole with Parmesan cheese. Replace the wax paper and microwave on high power for 2 to 3 minutes or until the tomatoes soften and the cheese melts.

REYNOLDS KITCHENS TIP

Wax paper is a terrific cover for foods during microwaving. It holds in moisture but does not seal tightly, and so is self-venting. Tear off the amount you need and lay it over the top of the casserole or other microwave-safe dish.

Italian Vegetable Toss

Teriyaki Roasted Vegetables

PREP TIME
20 minutes

COOK TIME
35 minutes

MAKES
8 to 10
servings

$^1\!/_3$ cup teriyaki sauce

2 tablespoons balsamic vinegar

1 tablespoon olive oil

$^1\!/_2$ teaspoon garlic salt

$^1\!/_4$ teaspoon freshly ground pepper

3 medium yellow squash, sliced $^1\!/_2$-inch thick

1 medium red bell pepper, cut in 1-inch dice

1 medium green bell pepper, cut in 1-inch dice

2 large portobello mushrooms, sliced in $^1\!/_4$-inch slices

1 large onion, cut in thin wedges

1 Preheat the oven to 450°F. Position the oven racks so that one is in the top third and one in the bottom third of the oven. Line two 10$^1\!/_2$-by-15$^1\!/_2$-by-1-inch pans with non-stick aluminum foil, non-stick (dull) side facing up.

2 In a large mixing bowl, stir together the teriyaki sauce, vinegar, oil, garlic salt, and pepper. Reserve and set aside 2 tablespoons for drizzling.

3 Put the squash, peppers, mushrooms, and onion in the bowl, and turn to coat. Divide the ingredients between the pans and spread evenly.

4 Bake for 35 to 40 minutes, or until the vegetables are browned and tender, stirring and switching racks after 20 minutes. Drizzle each pan with the reserved sauce before serving.

> **REYNOLDS KITCHENS TIP**
>
> *Slow roasting vegetables in the oven cooks them gently and brings out their natural sugars so that they caramelize very slightly and taste deep, rich, and sweet. The vegetables need little tending and won't stick to the pan when you line it with non-stick aluminum foil.*

. . .

Oriental Vegetable Packet

PREP TIME
12 minutes

COOK TIME
20 minutes

MAKES
4 to 6
servings

2 cups broccoli florets

2 cups snow peas

1 medium onion, sliced

1 medium red bell pepper, cut in strips

2 cloves garlic, minced

2 tablespoons soy sauce

1 tablespoon sesame oil or vegetable oil

$^1\!/_2$ teaspoon minced fresh ginger (optional)

$^1\!/_4$ teaspoon crushed red pepper flakes (optional)

1 Preheat the oven to 450°F or prepare a charcoal or gas grill so that the coals are medium-hot.

2 Lay an 18-by-24-inch sheet of heavy duty aluminum foil on the countertop. Arrange the broccoli, snow peas, onion, and bell pepper in the center of the foil. Top with garlic, soy sauce, and sesame oil. Sprinkle with ginger and red pepper flakes, if desired.

3 Bring up the sides of the foil. Double fold the top and ends to seal the packet, leaving room for heat circulation inside. If using the oven, put the packet on a cookie sheet.

4 Put the cookie sheet in the oven or slide the packet onto the grill rack. Bake for 20 to 25 minutes or grill for 10 to 12 minutes in a covered grill, or until the vegetables are crisp-tender.

> **REYNOLDS KITCHENS TIP**
>
> *Vegetables cooked in packets are super moist and cooked until crisp-tender. The enclosed environment seals in nutrients, as well.*

Center ingredients on a sheet (12 x 18 inches) of Reynolds Wrap Heavy Duty Aluminum Foil.

Bring up foil sides. Double fold top and ends to seal making one large packet, leaving room for heat circulation inside.

Bake on a cookie sheet in preheated 450°F oven, *or* grill on medium-high in covered grill until vegetables are crisp-tender.

After cooking, open end of foil packet first to allow steam to escape. Then open top of foil packet.

Herbed Vegetable Packet

3 cups broccoli florets

2 medium carrots, thinly sliced

1 small onion, thinly sliced

1 medium yellow squash or zucchini, sliced

1 teaspoon dried basil

1 teaspoon garlic salt

2 tablespoons butter or margarine

2 ice cubes

PREP TIME
12 minutes

COOK TIME
20 minutes

MAKES
4 to 6 servings

1 Preheat the oven to 450°F or prepare a charcoal or gas grill so that the coals are medium-hot.

2 Lay an 18-by-24-inch sheet of heavy duty aluminum foil on the countertop. Arrange the broccoli, carrots, onion, and squash in the center of the foil. Sprinkle with basil and garlic salt, and top with butter and ice cubes.

Herbed Vegetable Packet

3 Bring up the sides of the foil. Double fold the top and ends to seal the packet, leaving room for heat circulation inside. If using the oven, put the packet on a cookie sheet.

4 Put the cookie sheet in the oven or slide the packet onto the grill rack. Bake for 20 to 25 minutes or grill for 15 to 20 minutes in a covered grill, or until the vegetables are crisp-tender.

· · ·

Lemon-Dill Vegetables

2½ cups broccoli florets	1 teaspoon dried dill
2½ cups cauliflower florets	1 teaspoon olive oil
1 cup peeled baby carrots	½ teaspoon salt
1 clove garlic, minced	2 ice cubes
1 tablespoon grated lemon peel	Fresh lemon juice

PREP TIME
9 minutes

COOK TIME
20 minutes

MAKES
6 servings

1 Preheat the oven to 450°F or prepare a charcoal or gas grill so that the coals are medium-hot.

2 Lay an 18-by-24-inch sheet of heavy duty aluminum foil on the countertop. Arrange the broccoli, cauliflower, and carrots in the center of the foil. Sprinkle with garlic, lemon peel, dill, oil, and salt. Top with ice cubes.

3 Bring up the sides of the foil. Double fold the top and ends to seal the packet, leaving room for heat circulation inside. If using the oven, put the packet on a cookie sheet.

4 Put the cookie sheet in the oven or slide the packet onto the grill rack. Bake for 20 to 25 minutes or grill for 10 to 12 minutes in a covered grill, or until the vegetables are crisp-tender. Squeeze fresh lemon juice over the vegetables and stir just before serving.

Garden Vegetables

3 cups broccoli florets

2 cups cauliflower florets

1/2 medium red bell pepper, cut in 1-inch pieces

1 teaspoon dried basil

1/2 teaspoon salt

1/8 teaspoon pepper

2 ice cubes

PREP TIME
10 minutes

COOK TIME
20 minutes

MAKES
4 to 6
servings

1 Preheat the oven to 450°F or prepare a charcoal or gas grill so that the coals are medium-hot.

2 Lay an 18-by-24-inch sheet of heavy duty aluminum foil on the countertop. Arrange the broccoli, cauliflower, and bell pepper in the center of the foil. Sprinkle with basil, salt, and pepper. Top with ice cubes.

Garden Vegetables

3 Bring up the sides of the foil. Double fold the top and ends to seal the packet, leaving room for heat circulation inside. If using the oven, put the packet on a cookie sheet.

4 Put the cookie sheet in the oven or slide the packet onto the grill rack. Bake for 20 to 25 minutes or grill for 15 to 18 minutes in a covered grill, or until the vegetables are crisp-tender.

...

Greek Garden Vegetables

4 cups broccoli florets

2½ cups cauliflower florets

1 pint cherry tomatoes

¼ cup pitted, sliced Kalamata olives or sliced ripe olives

1½ teaspoons dried oregano

Salt and pepper

2 ice cubes

¼ cup crumbled feta cheese

PREP TIME
8 minutes
COOK TIME
20 minutes
MAKES
8 servings

Greek Garden Vegetables

1 Preheat the oven to 450°F or prepare a charcoal or gas grill so that the coals are medium-hot.

2 Lay an 18-by-24-inch sheet of heavy duty aluminum foil on the countertop. Arrange the broccoli, cauliflower, tomatoes, and olives in the center of the foil. Sprinkle with oregano, salt, and pepper. Top with ice cubes.

3 Bring up the sides of the foil. Double fold the top and ends to seal the packet, leaving room for heat circulation inside. If using the oven, put the packet on a cookie sheet.

4 Put the cookie sheet in the oven or slide the packet onto the grill rack. Bake for 20 to 25 minutes or grill for 12 to 14 minutes in a covered grill, or until the vegetables are crisp-tender. Sprinkle with feta cheese before serving.

> **REYNOLDS KITCHENS TIP**
>
> *Heavy duty aluminum foil forms a sturdy packet for enough vegetables for eight servings. If you don't have heavy duty foil, substitute a double layer of regular aluminum foil.*

. . .

Green Bean Casserole

Two 32-ounce packages frozen cut green beans, cooked and drained

Two 10¾-ounce cans cream of mushroom soup, undiluted

1 cup milk

2 teaspoons soy sauce or Worcestershire sauce

2 cups French fried onions

One 4-ounce jar diced pimiento, drained

½ teaspoon salt

¼ to ½ teaspoon pepper

PREP TIME
16 minutes

COOK TIME
40 minutes

MAKES
18 to 20
servings

1 Preheat the oven to 350°F for at least 20 minutes and arrange an oven rack so that it is in the center of the oven. Put a 9-by-12½-inch disposable plastic cookware pan on a cookie sheet, so that the pan does not hang over the sides.

2 Place half of the beans in an even layer in the pan.

3 In a mixing bowl, stir together the soup, milk, soy sauce, 1 cup of the onions,

pimiento, and salt. Add pepper to taste. Spread half of the sauce over the beans. Top with the remaining beans and then with the rest of the sauce.

4 Bake, uncovered, on the cookie sheet for 30 minutes. Use the cookie sheet to remove the pan from the oven and sprinkle with the remaining cup of onions. Bake for about 10 minutes longer, or until heated through and bubbling around the edges. Use the cookie sheet to remove the pan from the oven and let the casserole stand on the sheet for at least 2 minutes before lifting it by the handles.

REYNOLDS KITCHENS TIP

Disposable plastic cookware pans are reusable and can be run through the dishwasher on the top rack. Save them and use them for heating food in the microwave.

. . .

Asparagus with Mustard Sauce

2 pounds asparagus, trimmed

3 tablespoons butter or margarine

Salt and pepper

1 cup light sour cream

2 tablespoons red wine vinegar

¼ cup Dijon mustard

2 teaspoons sugar

⅛ teaspoon crushed red pepper flakes

PREP TIME
8 minutes

COOK TIME
14 minutes

MAKES
6 to 8 servings

1 Preheat the oven to 450°F or prepare a charcoal or gas grill so that the coals are medium-hot.

2 Lay an 18-by-24-inch sheet of heavy duty aluminum foil on the countertop. Lay the asparagus in the center of the foil and top with butter.

3 Bring up the sides of the foil. Double fold the top and ends to seal the packet, leaving room for heat circulation inside. If using the oven, put the packet on a cookie sheet.

4 Put the cookie sheet in the oven or slide the packet onto the grill rack. Bake for 14 to 16 minutes or grill for 7 to 9 minutes in a covered grill, or until the vegetables are crisp-tender. Open the foil and season to taste with salt and pepper.

REYNOLDS KITCHENS TIP

You don't need a knife to trim asparagus. Rinse them and then hold the stalk loosely with both hands and gently bend it. The asparagus stalk will break naturally where it should be trimmed.

5 Meanwhile, in a small microwave-safe bowl, stir together the sour cream, vinegar, mustard, sugar, and red pepper flakes until blended. Microwave on high power for 1½ to 2 minutes or until warm. Spoon the sauce over the asparagus.

Asparagus with Mustard Sauce

Herbed Corn on the Cob

PREP TIME
8 minutes

GRILL TIME
20 minutes

MAKES
6 servings

6 ears fresh corn, husked

1/3 cup butter or margarine, melted

1 teaspoon dried rosemary, crushed

1/4 teaspoon salt

1/4 teaspoon pepper

2 ice cubes

1 Prepare a charcoal or gas grill or preheat the oven to 450°F. The coals should be medium-hot. Put a large extra heavy duty foil bag in a 1-inch-deep pan.

2 Arrange the corn in an even layer in the bag.

3 In a small bowl, stir together the butter, rosemary, salt, and pepper. Spoon evenly over each ear of corn and then roll the corn to coat. Put the ice cubes in the bag. Double fold the bag to seal.

4 Slide the bag onto the grill or leave it in the pan and place it in the oven. Grill for 10 minutes in a covered grill, turn the bag over using oven mitts, and grill for about 10 minutes longer. If baking, bake for 35 to 40 minutes, or until the corn is tender.

5 Hold the bag with oven mitts and cut it open with a knife. Carefully fold back the top of the bag so that steam can escape.

> **REYNOLDS KITCHENS TIP**
>
> *For Spicy Lime Corn on the Cob, combine 3 tablespoons of fresh lime juice, 2 teaspoons of olive oil, 3/4 teaspoon of ground chili powder, and 1/2 teaspoon ground cumin. Spoon this mixture over corn (instead of herbed butter) and roll the corn to coat. Sprinkle with 2 tablespoons of chopped fresh cilantro and then grill or bake as instructed in the recipe for Herbed Corn on the Cob.*

· · ·

Cajun Spiced Corn

PREP TIME
12 minutes

COOK TIME
20 minutes

MAKES
4 servings

One 10-ounce package frozen whole kernel corn

1 small onion, chopped

1 cup chopped tomatoes

3/4 cup chopped green bell pepper

2 teaspoons Cajun seasoning

1 tablespoon butter or margarine

1 Preheat the oven to 450°F or prepare a charcoal or gas grill so that the coals are medium-hot.

2 Lay an 18-by-24-inch sheet of heavy duty aluminum foil on the countertop. Arrange the corn, onion, tomatoes, and bell pepper in the center of the foil. Sprinkle with Cajun seasoning and stir to blend. Top with butter.

3 Bring up the sides of the foil. Double fold the top and ends to seal the packet, leaving room for heat circulation inside. If using the oven, put the packet on a cookie sheet.

4 Put the cookie sheet in the oven or slide the packet onto the grill rack. Bake for 20 to 25 minutes or grill for 12 to 14 minutes in a covered grill, or until the vegetables are crisp-tender.

Cajun Spiced Corn

Zucchini-Tomato Vegetable Packet

PREP TIME
10 minutes

COOK TIME
20 minutes

MAKES
4 to 6 servings

2 small zucchini, sliced

1 medium onion, sliced

1 large tomato, cut in chunks

1 tablespoon olive oil or vegetable oil

¾ teaspoon lemon-pepper seasoning

½ teaspoon dried oregano

½ teaspoon salt

1 Preheat the oven to 450°F or prepare a charcoal or gas grill so that the coals are medium-hot.

2 Lay an 18-by-24-inch sheet of heavy duty aluminum foil on the countertop. Arrange the zucchini, onion, and tomato in the center of the foil. Drizzle with oil and sprinkle with the lemon-pepper seasoning, oregano, and salt.

3 Bring up the sides of the foil. Double fold the top and ends to seal the packet, leaving room for heat circulation inside. If using the oven, put the packet on a cookie sheet.

Zucchini-Tomato Vegetable Packet

4 Put the cookie sheet in the oven or slide the packet onto the grill rack. Bake for 20 to 25 minutes or grill for 12 to 14 minutes in a covered grill, or until the vegetables are crisp-tender.

. . .

Yellow Squash, Tomato, and Onion Packet

1 medium onion, chopped

2 medium yellow squash, cut in ¼ -inch slices

4 large Roma tomatoes, quartered

¼ cup chopped fresh basil

Salt and pepper

⅓ cup shredded Parmesan cheese

PREP TIME
16 minutes

COOK TIME
18 minutes

MAKES
6 servings

Yellow Squash, Tomato, and Onion Packet

1 Preheat the oven to 450°F or prepare a charcoal or gas grill so that the coals are medium-hot.

2 Lay an 18-by-24-inch sheet of heavy duty aluminum foil on the countertop. Put the onion in the center of the foil and top with the squash and tomatoes. Sprinkle with basil, salt, and pepper.

3 Bring up the sides of the foil. Double fold the top and ends to seal the packet, leaving room for heat circulation inside. If using the oven, put the packet on a cookie sheet.

4 Put the cookie sheet in the oven or slide the packet onto the grill rack. Bake for 18 to 22 minutes or grill for 13 to 15 minutes in a covered grill, or until the vegetables are crisp-tender. Open the foil packet and sprinkle with cheese. Let stand for about 3 minutes or until the cheese melts.

. . .

Sesame-Broccoli Packet

6 cups broccoli florets

One 8-ounce package sliced fresh mushrooms

2 tablespoons soy sauce

2 cloves garlic, minced

1 tablespoon dark sesame oil

½ teaspoon ground ginger

¼ teaspoon crushed red pepper flakes

Toasted sesame seeds (optional)

PREP TIME
5 minutes

COOK TIME
16 minutes

MAKES
4 servings

1 Preheat the oven to 450°F or prepare a charcoal or gas grill so that the coals are medium-hot.

2 In a large bowl, toss the broccoli and mushrooms with the soy sauce, garlic, sesame oil, ginger, and red pepper flakes.

3 Lay an 18-by-24-inch sheet of heavy duty aluminum foil on the countertop. Arrange the vegetable mixture in the center of the foil.

4 Bring up the sides of the foil. Double fold the top and ends to seal the packet, leaving room for heat circulation inside. If using the oven, put the packet on a cookie sheet.

5 Put the cookie sheet in the oven or slide the packet onto the grill rack. Bake for 16 to 18 minutes or grill for 8 to 10 minutes in a covered grill, or until the vegetables are crisp-tender. Sprinkle with sesame seeds before serving, if desired.

• • •

Broccoli and Carrots with Oranges

¼ cup orange marmalade spreadable fruit

½ teaspoon salt

6 cups broccoli florets

1½ cups peeled baby carrots, halved lengthwise

One 11-ounce can mandarin oranges, drained

¼ cup cashews

PREP TIME
10 minutes

COOK TIME
15 minutes

MAKES
6 to 8 servings

Broccoli and Carrots with Oranges

1 Preheat the oven to 450°F or prepare a charcoal or gas grill so that the coals are medium-hot.

2 In a large bowl, stir the marmalade and salt together. Add the broccoli and carrots and toss to coat.

3 Lay an 18-by-24-inch sheet of heavy duty aluminum foil on the countertop. Arrange the vegetable mixture in the center of the foil.

4 Bring up the sides of the foil. Double fold the top and ends to seal the packet, leaving room for heat circulation inside. If using the oven, put the packet on a cookie sheet.

5 Put the cookie sheet in the oven or slide the packet onto the grill rack. Bake for 15 to 20 minutes or grill for 8 to 10 minutes in a covered grill, or until the vegetables are crisp-tender. Open the packet, add the oranges, and stir. Sprinkle with cashews before serving.

. . .

Seasoned Broccoli and Mushrooms

6 cups broccoli florets

2 cups sliced mushrooms

1 medium red bell pepper, cut in strips

1 1/2 teaspoons dried basil

1 teaspoon garlic salt

1/2 cup water

PREP TIME

10 minutes

GRILL TIME

8 minutes

MAKES

6 servings

1 Prepare a charcoal or gas grill or preheat the oven to 450°F. The coals should be medium-hot. Put a large extra heavy duty foil bag in a 1-inch-deep pan.

2 Arrange the broccoli, mushrooms, and bell pepper in the bag in an even layer. Sprinkle with basil and garlic salt, and drizzle with water. Double fold the bag to seal.

3 Slide the bag onto the grill or leave it in the pan and place it in the oven. Grill for 8 to 10 minutes in a covered grill or bake for 20 to 25 minutes, or until the vegetables are crisp-tender.

4 Hold the bag with oven mitts and cut it open with a knife. Carefully fold back the top of the bag so that steam can escape.

REYNOLDS KITCHENS TIP

Using foil bags keeps low-fat foods such as boneless chicken, fish, and vegetables from sticking to the grill. Small delicate foods won't fall through the grill rack. Plus there's no need to scrape the grill rack clean after cooking.

Cauliflower with Fiery Cheese Sauce

PREP TIME
5 minutes

COOK TIME
25 minutes

MAKES
4 servings

4 cups cauliflower florets

½ cup pasteurized process cheese sauce (half of an 8-ounce jar)

1 teaspoon hot pepper sauce

¼ teaspoon crushed red pepper flakes (optional)

1 Preheat the oven to 450°F or prepare a charcoal or gas grill so that the coals are medium-hot.

2 Lay an 18-by-24-inch sheet of heavy duty aluminum foil on the countertop. Arrange the cauliflower in the center of the foil.

Cauliflower with Fiery Cheese Sauce

3   In a small bowl, stir together the cheese sauce, hot pepper sauce, and red pepper flakes, if desired. Spoon the sauce over the cauliflower.

4   Bring up the sides of the foil. Double fold the top and ends to seal the packet, leaving room for heat circulation inside. If using the oven, put the packet on a cookie sheet.

5   Put the cookie sheet in the oven or slide the packet onto the grill rack. Bake for 25 to 30 minutes or grill for 8 to 10 minutes in a covered grill, or until the cauliflower is crisp-tender.

REYNOLDS KITCHENS TIP

Jars of cheese sauce are easy to find in the supermarket. Kraft® Cheez Whiz® cheese sauce is a popular brand. It blends easily and smoothly.

...

Easy Homestyle Vegetables

6 medium red potatoes, cut in eighths

One 16-ounce package peeled baby carrots

1 medium onion, sliced in rings

1 medium green or red bell pepper, cut into large dice

Seasoned salt

Black pepper

½ cup water

PREP TIME
10 minutes

GRILL TIME
18 minutes

MAKES
5 to 6 servings

1   Prepare a charcoal or gas grill or preheat the oven to 450°F. The coals should be medium-hot. Put a large extra heavy duty foil bag in a 1-inch-deep pan. Spray the inside of the bag with cooking spray.

2   Arrange the potatoes, carrots, onion, and bell pepper in the bag in an even layer. Sprinkle with salt and pepper. Drizzle with water. Double fold the bag to seal.

3   Slide the bag onto the grill or leave it in the pan and place it in the oven. Grill for 18 to 20 minutes in a covered grill or bake for 45 to 50 minutes, or until vegetables are crisp-tender.

4   Hold the bag with oven mitts and cut it open with a knife. Carefully fold back the top of the bag so that steam can escape.

REYNOLDS KITCHENS TIP

After cooking, let the steam escape from the bag and then spoon out the vegetables. Take care, as the steam is very hot.

Honey Carrots

One 16-ounce package peeled baby carrots

2 tablespoons packed brown sugar

2 tablespoons honey

2 teaspoons lemon or lime juice

2 tablespoons butter or margarine

2 tablespoons dried parsley flakes (optional)

PREP TIME
5 minutes

COOK TIME
20 minutes

MAKES
5 to 6 servings

1 Preheat the oven to 450°F or prepare a charcoal or gas grill so that the coals are medium-hot.

2 Lay an 18-by-24-inch sheet of heavy duty aluminum foil on the countertop. Put the carrots in the center of the foil. Sprinkle with brown sugar and drizzle with honey and lemon juice. Top with butter.

Honey Carrots

3 Bring up the sides of the foil. Double fold the top and ends to seal the packet, leaving room for heat circulation inside. If using the oven, put the packet on a cookie sheet.

4 Put the cookie sheet in the oven or slide the packet onto the grill rack. Bake for 20 to 25 minutes or grill for 11 to 13 minutes in a covered grill, or until the vegetables are crisp-tender. Sprinkle with parsley flakes before serving, if desired.

REYNOLDS KITCHENS TIP

For Glazed Cranberry Carrots, combine ¼ cup of packed brown sugar, ¼ teaspoon of ground nutmeg, 2 teaspoons of lemon juice, and 2 tablespoons of melted butter. Pour this over the carrots and add ½ cup of dried cranberries to the packet. Cook as instructed in the recipe.

...

New England Baked Beans

2 slices bacon, cut in small pieces

1 medium onion, finely chopped

½ cup packed brown sugar

⅓ cup barbecue sauce

1 tablespoon prepared mustard

2 teaspoons Worcestershire sauce

Three 19¾-ounce cans pork and beans, drained

2 whole slices bacon, cooked until crisp and drained (optional)

PREP TIME
15 minutes

COOK TIME
40 minutes

MAKES
10 servings

1 Preheat the oven to 350°F for at least 20 minutes and arrange an oven rack so that it is in the center of the oven. Put a 1½-quart disposable plastic cookware pan on a cookie sheet, so that the pan does not hang over the sides.

2 Cook the bacon and onion in a skillet over medium-high heat, stirring constantly, for 3 to 5 minutes, or until the bacon is crisp. Cool for 1 to 2 minutes and then carefully pour the bacon, onion and bacon fat into the pan.

3 Add the brown sugar, barbecue sauce, mustard, and

REYNOLDS KITCHENS TIP

Disposable plastic cookware pans can withstand oven temperatures up to 400°F. If the recipe calls for covering the food during cooking, use aluminum foil. The lid that comes with the pan is not oven safe. It is microwave safe, however, and is great for fitting over the pan for storing or transporting.

Worcestershire sauce to the pan and stir until well blended. Add the pork and beans, stir to mix, and then spread evenly in the pan.

4 Bake, uncovered, on the cookie sheet for 40 to 45 minutes or until heated through and bubbling around the edges. Use the cookie sheet to remove the pan from the oven and let it stand on the sheet for at least 2 minutes before lifting it by the handles.

5 Garnish with the crisp bacon slices, if desired.

. . .

Triple-Cheese Potato Bake

Two 10¾-ounce cans cream of chicken soup, undiluted

One 8-ounce container sour cream

½ teaspoon pepper

One 30- to 32-ounce package frozen hash brown potatoes

¾ cup sliced green onions

One 2-ounce jar diced pimientos

¾ cup shredded sharp Cheddar cheese

¾ cup shredded Swiss cheese

¼ cup grated Parmesan cheese

PREP TIME
10 minutes

COOK TIME
1 hour

MAKES
8 to 10 servings

1 Preheat the oven to 375°F for at least 20 minutes and arrange an oven rack so that it is in the center of the oven. Put an 8-inch square disposable plastic cookware pan on a cookie sheet, so that the pan does not hang over the sides.

2 In a large mixing bowl, stir together the soup, sour cream, and pepper until well blended. Stir in the potatoes, onions, pimientos, Cheddar cheese, and Swiss cheese. Spoon into the pan and smooth in an even layer. Sprinkle with Parmesan cheese.

REYNOLDS KITCHENS TIPS

■ *To freeze, let the casserole cool for 15 to 20 minutes. Cover with non-stick aluminum foil, with non-stick (dull) side facing down. Then, freeze for up to 1 month.*

■ *To reheat a frozen casserole, thaw, still covered with foil, in the refrigerator. Preheat the oven to 350°F for at least 20 minutes and arrange an oven rack so that it is in the center of the oven. Place the covered pan on a cookie sheet and reheat for 45 minutes to 1 hour or until heated through. Remove the foil after the first 30 minutes of heating so the casserole can crisp.*

3 Bake, uncovered, on the cookie sheet for 1 to 1¼ hours or until bubbling and heated through. Use the cookie sheet to remove the pan from the oven and let it stand on the sheet for at least 2 minutes before lifting it by the handles. Serve immediately.

...

Glazed Sweet Potatoes

3 to 3½ pounds sweet potatoes (4 to 6 potatoes)

1 cup packed brown sugar

⅓ cup butter, melted

¼ cup light corn syrup

½ teaspoon salt

½ teaspoon ground cinnamon

¼ teaspoon ground nutmeg

½ cup chopped pecans, toasted

PREP TIME
25 minutes

COOK TIME
1 hour

MAKES
8 to 10 servings

1 Preheat the oven to 400°F. Line a 9-by-13-by-2-inch baking pan with non-stick aluminum foil, non-stick (dull) side facing up.

2 Put the potatoes in a 3-quart saucepan and add enough cold water to cover by an inch or so. Cover and bring to a boil over medium-high heat. Cook for about 20 minutes or until the potatoes are tender but still firm. Drain and set aside to cool. When cool enough to handle, peel and slice into ½-inch thick slices. Layer the slices in the foil-lined pan.

3 In a microwave-safe bowl, combine the brown sugar, butter, syrup, salt, cinnamon, and nutmeg. Microwave on high power for 1 minute or until the sugar dissolves. Stir the mixture once during microwaving. Drizzle a third of this syrup over the potatoes.

4 Bake, uncovered, for 40 to 50 minutes, or until

REYNOLDS KITCHENS TIP

Toasting nuts before adding them to a recipe makes them crispy and intensifies their flavor—which means you may be able to use less without any loss of flavor.

To toast, line a shallow baking pan with aluminum foil. Spread shelled nuts in a single layer in the pan and toast in a preheated 350°F oven for 8 to 10 minutes, stirring occasionally, or until the nuts are fragrant and light brown. Watch closely so that they don't burn. Different kinds of nuts may brown at slightly different rates.

Slide the nuts onto a fresh sheet of foil or a plate to halt the cooking. Let them cool completely before using. Toasted nuts can be stored, wrapped tightly, in a cool, dry place for up to 2 weeks.

the potatoes are tender. Drizzle the potatoes with the syrup every 10 minutes. (If the glaze becomes too thick, microwave it for about 30 seconds.) Sprinkle with pecans and spoon the last of the glaze over the potatoes and pecans before serving.

· · ·

Homestyle Fries with Salsa

3 medium baking potatoes

2 tablespoons olive oil

1 teaspoon chili powder

$\frac{1}{2}$ teaspoon salt

$\frac{1}{4}$ teaspoon ground cumin

1 cup thick and chunky salsa

$\frac{1}{4}$ cup light sour cream

PREP TIME
12 minutes

COOK TIME
30 minutes

MAKES
4 servings

Homestyle Fries with Salsa

1 Preheat the oven to 450°F. Line a 10½-by-15½-by-1-inch baking pan with non-stick aluminum foil, non-stick (dull) side facing up.

2 Without peeling, cut the potatoes into ½-inch-thick sticks.

3 In a large bowl, mix together the oil, chili powder, salt, and cumin. Add the potato sticks and toss to coat with the seasoned oil. Lay the potatoes in an even layer in the foil-lined pan.

4 Bake, uncovered, for 30 to 35 minutes, or until the potatoes are tender and beginning to brown. Turn the potatoes twice during baking.

5 In a small bowl, stir the salsa into the sour cream. Serve the potatoes with the dipping sauce.

> **REYNOLDS KITCHENS TIP**
>
> *For plain roasted potatoes, substitute 2 teaspoons of seasoned salt and ¼ teaspoon pepper for the chili powder, salt, and cumin. Cook as instructed in this recipe.*

· · ·

Packet Potatoes

PREP TIME
12 minutes

COOK TIME
30 minutes

MAKES
4 servings

I small onion, thinly sliced

1⅓ pounds red-skinned, all-purpose potatoes (4 medium potatoes), cut in bite-size pieces

2 tablespoons olive oil or vegetable oil

I teaspoon seasoned salt

½ teaspoon dried dill (optional)

¼ teaspoon pepper

1 Preheat the oven to 450°F or prepare a charcoal or gas grill so that the coals are medium-hot.

2 Lay an 18-by-24-inch sheet of non-stick aluminum foil on the countertop, non-stick (dull) side facing up. Put the onion in the center of the foil and layer the potatoes evenly on top. Drizzle with oil and sprinkle with salt, dill, and pepper.

> **REYNOLDS KITCHENS TIP**
>
> *Know your potatoes. Red or white potatoes, sometimes called boiling or all-purpose potatoes, are rounded with thin skin (unlike russet potatoes, the classic baking potato with thick skin). All-purpose potatoes have waxy flesh that keeps its shape during cooking.*

3 Bring up the sides of the foil. Double fold the top and ends to seal the packet, leaving room for heat circulation inside. If using the oven, put the packet on a cookie sheet.

4 Put the cookie sheet in the oven or slide the packet onto the grill rack. Bake for 30 to 35 minutes or grill for 15 to 20 minutes in a covered grill, or until the potatoes are tender.

Packet Potatoes

Southwestern Potato Packet

PREP TIME
15 minutes

COOK TIME
30 minutes

MAKES
4 servings

1 medium onion, thinly sliced

1 1/3 pounds all-purpose potatoes (4 medium potatoes), cut in 1/2-inch cubes

1 teaspoon seasoned salt

1/2 teaspoon chili powder

1/4 teaspoon ground cumin

One 4 1/2-ounce can chopped green chiles, undrained

1 cup shredded Cheddar cheese

Salsa

Sour cream

Chopped fresh cilantro

1 Preheat the oven to 450°F or prepare a charcoal or gas grill so that the coals are medium-hot.

2 Lay an 18-by-24-inch sheet of non-stick aluminum foil on the countertop, non-

Southwestern Potato Packet

stick (dull) side facing up. Put the onion in the center of the foil and top with the potatoes.

3 In a small bowl, stir together the seasoned salt, chili powder, and cumin. Sprinkle over the potatoes and top with the green chiles.

4 Bring up the sides of the foil. Double fold the top and ends to seal the packet, leaving room for heat circulation inside. If using the oven, put the packet on a cookie sheet.

5 Put the cookie sheet in the oven or slide the packet onto the grill rack. Bake for 30 to 35 minutes or grill for 15 to 18 minutes in a covered grill, or until the potatoes are tender. Sprinkle the potatoes with cheese. Let stand for about 2 minutes or until the cheese melts.

6 Serve the potatoes with salsa, sour cream, and cilantro.

REYNOLDS KITCHENS TIP

When the food is cooked, open both ends of the packet first and let the steam escape. Next, open the top of the foil packet to remove the food.

Roasted Garlic Mashed Potatoes

2 large bulbs garlic

1 teaspoon olive oil

3 pounds all-purpose potatoes, peeled and cubed

$\frac{1}{4}$ cup milk, heated

$\frac{1}{4}$ cup butter or margarine, softened

Salt and pepper

1 tablespoon chopped fresh parsley

PREP TIME
12 minutes

COOK TIME
25 minutes

MAKES
6 to 8 servings

1 Preheat the oven to 400°F.

2 Slice the tops off the unpeeled garlic bulbs. Remove the papery outer layer of skin. Set the bulbs on a sheet of aluminum foil large enough to enclose them and drizzle with the olive oil. Wrap the bulbs in the foil. Put the packet on a cookie sheet.

3 Roast for 25 minutes or until the garlic is soft. Unwrap the foil and let the garlic bulbs cool. Squeeze the garlic pulp from the bulbs, discard the skins, and mash the pulp.

4 Put the potatoes in a large saucepan. Pour enough cold water into the pan to cover the potatoes by several inches. Add a pinch of salt to the water. Cover the pan and bring to a boil over medium-high heat. Cook for 20 to 25 minutes or until the potatoes are tender. Drain.

5 Transfer the potatoes to a bowl and mash with a potato masher or with an electric mixer set on low speed. Add the mashed garlic, milk, butter, and salt and pepper to taste. Beat until light and fluffy. Stir in the parsley and serve immediately.

> **REYNOLDS KITCHENS TIP**
>
> *One of the best ways to roast whole heads of garlic is to wrap them in aluminum foil and roast them for about 25 minutes in a 400°F oven. Drizzle with a little oil first to moisten and flavor them.*

Creamy Macaroni and Cheese

Creamy Macaroni and Cheese

PREP TIME
12 minutes

COOK TIME
30 minutes

MAKES
6 servings

2 tablespoons butter or margarine

2 tablespoons finely chopped onion

2 tablespoons flour

$\frac{1}{2}$ teaspoon salt

$\frac{1}{4}$ teaspoon pepper

2 cups milk

8 ounces pasteurized prepared cheese product, coarsely chopped

$1\frac{1}{2}$ cups shredded sharp Cheddar cheese

One 8-ounce package elbow macaroni, cooked and drained

Paprika

Tomato wedges, fresh parsley

1 Preheat the oven to 350°F for at least 20 minutes and arrange an oven rack so that it is in the center of the oven.

2 Put the butter in a 1½-quart disposable plastic cookware pan. Cover with wax paper and microwave on high power for 20 to 30 seconds or until the butter melts. Add the onion, recover with wax paper, and microwave on high power for 1 minute or until the onion softens.

3 Add the flour, salt, and pepper and stir until smooth. Recover with wax paper and microwave on high power for 30 seconds or until heated. Using a spoon or whisk, blend the milk into the sauce. Recover with wax paper and microwave on high power for 5 to 6 minutes, stirring every minute, until thick and smooth.

4 Remove the pan from the microwave. Add the cheese product and Cheddar cheese. Stir until the cheese melts and the sauce is smooth.

5 Stir in the macaroni and sprinkle with paprika.

6 Set the pan on a cookie sheet so the pan does not hang over the sides.

7 Bake, uncovered, on the cookie sheet for 25 to 30 minutes, or until browned and bubbly. Use the cookie sheet to remove the pan from the oven and let it stand on the sheet for at least 2 minutes before lifting it by the handles. Garnish with tomato wedges and parsley and serve immediately.

REYNOLDS KITCHENS TIP

Pasteurized cheese products, such as Kraft® Velveeta® cheese product, melt extremely well and blend with the Cheddar cheese to make an easy, smooth sauce.

Cakes, Cupcakes, and Cookies

Apple-Cinnamon Coffee Cake

Water Fun Cake

Turtle Sundae Chocolate Cake

Peach Upside-Down Cake

Carrot-Pineapple Cake

Almond Mocha Cake

Cookies 'N' Mint Cake

Pound Cake

Rose-Wrapped Pound Cake

Merry-Go-Round Cake

Slumber Party Cake

Cupcake Critters

Flutterby Butterfly Cupcakes

Chocolate Cappuccino Cupcakes

Smiling Sunshine Cupcakes

Friendly Frog Cupcakes

Frizzy-the-Clown Cupcakes

Winter Wonderland Cupcakes

Snowman Cupcakes

Birthday Cupcake Tray

Marble-Frosted Macadamia
Brownies

Peppermint-Surprise Brownies

Brownie Pizza

Triple-Chocolate Brownie Cake

Star-Spangled Brownies

Buttery Sugar Cookies

Jam-Filled Sugar Cookies

Chocolate-Chunk Orange Cookies

Lemon-Blueberry Cookies

Mexican Wedding Cakes

Maple Leaf Cookie Basket

Chocolate-Dipped Cookie Bundles

Oatmeal-Raisin Cookies

Stained Glass Butter Cookies

Almond-Apricot Bars

Nutty Cranberry-Orange Bars

Favorite Chocolate Chip Cookies

When you bring out the cupcakes,
you know you're going to have
some fun!
—Pat

Whenever I can get my hands on a
good oatmeal-raisin cookie I am
happy. I evaluate them constantly. I
am on the search for the perfect one.
—Betty

WHEN THE REYNOLDS KITCHENS ARE filled with the warm fragrance of cakes and cookies baking in the ovens, everyone in our office is happy because we share the goodies. For many, baking is relaxing and rewarding. Carry a tray of cupcakes or cookies into a room and you just might make instant friends. Betty's nephew was a prime example. He was having difficulty adjusting to a new school so his mom baked a batch of cupcakes, wrapped them up in color plastic wrap, and sent them with him to class. He was the star of the day!

Cakes

We take shortcuts wherever we can and still get great results. Cakes are the perfect example. Use a packaged cake mix as the starting point and let your creativity go. You can stir in additional ingredients to change the flavor or get crazy with the decorations. Sheet cakes are easy to bake when there's a last-minute dessert request and transport to a bake sale or neighbor's house, but they also present a large canvas for decorating.

We use candies, frosting, and Reynolds Clear and Color Plastic Wrap with abandon. The results are fun, whimsical, colorful, and designed to charm children and their parents alike. We hope you'll use our ideas to come up with your own so you can have as much fun as we do!

Some of our cakes are baked in traditional 9-by-13-inch pans, while others are baked in Reynolds Pot Lux Disposable Cookware. These attractive, sturdy pans are terrific for transporting food. Plus, cakes such as the Carrot-Pineapple Cake can be refrigerated right in the pan, with the lid snapped in place.

When Pat brought a cake baked in a Pot Lux pan to a gathering at a neighbor's house, she took along the label from the box so that her neighbor, who had just had a new baby, would know how to reuse the handy container. The package is designed so that you can easily detach the pertinent part of the label.

You're guaranteed success with a cake mix. It takes practice to be a good baker, and if you haven't made a cake from scratch in a while, a cake mix is practically foolproof. We look for ways for people to add their own special touch and feel good about the cake.

For example, Pat started with a basic white cake mix when she developed the Cookies 'N' Mint Cake and then stirred cookie crumbs into the batter.

She decided to use chocolate fudge mint cookies because she loves the combination of mint and chocolate.

At the other end of the spectrum is Betty's famous "from scratch" pound cake. For her, growing up in North Carolina meant regular family and church gatherings, where there were always one, two, or more pound cakes. This is her favorite. She uses vanilla yogurt instead of the sour cream used in many pound cake recipes. We bake it in a bundt pan for a pretty presentation, but it would be just as delectable baked in a tube pan.

Our extra-wide plastic wrap comes in handy to cover cakes or the cardboard sheets or other trays they're served on. Covering cakes with plastic wrap helps keep them fresh.

Cupcakes

Cupcakes are extremely popular in our kitchens and, as we've noticed, all across America. They're showing up on menus in fine restaurants, dessert cafés, and office parties, and are no longer the stuff of kids' birthday parties alone. They couldn't be easier to make with our paper or foil baking cups, and dessert lovers like them for their innate charm. And, let's face it, portion control is a real plus!

Our paper baking cups are available in a number of designs to fit any occasion—party, spring, holiday, hearts, and Halloween to name a few.

We think it's fun to get kids into the kitchen to decorate cupcakes, plus it's a good introduction to cooking and baking. Children do best with simple decorations, and go wild with brightly colored candies and sprinkles. Don't forget to line the countertops with wax paper before decorating, to catch all the stray sprinkles. When they're done decorating, we suggest arranging the cupcakes on a tray and covering with the color plastic wrap for a superb and easy presentation.

We offer lots of recipes for cupcakes, and as you'll see as you thumb through the pages, we have enormous fun coming up with decorations for them. Check out our Friendly Frog Cupcakes, Smiling Sunshine Cupcakes, and Frizzy-the-Clown Cupcakes to see what we mean.

Cookies

Not only are brownies, cookies, and bars great favorites, they are endlessly versatile; we can never have too many recipes. In these recipes, it's clear why so many home bakers rely on our products. They work so very well!

For instance, we line baking pans with Reynolds Wrap Release Non-Stick Aluminum Foil, leaving a little excess foil on each end. Use the foil to lift

brownies or bar cookies right out onto a cutting board. Fold the foil back and you can easily cut them in squares. When we line cookie sheets with non-stick foil or parchment paper, there's no need to grease the pans.

Parchment paper is superb for sandwiching cookie dough that needs to be rolled out. The paper stays in place, and the dough doesn't stick to the rolling pin or the work surface. We also use parchment paper to line the pans for our Brownie Pizza, Jam-Filled Sugar Cookies, and Favorite Chocolate Chip Cookies, which happen to be chocoholic Pat's choice. Betty is partial to Oatmeal-Raisin Cookies, so we included a recipe for those, too.

Perhaps it's the influence of celebrity television chefs who use it (we have our favorites), but the demand for parchment paper has dramatically increased. We were pleased when it was added to our product line. It's excellent for lining cookie sheets for delicate cookies and for those you don't want to spread, while non-stick foil is great for more rustic cookies. Our parchment paper is oven safe up to 420°F, although we never recommend baking our recipes at that high temperature.

Words of Wisdom

Like most bakers, we use quality ingredients. We use real butter for its consistency and flavor and suggest that our consumers stay away from reduced-calorie margarine or whipped butter for baking. These products are fine for spreading on toast or an English muffin, but they have too much added moisture to do well in baking.

We use large eggs and all-purpose flour, and always take care to measure accurately and preheat the oven to the correct temperature. When you take a little care, we promise you'll have sweet success with baked goods!

like most bakers, we use

quality ingredients

Apple-Cinnamon Coffee Cake

PREP TIME
20 minutes

COOK TIME
30 minutes

MAKES
8 to 10 servings

CAKE

2 cups flour

1 teaspoon baking powder

1 teaspoon baking soda

1 teaspoon ground cinnamon

1/4 teaspoon salt

1/2 cup butter or margarine, softened

1 cup sugar

2 eggs

1 teaspoon vanilla extract

One 8-ounce carton vanilla yogurt

2 medium apples, peeled and coarsely chopped (about 2 cups)

TOPPING

1/4 cup flour

1/4 cup sugar

1/4 teaspoon ground cinnamon

1/4 cup chopped pecans

2 tablespoons butter or margarine, softened

1 Preheat the oven to 350°F for at least 20 minutes and arrange an oven rack so that it is in the center of the oven. Put a 9-by-12½-inch disposable plastic cookware pan on a cookie sheet so that the pan does not hang over the sides.

2 To make the cake: Combine the flour, baking powder, baking soda, cinnamon, and salt on a sheet of wax paper.

3 In the bowl of an electric mixer set on medium speed, cream the butter and sugar for 2 to 3 minutes or until light and fluffy. Add the eggs one at a time, beating after each addition. Add the vanilla and beat until well mixed.

4 Beginning and ending with the flour, add the flour to the batter alternating with the yogurt. Beat on medium speed for 1 to 2 minutes or until the batter is smooth.

5 Remove the bowl from the mixer and stir in the apples with a wooden spoon or spatula. Pour the batter into the pan and smooth the surface.

6 To make the topping: In a small bowl, combine the flour, sugar, cinnamon, pecans, and butter. Work with

> **REYNOLDS KITCHENS TIP**
>
> *Disposable plastic cookware pans can withstand oven heat up to 400°F. When you take the pan from the oven, still supported on the cookie sheet, let it stand for a few minutes before lifting it.*
>
> *Baking a coffee cake in a disposable pan makes it easy to carry to a bake sale, meeting, or potluck supper. Snap the lid on the cooled cake and go!*

your fingers or a fork until the mixture is crumbly. Sprinkle the topping over the cake.

7 Bake on the cookie sheet for 30 to 35 minutes or until golden brown. Use the cookie sheet to remove the pan from the oven. Let stand for at least 2 minutes before lifting the pan by the handles. Set on a wire rack to cool completely.

. . .

Water Fun Cake

PREP TIME
30 minutes

COOK TIME
15 minutes

MAKES
24 servings

One 18-ounce package of your favorite cake mix

One 25-by-16-inch sheet of sturdy white cardboard or purchased sheet cake board

Extra-wide teal plastic wrap

One and a half 16-ounce containers vanilla ready-to-spread frosting

1 to 2 tablespoons graham cracker crumbs

6 fish graham snacks or gummy fish candies

12 teddy bear graham snacks

5 gummy ring-shaped candies

2 sticks fruit-striped chewing gum

2 sugar wafers

4 pull-apart licorice strings

1 fruit roll-up

Green plastic wrap

1 licorice twist, cut in half

Gum balls

2 paper drink umbrellas

1 Preheat the oven to 350°F. Spray a 10½-by-15½-by-1-inch baking pan with cooking spray.

2 Prepare the cake mix following the package directions and pour evenly into the pan.

3 Bake for 15 to 20 minutes or until firm and a toothpick inserted in the center comes out clean. Set on a wire rack to cool completely.

4 Cover the cardboard sheet with extra-wide teal plastic wrap. Tape the plastic wrap to the back of the cardboard. Invert the cake onto the cardboard so that it is centered on the sheet. Lift off the pan. Spread most of the frosting over the top and sides of the cake. Reserve the remaining frosting.

5 To make the beach, sprinkle half of the cake very lightly with graham cracker crumbs. For water, cover the remaining half of the cake with teal plastic wrap. Arrange fish on top of the plastic wrap. Cover the fish with another layer of teal plastic wrap.

6 Decorate the cake as desired for water fun. Use teddy bear graham snacks for swimmers. Use gummy ring-shaped candies for inner tubes. Cut fruit-striped chewing gum for beach towels.

7 Use two sugar wafers for a diving board and glue them together with frosting. Add licorice strings for handrails; attach to diving board with frosting. For a sliding board, press pull-apart licorice strings to the long edges of a 3-inch-long strip of fruit roll-up. Bend and insert into cake.

8 For a palm tree, tear off two 12-inch sheets of green plastic wrap. Fold each into a 2-inch-wide strip and trim and cut the fringe to make leaves. Crisscross strips, cut an X in the center, and slide over the end of the licorice twist. Insert into the cake. Add gum balls and paper umbrellas.

Water Fun Cake

Turtle Sundae Chocolate Cake

PREP TIME
20 minutes

COOK TIME
15 minutes

MAKES
24 servings

One 18-ounce package chocolate cake mix

1/2 cup mini semi-sweet chocolate morsels

1/2 cup chopped pecans

1/2 cup flaked sweetened coconut

One 16-ounce container vanilla ready-to-spread frosting

24 caramel candies, unwrapped

2 teaspoons milk

Colored sprinkles

24 chocolate candy kisses, gummy candies, pecan halves, cherry halves, or gumdrops

1 Preheat the oven to 350°F. Spray a 10½-by-15½-by-1-inch baking pan with cooking spray.

2 Prepare the cake mix following the package directions. Stir in the chocolate morsels, pecans, and coconut. Spoon the batter into the pan and smooth the surface.

3 Bake for 15 to 20 minutes or until firm and a toothpick inserted in the center comes out clean. Set on a wire rack to cool completely.

4 Frost the top of the cake with vanilla frosting. Cut into 24 squares.

5 Put the caramels and milk in a small microwave-safe bowl and microwave for 30 seconds on high power. Stir and microwave for about 15 seconds longer or until the caramels melt and the mixture is smooth.

6 Drizzle the caramel over each square. Decorate with colored sprinkles and center 1 chocolate candy kiss on each square. Let stand until the caramel is set.

7 Cover the cake with extra-wide plastic wrap.

REYNOLDS KITCHENS TIP

To prepare items for bake sales, wrap them in color plastic wrap to grab attention and make eye-catching displays. Compared to the ordinary bake sale treats offered by others, yours will stand out.

Peach Upside-Down Cake

PREP TIME
15 minutes

COOK TIME
35 minutes

MAKES
24 servings

2 tablespoons butter or margarine, melted

½ cup packed brown sugar

3 to 4 medium fresh peaches, peeled and sliced, or one 30-ounce can sliced peaches, drained

⅓ cup whole maraschino cherries

½ cup chopped pecans

One 20-ounce package yellow cake mix

One 4-ounce package vanilla instant pudding and pie filling mix

4 eggs

1 cup water

⅓ cup vegetable oil

1 teaspoon vanilla extract

1 teaspoon ground cinnamon

Ice cream or whipped topping (optional)

1 Preheat the oven to 350°F. Line a 9-by-13-by-2-inch baking pan with non-stick aluminum foil, non-stick (dull) side facing up.

2 Pour the melted butter in the bottom of the pan and tilt to coat the bottom. Sprinkle the brown sugar over the butter. Arrange the peach slices and cherries in an even layer and then sprinkle the pecans over the fruit.

3 In the bowl of an electric mixer set on medium speed, beat the cake mix, pudding mix, eggs, water, oil, vanilla extract, and cinnamon for 2 minutes. Spoon the batter over the fruit in the pan and spread it in an even layer.

4 Bake for 35 to 40 minutes or until golden brown and a toothpick inserted in the center of the cake comes out clean. Immediately invert the pan on a flat serving platter or tray. Lift off the pan and remove the foil. Let the cake stand for at least 10 minutes.

5 Serve warm with ice cream or whipped topping, if desired.

> **REYNOLDS KITCHENS TIP**
>
> *Upside-down cake was never easier! When you line the pan with non-stick aluminum foil, the butter, sugar, fruit, and nuts don't stick to the foil or the pan.*

Carrot-Pineapple Cake

PREP TIME
15 minutes

COOK TIME
35 minutes

MAKES
12 to 15
servings

2 cups flour

1½ cups sugar

2 teaspoons baking powder

2 teaspoons ground cinnamon

½ teaspoon ground nutmeg

½ teaspoon salt

1 cup vegetable oil

One 8-ounce can crushed pineapple, undrained

4 eggs

1 teaspoon vanilla extract

2 cups shredded carrots

1 cup chopped nuts

One 16-ounce container cream cheese ready-to-spread frosting

1 Preheat the oven to 350°F for at least 20 minutes and arrange an oven rack so that it is in the center of the oven. Put a 9-by-12½-inch disposable plastic cookware pan

Carrot-Pineapple Cake

on a cookie sheet so that the pan does not hang over the sides. Spray the bottom of the pan with cooking spray.

2 In a large bowl, stir together the flour, sugar, baking powder, cinnamon, nutmeg, and salt. Add the oil, pineapple and its juice, eggs, and vanilla. Stir until well blended.

3 Stir in the carrots and ¾ cup of the nuts. Pour the batter into the pan and smooth the surface.

4 Bake on the cookie sheet for 35 to 40 minutes or until firm and a toothpick inserted in the center comes out clean. Use the cookie sheet to remove the pan from the oven. Let stand for at least 2 minutes before lifting the pan by the handles. Set on a wire rack to cool completely.

5 When cool, frost the top of the cake with cream cheese frosting and sprinkle with the remaining ¼ cup of nuts.

6 To store, cover the pan with its lid and refrigerate the cake.

> **REYNOLDS KITCHENS TIP**
>
> *It's easy to store a rich, dense, moist carrot cake made in a disposable plastic cookware pan. Just snap the lid on the pan and put in the refrigerator.*

. . .

Almond Mocha Cake

2 tablespoons instant coffee

½ cup boiling water

One 18-ounce package chocolate fudge cake mix

1½ teaspoons almond extract

One 16-ounce container chocolate ready-to-spread frosting

½ cup sliced almonds

PREP TIME
15 minutes

COOK TIME
40 minutes

MAKES
24 servings

1 Preheat the oven to 350°F for at least 20 minutes and arrange an oven rack so that it is in the center of the oven. Put a 9-by-12½-inch disposable plastic cookware pan on a cookie sheet so that the pan does not hang over the sides. Spray the bottom of the pan with cooking spray.

2 In a heatproof measuring cup, stir the coffee into the boiling water until dissolved. Add enough cold water to equal the amount of liquid called for in the package directions.

3 Prepare the cake mix following the package directions, using the coffee in place of water. Add 1 teaspoon of the almond extract and mix well. Spoon the batter into the pan and smooth the surface.

4 Bake on the cookie sheet for 40 to 45 minutes or until a toothpick inserted in the center comes out with a few moist crumbs clinging to it. Use the cookie sheet to remove the pan from the oven. Let stand for at least 2 minutes before lifting the pan by the handles. Set on a wire rack to cool completely.

5 In a mixing bowl, stir the frosting with the remaining ½ teaspoon of almond extract until smooth. Spread the top of the cake with frosting. Decorate with sliced almonds.

6 To store, cover the pan with its lid and refrigerate the cake.

. . .

Cookies 'N' Mint Cake

One 18-ounce package white cake mix

¾ cup coarsely crushed chocolate fudge mint cookies

3½ ounces marshmallow creme (from a 7-ounce jar)

¼ teaspoon peppermint extract

1 teaspoon milk

3 drops green food coloring

4 ounces frozen whipped topping (from one 8-ounce carton), thawed

Chocolate fudge mint cookies, cut in half

¼ cup chocolate ready-to-spread frosting (optional)

PREP TIME
25 minutes

COOK TIME
38 minutes

MAKES
24 servings

1 Preheat the oven to 350°F for at least 20 minutes and arrange an oven rack so that it is in the center of the oven. Put a 9-by-12½-inch disposable plastic cookware pan on a cookie sheet so that the pan does not hang over the sides. Spray the inside of the pan with cooking spray.

2 Prepare the cake mix following the package directions. Reserve 1 tablespoon of the crushed cookies for garnish and then stir the remaining cookie crumbs into the batter. Pour the batter into the pan and smooth the surface.

3 Bake on the cookie sheet for 38 to 43 minutes or until firm and a toothpick

inserted in the center comes out with a few moist crumbs clinging to it. Use the cookie sheet to remove the pan from the oven. Let stand for at least 2 minutes before lifting the pan by the handles. Set on a wire rack to cool completely.

4 In a mixing bowl, combine the marshmallow creme, peppermint extract, milk, and food coloring. Gently stir in the whipped topping and spread over the cake. Sprinkle with the reserved tablespoon of crushed cookies. Garnish with cookie halves. Drizzle with softened chocolate frosting, if desired. Cover with the pan lid and refrigerate.

REYNOLDS KITCHENS TIP

To make the chocolate frosting liquid enough to drizzle, spoon the frosting into a small plastic food storage bag. Leave the bag unsealed and microwave on high power for 5 seconds. Squeeze the bag to remove any air pockets. Seal, snip a bottom corner with scissors, and gently squeeze the frosting through the snipped opening to drizzle frosting on a cake.

Cookies 'N' Mint Cake

Pound Cake

1 cup (2 sticks) butter or margarine, softened

2½ cups sugar

4 eggs

3 cups flour

1 teaspoon baking powder

¼ teaspoon salt

One 8-ounce container vanilla yogurt

½ cup milk

1 teaspoon vanilla extract

1 teaspoon lemon extract

1 teaspoon almond extract

Juice of 1 lemon

Powdered sugar

PREP TIME
25 minutes

COOK TIME
1 hour 15 minutes

MAKES
18 to 20 servings

1 Preheat the oven to 325°F. Spray a 10-inch bundt or tube cake pan with cooking spray. Coat the pan with flour and tap out the excess.

2 In the bowl of an electric mixer set on medium speed, cream the butter and sugar for 2 to 3 minutes or until light and fluffy. Add the eggs one at a time, beating well after each addition.

3 On a sheet of wax paper, combine the flour, baking powder, and salt.

4 In a small bowl, stir together the yogurt, milk, and extracts.

5 Beginning and ending with the flour, add the flour to the batter alternating with the yogurt mixture and beat on medium speed after each addition until blended. Beat on medium speed for 1 to 2 minutes or until the batter is smooth.

6 Pour the batter into the pan and smooth the surface.

7 Bake for 1 to 1¼ hours or until lightly browned and a toothpick inserted halfway between the edge of the pan and center tube comes out clean. Let the pan sit on a wire rack for 10 minutes.

8 Gently loosen the sides of the cake by sliding a kitchen knife around the pan. Invert the cake onto a wire rack to cool completely.

9 Drizzle the cake with lemon juice and sprinkle with powdered sugar for serving.

10 For gift giving, wrap the cake in color plastic wrap.

> **REYNOLDS KITCHENS TIP**
>
> *Combining dry ingredients such as flour, baking powder, and salt on a sheet of wax paper or parchment paper makes it easy to funnel into the mixing bowl.*

Rose-Wrapped Pound Cake

PREP TIME

25 minutes

MAKES

18 to 20
servings

1 homemade or prepared bundt-shaped pound cake, page 259

Rose plastic wrap

Pencil

Scissors

Transparent tape

Green plastic wrap

1 Put the bundt cake on a cake plate or stand. Cover with rose plastic wrap to seal in freshness.

2 To make roses, gather an 18-inch sheet of rose plastic wrap into a strip. Lay 2 to 3 inches along the side of a pencil. Loosely twist and wind the strip around tip of the pencil, leaving 2 inches at end.

3 Slip the rose off the pencil and adhere a strip of folded tape to the back of the rose so it sticks to itself and will attach the roses to the cake. Twist the ends of the strip together to make the stem.

4 Repeat for as many roses as desired. Attach the roses to the plastic wrap covering the cake.

5 To make leaves, fold a 12-inch-wide sheet of green plastic wrap in half three times, keeping each layer as smooth as possible. With scissors, cut out leaf shapes, keeping the end rather wide. Pinch the ends together and tape in place beside the roses on the cake.

Rose-Wrapped Pound Cake

Merry-Go-Round Cake

PREP TIME

30 minutes

MAKES

18 to 20 servings

1 homemade or commercially prepared pound cake, page 259

½ cup vanilla ready-to-spread frosting

Multicolored sprinkles

½ cup premium white morsels

8 animal cookies

8 plastic drinking straws

1 empty paper towel tube

Color plastic wrap

One 7-ounce paper cup

1 Center the pound cake on a 12-inch round platter.

2 Put the frosting in a small microwave-safe bowl and microwave on high power for 5 to 10 seconds or until the frosting is softened but not melted.

3 Drizzle the frosting over the pound cake. Top with sprinkles.

4 Put the white morsels in a small microwave-safe bowl and microwave on high power for 30 to 60 seconds until softened. Stir until smooth.

5 Spoon the melted white morsels on the back of the animal cookies. To attach cookies to straws, roll the straws in the melted morsels. Lay on parchment or wax paper to set. Trim the bottom of the straw, if desired, and arrange in the top of the cake.

6 To make the striped center pole, cut the paper towel tube to 10 inches long. Wrap in color plastic wrap. Cut an X in the bottom of the paper cup. Cover the cup with color plastic wrap and place upside down in center of cake. Insert the tube through the X. Twist a long sheet of color plastic wrap into a string and wrap around the tube to make a striped pole. Tuck the end into the top of the tube.

7 To make spokes, twist a 3½-foot sheet of color plastic wrap and pull to stretch into a tight string. Loop the string under the platter and tuck the ends into the top of the tube to make 2 spokes. Repeat to make 8 spokes.

8 To make the fluffy top, pinch the center of a 12-inch sheet of color plastic wrap. Twist the center to make a small stem. Repeat with 2 more sheets of color plastic wrap. Hold the stems together like a bouquet of flowers and tuck them into the top of the pole.

> **REYNOLDS KITCHENS TIP**
>
> *When melted premium white morsels or semisweet morsels are allowed to harden on sheets of wax or parchment paper, they are easy to lift from the paper without sticking.*

Slumber Party Cake

PREP TIME
25 minutes

COOK TIME
30 minutes

MAKES
24 servings

Color plastic wrap

One 18-ounce package of your favorite flavor cake mix

One 16-ounce container vanilla ready-to-spread frosting

Assorted food coloring

2 or 3 vanilla-flavored wafers

2 or 3 chocolate-flavored wafers

10 to 12 mini semi-sweet chocolate baking bits

Powdered sugar

5 to 6 sugar wafers

1 To make a cake platter, cover a sturdy piece of cardboard with your choice of color plastic wrap.

2 Prepare the cake mix following the package directions for a 9-by-13-by-2-inch pan.

Slumber Party Cake

3   Invert the baked cake onto a wire rack to cool completely. When cool, transfer to the prepared platter. Spread with frosting. Reserve the leftover frosting for piping.

4   To make cookie kids, decorate vanilla or chocolate wafers to represent the faces of each party guest by using mini baking bits for eyes and piped frosting for smiles.

5   Add powdered sugar to remaining frosting. Divide and tint the frosting for hair. To make hair, squeeze the frosting through a garlic press and adhere to the cookie faces.

6   Arrange the decorated faces on the cake at the head of the "bed."

7   To make bodies for the cookie kids, place sugar wafers on the cake below the faces. Cover the bodies of the cookie kids with a sheet of color plastic wrap for a blanket.

• • •

Cupcake Critters

One 18-ounce package chocolate cake mix

One 16-ounce container vanilla or chocolate ready-to-spread frosting

48 pecan halves

48 candy-coated plain chocolate candies

24 mini red candy-coated plain chocolate candies

96 pretzel sticks

PREP TIME
10 minutes

COOK TIME
18 minutes

MAKES
24 cupcakes

1   Preheat the oven to 350°F. Place 24 baking cups in two 12-cup muffin pans.

2   Prepare the cake mix following the package directions for 24 cupcakes. Spoon the batter into the baking cups, filling each about two-thirds full.

3   Bake for 18 to 23 minutes or until a toothpick inserted in the center of a cupcake comes out clean. Set the muffin pans on wire racks to cool.

4   Frost the cooled cupcakes. Decorate with pecan halves for ears, chocolate candies for eyes, a mini red chocolate candy for the nose, and pretzel sticks for whiskers.

> **REYNOLDS KITCHENS TIP**
>
> *Baking cups provide easy cleanup. There's no need to grease the muffin pans.*

Flutterby Butterfly Cupcakes

One 18-ounce package white cake mix

One 16-ounce container vanilla ready-to-spread frosting

Green food coloring

Mini pretzels

One 12-ounce package premium white morsels, melted

Colored sprinkles

Red string licorice

PREP TIME
10 minutes

COOK TIME
18 minutes

MAKES
24 cupcakes

1 Preheat the oven to 350°F. Place 24 baking cups in two 12-cup muffin pans.

2 Prepare the cake mix following the package directions for 24 cupcakes. Spoon the batter into the baking cups, filling each about two-thirds full.

3 Bake for 18 to 23 minutes or until a toothpick inserted in the center of a cupcake comes out clean. Set the muffin pans on wire racks to cool.

Flutterby Butterfly Cupcakes

4 In a small bowl, tint the frosting with green food coloring. Frost the cupcakes.

5 For each butterfly, dip 2 mini pretzels in the melted white morsels. Put the candy-coated pretzels on wax paper, with bottom sides touching each other. Use 2 small balls of wax paper to lift butterfly "wings" up.

6 Drizzle more melted white morsels between the pretzels to cover them more completely to make the body. Sprinkle with colored sprinkles.

7 For the antenna, insert 2 pieces of licorice into the melted white morsels. Repeat to make 24 butterflies.

8 Refrigerate to set. When set, stand a butterfly on top of each cupcake.

. . .

Chocolate Cappuccino Cupcakes

One 18-ounce package chocolate cake mix

¼ cup instant coffee

2 teaspoons hot water

One 16-ounce container cream cheese ready-to-spread frosting

½ cup semi-sweet chocolate morsels

2 teaspoons vegetable oil

PREP TIME
10 minutes

COOK TIME
18 minutes

MAKES
24 cupcakes

1 Preheat the oven to 350°F. Place 24 baking cups in two 12-cup muffin pans.

2 Prepare the cake mix following the package directions for 24 cupcakes. Add 2 tablespoons of the instant coffee granules before mixing the cake batter. Spoon the batter into the baking cups, filling each about two-thirds full.

3 Bake for 18 to 23 minutes or until a toothpick inserted in the center of a cupcake comes out clean. Set the muffin pans on wire racks to cool.

4 Dissolve the remaining 2 tablespoons of coffee in the hot water. Add to the frosting and stir until smooth. Frost the cupcakes.

5 In a small microwave-safe dish, melt the chocolate morsels and oil on high power for 1 to 1½ minutes, stirring once, until the chocolate melts and the mixture is smooth.

6 Drizzle the melted chocolate over the frosted cupcakes in a decorative pattern. Let stand until the chocolate sets.

Chocolate Cappuccino Cupcakes

Smiling Sunshine Cupcakes

One 18-ounce package white cake mix

One 16-ounce container white ready-to-spread frosting

Yellow food coloring

Candy corn

Red cinnamon candies

Red string licorice

PREP TIME
10 minutes

COOK TIME
18 minutes

MAKES
24 cupcakes

1 Preheat the oven to 350°F. Place 24 baking cups in two 12-cup muffin pans.

2 Prepare the cake mix following the package directions for 24 cupcakes. Spoon the batter into the baking cups, filling each about two-thirds full.

3 Bake for 18 to 23 minutes or until a toothpick inserted in the center of a cupcake comes out clean. Set the muffin pans on wire racks to cool.

4 Tint the frosting with yellow food coloring. Frost the cupcakes.

5 Decorate each cupcake by arranging the candy corn around the cupcake's edge with the points facing outward. Make eyes with red cinnamon candies, and a smile with red string licorice.

REYNOLDS KITCHENS TIP

Once you start investigating the candy and baking aisles of the supermarket, you will find dozens of creative ways to use candy and manufactured cake decorations. Cupcakes are great places to test your imagination.

Smiling Sunshine Cupcakes

Friendly Frog Cupcakes

PREP TIME
10 minutes

COOK TIME
18 minutes

MAKES
24 cupcakes

One 18-ounce package
chocolate cake mix

One 16-ounce container vanilla
ready-to-spread frosting

Blue food coloring

24 large spearmint gumdrops

48 mini yellow hard candies

Melted chocolate

Red gumdrops

Green fruit roll-ups

1 Preheat the oven to 350°F. Place 24 baking cups in two 12-cup muffin pans.

2 Prepare the cake mix following the package directions for 24 cupcakes. Spoon the batter into the baking cups, filling each about two-thirds full.

3 Bake for 18 to 23 minutes or until a toothpick inserted in the center of a cupcake comes out clean. Set the muffin pans on wire racks to cool.

4 Tint the frosting with blue food coloring. Frost the cupcakes.

5 Decorate each cupcake by using a spearmint gumdrop for the frog's body. For the eyes, press the small yellow hard candies into the gumdrop. Using a toothpick, put a dot of melted chocolate in the center of each yellow eye. For the mouth, cut a red gumdrop slice with scissors and press into the spearmint gumdrop. Cut the fruit roll-ups to make feet.

...

Frizzy-the-Clown Cupcakes

PREP TIME
15 minutes

COOK TIME
18 minutes

MAKES
24 cupcakes

One 18-ounce package cake mix

One 16-ounce container vanilla
ready-to-spread frosting

Orange food coloring

Powdered sugar

12 gummy fruit-flavored ring
candies

24 small gumdrops

48 mini candy-coated plain
chocolate candies

Red string licorice

1 Preheat the oven to 350°F. Place 24 baking cups in two 12-cup muffin pans.

2 Prepare the cake mix following the package directions for 24 cupcakes. Spoon the batter into the baking cups, filling each about two-thirds full.

3 Bake for 18 to 23 minutes or until a toothpick inserted in the center of a cupcake comes out clean.

4 Frost the cupcakes with vanilla frosting.

5 Tint a small amount of the remaining frosting with orange food coloring for Frizzy's hair. Add powdered sugar to the frosting until it is no longer sticky and has the consistency of cookie dough. Press the orange frosting through a clean garlic press or fine-mesh sieve. Pinch strands of frosting together and press on top of a cupcake.

6 For the mouth, cut a section of a gummy fruit-flavored ring candy and press into the cupcake. Use a gumdrop for the nose, chocolate candies for the eyes, and red string licorice for eyebrows. Repeat to make 24 cupcakes.

Frizzy-the-Clown Cupcakes

Winter Wonderland Cupcakes

One 18-ounce package white
cake mix

One 16-ounce container vanilla
ready-to-spread frosting

Red and green colored sprinkles

Flaked sweetened coconut

Large green gumdrops

Sugar

PREP TIME
20 minutes

COOK TIME
18 minutes

MAKES
24 cupcakes

1 Preheat the oven to 350°F. Place 24 holiday designs baking cups in two 12-cup muffin pans.

2 Prepare the cake mix following the package directions for 24 cupcakes. Spoon the batter into the baking cups, filling each about two-thirds full.

Winter Wonderland Cupcakes

3 Bake for 18 to 23 minutes or until a toothpick inserted in the center of a cupcake comes out clean. Set the muffin pans on wire racks to cool.

4 Frost the cupcakes with the vanilla frosting.

5 Spread the red and green colored sprinkles on a sheet of wax paper. Roll the edge of the frosted cupcakes in the sprinkles. Sprinkle the coconut over the top of the cupcakes in a fluffy mound but without covering the sprinkles, holding the cupcakes over wax paper to catch the excess.

6 For trees, press several large gumdrops together with your fingers. Line the countertop with wax paper and sprinkle it with sugar.

7 Use a rolling pin to flatten the gumdrops into circles the size of a silver dollar. Cut out trees with a small cookie cutter. Stand 2 trees on top of each cupcake.

8 Wrap each cupcake in holiday designs printed plastic wrap and tie with a ribbon.

> **REYNOLDS KITCHENS TIP**
>
> *When you use wax paper as a decorating tool—to catch excess sprinkles and coconut—cleanup is simple. No sticky, messy countertops!*

. . .

Snowman Cupcakes

One 18-ounce package white cake mix

One 16-ounce container white whipped ready-to-spread frosting

Flaked coconut

48 large marshmallows

48 mini red or green candy-coated chocolate candies

24 red or green fruit-flavored roll-ups, cut in 7 1/2-inch-long strips

24 pretzel twists

1 tube black decorating icing

24 black hat-shaped gummy candies

PREP TIME
20 minutes

COOK TIME
18 minutes

MAKES
24 cupcakes

1 Preheat the oven to 350°F. Place 24 baking cups in two 12-cup muffin pans.

2 Prepare the cake mix following the package directions for 24 cupcakes. Spoon the batter into the baking cups, filling each about two-thirds full.

3 Bake for 18 to 23 minutes or until a toothpick inserted in the center of a cupcake comes out clean. Set the muffin pans on wire racks to cool.

4 Frost the cupcakes with the whipped frosting. Put the cupcakes on a sheet of wax paper and sprinkle each with a generous mound of coconut.

5 For the snowmen, spread the tops of 24 marshmallows with frosting. Stack another marshmallow on top of the frosted marshmallow. Press them together so they adhere to each other.

6 Using frosting, attach 2 green candies to the bottom marshmallows for buttons. For a scarf, wrap a fruit-flavored roll-up strip around the center of the snowman.

7 Cut or break the pretzel twists to make arms and insert into the sides of the marshmallow.

8 Make the eyes and smile with black decorating icing.

9 Attach the hat-shaped candy to the top of the marshmallow. Repeat to make 24 decorated marshmallow snowmen.

10 Center 1 decorated marshmallow snowman in the center of each frosted cupcake, pressing down to hold securely.

. . .

Birthday Cupcake Tray

One 18-ounce package white cake mix

One 16-ounce container vanilla ready-to-spread frosting

Neon colored sprinkles

Bright colored candy pieces

Color plastic wrap

PREP TIME
20 minutes
COOK TIME
18 minutes
MAKES
24 cupcakes

1 Preheat the oven to 350°F. Place 24 baking cups in two 12-cup muffin pans.

2 Prepare the cake mix following the package directions for 24 cupcakes. Spoon the batter into the baking cups, filling each about two-thirds full.

3 Bake for 18 to 23 minutes or until a toothpick inserted in the center of a cupcake comes out clean. Set the muffin pans on wire racks to cool.

4 Frost the cupcakes. Sprinkle with neon colored sprinkles.

5 Arrange the cupcakes on a Mylar or other tray and scatter bright colored candy around the cupcakes on the tray. Wrap the tray with color plastic wrap.

Step 1 Tear off 2 or more sheets of color plastic wrap, each about 3½ times the diameter of the tray. Crisscross the plastic wrap sheets on the countertop. Center the tray on the plastic wrap.

Step 2 Pull the plastic wrap tightly up and around the tray.

Step 3 Tie the plastic wrap at the top with ribbon. Trim the ends of the plastic wrap, if desired.

Birthday Cupcake Tray

Marble-Frosted Macadamia Brownies

PREP TIME
10 minutes

COOK TIME
brownie mix package directions

MAKES
16 brownies

One 15-ounce package rich and moist fudge brownie mix

One 3¼-ounce jar macadamia nuts, coarsely chopped

½ cup flaked sweetened coconut

1 cup chocolate ready-to-spread frosting

¼ cup vanilla ready-to-spread frosting, softened

| Preheat the oven to the temperature on the brownie mix package directions for at least 20 minutes. Arrange an oven rack so that it is in the center of the oven. Put an 8-inch square disposable plastic cookware pan on a cookie sheet so that the pan does not hang over the sides.

Marble-Frosted Macadamia Brownies

2 Mix the brownie batter following the package directions. Stir in the nuts and coconut. Spoon the batter into the pan and spread the surface so it is smooth.

3 Bake on the cookie sheet according to the package directions. Use the cookie sheet to remove the pan from the oven. Let stand for at least 2 minutes before lifting the pan by the handles. Set on a wire rack to cool completely.

4 Spread the chocolate frosting over the cooled brownies. Squeeze softened vanilla frosting in six to eight lines over the chocolate frosting, leaving about 1 inch between each line. Using a toothpick or wooden skewer, draw lines through frosting to create a marble pattern. Cut into bars, cover with the lid, and store.

> **REYNOLDS KITCHENS TIP**
>
> *To make the vanilla frosting liquid enough to make lines, spoon the frosting into a small plastic food storage bag. Leave the bag unsealed and microwave on high power for 5 seconds. Squeeze the bag to remove any air pockets. Seal, snip a bottom corner with scissors, and gently squeeze the frosting through the snipped opening.*

. . .

Peppermint-Surprise Brownies

One 19-ounce package brownie mix

27 chocolate-covered peppermint patties, unwrapped (one 13-ounce package)

1 cup semi-sweet chocolate morsels

2 tablespoons light corn syrup

2 tablespoons milk

Chocolate and mint colored sprinkles

PREP TIME
10 minutes

COOK TIME
brownie mix package directions

MAKES
24 brownies

1 Preheat the oven to the temperature on the brownie mix package directions. Line a 9-by-13-by-2-inch baking pan with non-stick aluminum foil, non-stick (dull) side facing up.

2 Prepare the brownie mix following the package directions for cakelike brownies. Spread half the batter in the foil-lined pan and arrange 24 of the peppermint patties (reserve 3 patties) over the batter in a single layer of 4 across and 6 down, so

that 1 patty will be in every brownie. Carefully spread the remaining batter over the patties. Smooth the surface.

3 Bake the brownies following the package directions. Place the pan on a wire rack.

4 To make the frosting, break the remaining 3 patties into pieces and transfer to a microwave-safe dish. Add the chocolate morsels, corn syrup, and milk and microwave on high power for 1 to 1½ minutes, or until the morsels are softened and shiny. Stir until smooth.

5 Spread the frosting over the warm brownies. Scatter the sprinkles over the frosting before it sets. Once the frosting sets and the brownies are cool, lift the brownies from the pan onto a cutting board, using the foil overhang as handles. Fold down the foil sides and cut the brownies into bars.

> **REYNOLDS KITCHENS TIP**
>
> *The chocolate morsels may not melt to a liquid pool in the microwave but will liquefy as soon as you stir them.*

. . .

Brownie Pizza

One 19-ounce package fudge brownie mix

One 16-ounce container of your favorite ready-to-spread frosting

Jelly beans, chocolate covered candies, colored sprinkles, mini marshmallows, or nuts

PREP TIME
15 minutes
COOK TIME
20 minutes
MAKES
12 servings

1 Preheat the oven to 350°F. Line a large cookie sheet with parchment paper and trace a 12-inch circle on it.

2 Prepare the brownie mix following the package directions for fudge brownies. Pour the batter into the center of the parchment paper and spread evenly to fill the circle.

3 Bake for 20 to 22 minutes or until a toothpick inserted in the center comes out clean. Cool the brownie, still on the cookie sheet, on a wire rack.

4 Frost the brownie, leaving a 1-inch border unfrosted as the pizza crust. Decorate with candies, sprinkles, marshmallows, and nuts, or any combination of these.

> **REYNOLDS KITCHENS TIP**
>
> *Using parchment paper as the base for this brownie pizza prevents it from sticking to the cookie sheet.*

Triple-Chocolate Brownie Cake

PREP TIME
15 minutes

COOK TIME
35 minutes

MAKES
12 to 16 servings

CAKE

Three 3-ounce squares unsweetened chocolate, chopped

½ cup (1 stick) butter

3 eggs

1½ cups sugar

1 teaspoon vanilla extract

¼ teaspoon salt

1 cup flour

1 cup premium white morsels

GLAZE

Four 4-ounce squares semi-sweet chocolate

3 tablespoons water

1½ tablespoons butter

2 teaspoons light corn syrup

I Preheat the oven to 350°F. Grease sides of a 9-inch round cake pan and line bottom with parchment paper.

Triple-Chocolate Brownie Cake

2 To make the cake, put the chocolate and butter in a microwave-safe bowl. Microwave on high power, stirring every 30 seconds, 1 to 1½ minutes or until the butter melts and the chocolate is soft and shiny. Stir until smooth. Let the chocolate cool.

3 In the bowl of an electric mixer set on medium, beat the eggs until frothy. Add the sugar, vanilla, and salt, and beat until smooth. Remove the bowl from the mixer and stir in the chocolate, flour, and white morsels. Pour the batter into the prepared pan and smooth the surface.

4 Bake for 35 to 37 minutes or until a toothpick inserted in the center comes out with a few moist crumbs clinging to it. Cool in the pan set on a wire rack for 15 minutes. Loosen the sides with a knife and invert the cake onto a plate. Peel off the parchment and let the cake cool completely. The cake will be dense and fudgy.

5 To make the glaze, put the chocolate, water, butter, and corn syrup in a microwave-safe bowl. Microwave on high power, stirring every 30 seconds, 1 to 1½ minutes or until the chocolate and butter melt and the chocolate is soft and shiny. Stir until smooth. Let the chocolate cool.

6 Slide 4 strips of parchment paper under the cake to shield the plate. Pour the glaze over the center of the cake and let the glaze spread over the cake. Using a spatula, spread the glaze over the top and down the sides of the cake. Remove the parchment. Refrigerate the cake until the glaze sets.

REYNOLDS KITCHENS TIP

The quickest and easiest way to line a cake pan with parchment paper is to place the cake pan on the parchment and then trace around the bottom of the pan with a pencil. Cut the parchment circle out and fit it into the greased pan.

Star-Spangled Brownies

PREP TIME
30 minutes

COOK TIME
brownie mix package directions

MAKES
48 brownies

Two 19-ounce packages fudge brownie mix

One 16-ounce container vanilla ready-to-spread frosting

Clear, rose, and blue plastic wrap

Red and blue sprinkles

White cardboard

9 miniature American flags (optional)

I Preheat the oven according to the brownie mix package directions. Line two 9-by-13-by-2-inch baking pans with non-stick aluminum foil, non-stick (dull) side facing up.

Star-Spangled Brownies

2 Prepare the brownie mixes following the package directions. Spoon into the foil-lined pans and smooth the surface.

3 Bake the brownies according to the package directions. Cool in the pans on wire racks. Use the foil to lift the brownies from the pans and transfer to a cutting board.

4 Frost the brownies. Cut into 2-inch squares. Wrap 11 brownies in clear plastic wrap.

5 Sprinkle 15 brownies with red sprinkles and wrap each in rose plastic wrap.

6 Sprinkle 9 brownies with blue sprinkles and wrap each in blue plastic wrap. Add paper stars.

7 Arrange the wrapped brownies in the shape of the American flag on a large tray or white cardboard covered with plastic wrap. Insert the miniature flags into the star brownies through the blue plastic wrap. Serve the leftover brownies separately.

. . .

Buttery Sugar Cookies

3 cups flour	1 cup sugar
1/2 teaspoon baking powder	1 egg
1/4 teaspoon salt	2 teaspoons vanilla extract
1 cup (2 sticks) butter, softened	Colored sprinkles and candies

PREP TIME
20 minutes

COOK TIME
8 minutes

MAKES
3 to 3 1/2 dozen cookies

1 Combine the flour, baking powder, and salt on a sheet of parchment paper.

2 In the bowl of an electric mixer set on medium speed, cream the butter and sugar for 4 to 5 minutes or until light and fluffy. Add the egg and vanilla and beat until blended.

3 Reduce the speed to low and gradually beat the flour mixture into the batter until smooth.

4 Turn the dough out onto a lightly floured sheet of parchment paper or lightly floured surface and divide in half. Form each half into a flattened disk and wrap each in plastic wrap. Refrigerate for 30 minutes to 1 hour or until firm enough to roll.

5 Preheat the oven to 375°F. Line 1 or 2 cookie sheets with parchment paper or non-stick aluminum foil, non-stick (dull) side facing up.

6 Set a disk between 2 lightly floured sheets of parchment paper or on a lightly floured surface. Roll out to a ⅛-inch-thick circle. Cut the dough with 2- to 6-inch cookie cutters and transfer the cookies to the prepared cookie sheets. Leave about 1 inch between the cookies. Repeat with the other disk.

7 Decorate the cookies with colored sprinkles or candies.

8 Bake for 8 to 10 minutes or until the cookies just begin to brown around the edges. Transfer the cookies to a wire rack until cool.

> **REYNOLDS KITCHENS TIP**
>
> *Rolling out cookie dough between 2 sheets of parchment prevents sticking and keeps your work surface clean. To hold the parchment in place, fold a few inches of the parchment sheets over the edge of the counter and lean against it while you are rolling the dough. If necessary, turn the parchment to roll the dough at different angles.*

...

Jam-Filled Sugar Cookies

PREP TIME
1½ hours
COOK TIME
6 minutes
MAKES
2½ to 3 dozen cookies

3 cups flour

1¼ teaspoons baking powder

¾ teaspoon salt

1½ cups sugar

¾ cup butter or margarine, softened

2 eggs

1 teaspoon vanilla extract

Raspberry, strawberry, or apricot jam or preserves

1 Combine the flour, baking powder, and salt on a sheet of parchment or wax paper.

2 In the bowl of an electric mixer set on medium speed, cream the sugar and butter for 2 to 3 minutes or until light and fluffy. Add the eggs one at a time, beating after each addition. Add the vanilla and beat until blended.

3 Reduce the speed to low and gradually beat the flour mixture into the batter until smooth.

4 Turn the dough out onto a lightly floured sheet of parchment paper or lightly floured surface and divide in half. Form each half into a flattened disk and wrap each in plastic wrap. Refrigerate for 30 minutes to 1 hour or until firm enough to roll.

Jam-Filled Sugar Cookies

5 Preheat the oven to 375°F. Line 1 or 2 cookie sheets with parchment paper or non-stick aluminum foil, non-stick (dull) side facing up.

6 Set a disk between 2 lightly floured sheets of parchment paper or on a lightly floured surface. Roll out to a ⅛-inch-thick circle. Cut the dough with 2½-inch cookie cutters and cut the centers from half the cookies with a 1-inch cookie cutter. Transfer the cookies to the cookie sheet. Leave about 1 inch between the cookies. Repeat with the other disk.

7 Bake for 6 to 8 minutes or until the cookies just begin to brown around the edges. Transfer the cookies to a wire rack until cool.

8 Spread the solid cookies with ½ to 1 teaspoon of jam. Top with the cut-out cookies and gently press together, sandwich-style.

> **REYNOLDS KITCHENS TIP**
>
> *When you line a cookie sheet with parchment paper, there's no need to wait between batches. You won't even have to wash the cookie sheet! Line the cookie sheet with parchment paper and while the first batch of cookies bakes, lay a second sheet of parchment paper on the countertop and arrange unbaked cookies on it. Slide the baked cookies and parchment paper off the sheet and slide on the second batch.*

...

Chocolate-Chunk Orange Cookies

PREP TIME
10 minutes
COOK TIME
10 minutes
MAKES
2½ dozen cookies

1½ cups flour

½ teaspoon baking soda

½ teaspoon salt

½ cup (1 stick) butter or margarine, softened

¾ cup sugar

2 tablespoons orange juice

1 egg

Four 4-ounce squares semi-sweet chocolate, coarsely chopped

2 tablespoons grated orange peel

1 Preheat the oven to 375°F. Line a cookie sheet with parchment paper or non-stick aluminum foil, non-stick (dull) side facing up.

2 Combine the flour, baking soda, and salt on a sheet of parchment paper.

3 In the bowl of an electric mixer set on medium speed, beat the butter, sugar, and orange juice for 2 to 3 minutes until fluffy. Beat in the egg.

4   Reduce the speed to low and gradually add the flour mixture, beating until blended. Remove the bowl from the mixer and stir in the chocolate and orange peel.

5   Drop the dough by level measuring tablespoons onto the prepared cookie sheet. Bake for 10 to 12 minutes or until the cookies are lightly browned. Cool on wire racks.

...

Lemon-Blueberry Cookies

PREP TIME
15 minutes

COOK TIME
12 minutes

MAKES
32 cookies

1 1/4 cups flour

1/4 cup cornstarch

1/4 teaspoon baking powder

1/4 teaspoon salt

1/2 cup (1 stick) butter, softened

1/3 cup sugar

2 egg yolks, at room temperature

1 teaspoon grated lemon peel

1/3 cup dried blueberries or dried sweetened cranberries

Sugar

1   Preheat the oven to 375°F. Line a cookie sheet with parchment paper or non-stick aluminum foil, non-stick (dull) side facing up.

2   Combine the flour, cornstarch, baking powder, and salt on a sheet of parchment or wax paper.

3   In the bowl of an electric mixer set at medium speed, cream the butter and sugar for 2 to 3 minutes or until light and fluffy. Beat in the egg yolks and lemon peel.

4   Reduce the speed to low and gradually add the flour mixture, beating just until crumbly. Remove the bowl from the mixer and stir in the blueberries.

5   Lay a sheet of parchment paper on the countertop. Scoop the dough onto the parchment and divide the dough in half. Knead each half until the dough holds together. Divide each half into 16 pieces. Roll each piece into a ball.

6 Put the cookies on the prepared cookie sheet. Dip the bottom of a small glass in sugar and then press it on a cookie ball to flatten to a ¼-inch thickness. Repeat with the other cookies.

7 Bake for 12 to 14 minutes or until the cookies are lightly browned around the edges. Transfer to wire racks to cool.

REYNOLDS KITCHENS TIP

Lining the kitchen counter with parchment paper protects it and keeps it clean while you work with the dough.

Lemon-Blueberry Cookies

Mexican Wedding Cakes

PREP TIME
30 minutes

CHILL TIME
1 hour

COOK TIME
8 minutes

MAKES
3½ to 4 dozen cookies

2 cups flour

⅛ teaspoon salt

¾ cup butter, softened

¼ cup powdered sugar

2 teaspoons vanilla extract

1 cup finely chopped pecans

Powdered sugar

1 Combine the flour and salt on a sheet of parchment paper.

2 In the bowl of an electric mixer on medium speed, cream the butter for 3 to 4 minutes or until fluffy. Add the sugar and vanilla and beat until blended.

3 Reduce the speed to low and gradually add the flour mixture, beating until blended. Remove the bowl from the mixer and stir in the pecans.

4 Turn the dough out onto the countertop and divide the dough in half and roll each into an 8-inch long roll. Wrap the rolls in non-stick aluminum foil, non-stick (dull) side facing the dough, and refrigerate for 1 to 2 hours or until firm.

5 Preheat the oven to 400°F. Line a cookie sheet with parchment paper or non-stick aluminum foil, non-stick (dull) side facing up.

6 Unwrap the rolls and cut them into ¼-inch-thick slices. Roll each into a 1-inch ball and place the balls, 1 inch apart, on the cookie sheet.

7 Bake for 8 to 10 minutes. Remove the hot cookies from the cookie sheet and roll in powdered sugar to coat. Place on a wire rack to cool. Roll again in more powdered sugar, if desired.

REYNOLDS KITCHENS TIP

When forming dough into 8-inch long rolls, use the non-stick foil with the dull side facing the dough to help you shape the rolls. From there, it's easy to wrap the rolls for chilling.

Maple Leaf Cookie Basket

One 18-ounce package
refrigerated sugar cookie dough

2 cups powdered sugar

2 tablespoons butter or
margarine, softened

1 tablespoon light corn syrup

1 teaspoon maple extract

2 to 3 tablespoons milk

1/2 cup finely chopped nuts
(optional)

Apples

Pears

PREP TIME
15 minutes

COOK TIME
7 minutes

MAKES
2 dozen
cookies

1 Preheat the oven to 350°F. Line a cookie sheet with parchment paper or non-stick
aluminum foil, non-stick (dull) side facing up.

Maple Leaf Cookie Basket

2 Working with half the dough, roll the dough out on a well floured sheet of parchment paper or well floured surface to a ¼-inch thickness. Cut out cookies with a 3-inch leaf cookie cutter and transfer the cookies to the cookie sheet.

3 Bake for 7 to 9 minutes or until the cookies begin to brown around the edges. Transfer to wire racks to cool. Repeat with the remaining cookie dough.

4 In a medium bowl, stir together the powdered sugar, butter, corn syrup, and maple extract. Add enough milk to make a frosting. Frost the cooled cookies and sprinkle with finely chopped nuts, if desired.

5 Wrap the cookies individually in color plastic wrap. Put the cookies in a small basket lined with fluffed color plastic wrap. Add a few apples and pears to basket, if desired.

> **REYNOLDS KITCHENS TIP**
>
> *With color plastic wrap, it's easy to dress up any food gift. Wrap individual cookies or cupcakes in color plastic wrap or place several items in a basket and wrap the entire basket in color plastic wrap. Add a bow and a note and your gift is ready.*

...

Chocolate-Dipped Cookie Bundles

One 18-ounce package refrigerated sugar cookie dough

One 8-ounce package semi-sweet chocolate chips

2 teaspoons vegetable shortening

PREP TIME
15 minutes

COOK TIME
cookie package directions

MAKES
10 to 12 cookie bundles

1 Preheat the oven according to the cookie package directions. Line a cookie sheet with parchment paper or non-stick aluminum foil, non-stick (dull) side facing up.

2 Working with half the dough, roll the dough out on a well-floured sheet of parchment paper to a ¼-inch thickness. Cut out cookies with holiday cookie cutters and transfer the cookies to the cookie sheet.

3 Bake according to the cookie package directions, or until the cookies begin to

brown around the edges. Transfer to wire racks to cool. Repeat with the remaining cookie dough.

4 Put the chocolate chips and shortening in a microwave-safe bowl. Microwave on high power, stirring every 30 seconds, 1 to 2 minutes or until the chocolate is soft and shiny. Stir until smooth.

5 Dip half of each cookie in the melted chocolate. Set on a sheet of parchment paper or wax paper.

6 When the chocolate is set, stack the cookies in baking cups. Wrap each in color plastic wrap. Tie the top of each bundle with ribbon. Put the bundles in a holiday container or gift basket.

Chocolate-Dipped Cookie Bundles

Oatmeal-Raisin Cookies

PREP TIME
10 minutes

COOK TIME
10 minutes

MAKES
2 dozen
cookies

$^1/_2$ cup flour

$^1/_4$ teaspoon baking soda

$^1/_4$ teaspoon salt

$^1/_4$ teaspoon ground cinnamon

$^1/_2$ cup (1 stick) butter or
margarine, softened

$^3/_4$ cup packed brown sugar

1 egg

$^1/_2$ teaspoon vanilla extract

1 $^1/_2$ cups quick oats, uncooked

$^1/_2$ cup raisins or dried
sweetened cranberries

1 Preheat the oven to 375°F. Line cookie sheets with parchment paper or non-stick aluminum foil, non-stick (dull) side facing up.

2 Combine the flour, baking soda, salt, and cinnamon on a sheet of parchment paper.

3 In the bowl of an electric mixer on medium speed, cream the butter and brown sugar for 2 to 3 minutes or until light and fluffy. Beat in the egg and vanilla until blended.

4 Reduce the speed to low and gradually add the flour mixture, beating until blended. Remove the bowl from the mixer and stir in the oats and raisins.

5 Drop by rounded teaspoons onto the cookie sheets.

6 Bake for 10 to 12 minutes or until the cookies begin to brown around the edges. Transfer to a wire rack to cool.

REYNOLDS KITCHENS TIP

To make ice cream sandwiches with these cookies, soften $^1/_4$ cup of your favorite flavor of ice cream or frozen yogurt. Sandwich the ice cream between two cookies and press the cookies together until the ice cream reaches the edges. With a knife, smooth the side of the ice cream between the cookies. Decorate the ice cream with colored sprinkles, mini chocolate morsels, or chopped candy bars. Repeat for each ice cream sandwich. Wrap individually in non-stick aluminum foil and freeze.

Stained Glass Butter Cookies

3 cups flour

1 1/4 teaspoons baking powder

3/4 teaspoon salt

3/4 cup butter or margarine, softened

1 1/2 cups sugar

2 eggs

1 teaspoon vanilla extract

5 rolls of ring-shaped hard candy

PREP TIME
15 minutes

CHILL TIME
1 hour

COOK TIME
6 minutes

MAKES
3 1/2 to 4 dozen cookies

1 Combine the flour, baking powder, and salt on a sheet of parchment paper.

2 In the bowl of an electric mixer set on medium speed, cream the butter and sugar for 2 to 3 minutes until light and fluffy. Add the eggs and vanilla and beat until blended.

3 Reduce the speed to low and gradually add the flour mixture. Beat until blended and a dough forms. Cover the dough with plastic wrap and refrigerate the dough for at least 1 hour.

4 Preheat the oven to 375°F. Line a cookie sheet with parchment paper or non-stick aluminum foil, non-stick (dull) side facing up.

5 On a lightly floured sheet of parchment paper, roll the dough to a 1/8-inch thickness. Using 3/4-inch round doughnut cookie cutters, cut out cookies. Transfer to the cookie sheet. Put a candy in center of each cookie.

6 Bake for 6 to 8 minutes or until cookies are just beginning to brown on edges and candy melts. Slide the parchment or non-stick aluminum foil off the cookie sheet. When completely cool, peel the parchment or foil from cookies.

REYNOLDS KITCHENS TIP

Plastic wrap stretches tightly to seal bowls and dishes to keep dough fresh during chilling.

Almond-Apricot Bars

PREP TIME
20 minutes

COOK TIME
35 minutes

MAKES
24 bars

$1\frac{3}{4}$ cups flour

$1\frac{1}{2}$ cups quick-cooking oats

1 cup packed brown sugar

1 teaspoon baking powder

$\frac{1}{2}$ teaspoon salt

1 cup (2 sticks) butter or margarine, melted

2 eggs

$\frac{1}{2}$ teaspoon almond extract

One 12-ounce jar apricot preserves

1 cup seedless raisins

$\frac{1}{2}$ cup sliced almonds

1 Preheat the oven to 350°F. Line a 9-by-13-by-2-inch baking pan with non-stick aluminum foil, non-stick (dull) side facing up.

2 In a large bowl, mix together the flour, oats, brown sugar, baking powder, and salt. Stir in the butter until the mixture is crumbly. Reserve 1 cup of the mixture.

3 Stir the eggs and almond extract into the flour mixture. Spread the batter in the prepared pan.

4 In a small bowl, stir the apricot preserves until smooth. Spread over the batter. Sprinkle with raisins.

5 Mix the almonds with the reserved oat mixture and sprinkle this over the raisins.

6 Bake for 35 to 40 minutes or until the center is set and almonds begin to brown. Cool in the pan set on a wire rack. Use the foil to lift the bars from the pan onto a cutting board. Cut into bars.

Nutty Cranberry-Orange Bars

PREP TIME

15 minutes

COOK TIME

30 minutes

MAKES

24 bars

2 cups flour

½ cup sugar

¾ teaspoon baking powder

¾ cup butter or margarine, softened

One 18-ounce jar orange marmalade

1 cup chopped nuts

1 cup sweetened dried cranberries

1 Preheat the oven to 350°F. Line a 9-by-13-by-2-inch baking pan with non-stick aluminum foil, non-stick (dull) side facing up.

2 In a large bowl, mix together the flour, sugar, and baking powder. Cut in the butter using a pastry cutter or two knives until the mixture is crumbly. Press into the pan.

3 Bake for 15 to 18 minutes or until firm.

4 In a small bowl, stir the marmalade until smooth. Spread half over the hot crust and sprinkle with nuts and cranberries. Spread the remaining marmalade over the top.

5 Bake for 15 to 20 minutes longer or until the marmalade begins to bubble. Cool in the pan set on a wire rack. Use the foil to lift the bars from the pan. Cut into bars.

> **REYNOLDS KITCHENS TIP**
>
> *Extensions of foil on lined pans transform into handy handles to lift the bars from pans.*

Favorite Chocolate Chip Cookies

2½ cups flour

1 teaspoon baking powder

1 teaspoon salt

½ teaspoon ground cinnamon (optional)

1 cup butter (2 sticks), softened

1 cup packed brown sugar

½ cup granulated sugar

2 eggs

2 teaspoons vanilla extract

One 12-ounce package or 2 cups semi-sweet chocolate morsels

1 cup coarsely chopped nuts

PREP TIME
15 minutes

COOK TIME
10 minutes

MAKES
3½ to 4 dozen cookies

1   Preheat the oven to 350°F. Line a cookie sheet with parchment paper or non-stick aluminum foil, non-stick (dull) side facing up.

2   Combine the flour, baking powder, salt, and cinnamon on a sheet of parchment paper.

3   In the bowl of an electric mixer set on medium speed, cream the butter, brown sugar, and granulated sugar for 2 to 3 minutes or until light and fluffy. Beat in the egg yolks, one at a time, beating until blended. Beat in the vanilla extract.

4   Reduce the speed to low and gradually add the flour mixture, beating until smooth. Remove the bowl from the mixer and stir in the chocolate morsels and nuts.

5   Drop by rounded tablespoons onto the cookie sheet.

6   Bake for 10 to 12 minutes or until the cookies are lightly browned around the edges. Transfer to wire racks to cool.

REYNOLDS KITCHENS TIP

It takes several minutes to cream butter and sugar so the batter is light and fluffy. Be patient.

carry a tray of cupcakes

or cookies into a room and

you just might make

instant friends

Desserts

Old-Fashioned Apple Pie

Apple Cobbler

Quick Apple Crisp

Chocolate-Raspberry Mousse

Cherry-Apple Crisp

Flower Pots and Shovels

Party Cheesecakes

All-American Ice Cream Cups

Caramel Cream Dessert

Chocolate-Mint Cups

Chocolate Dessert Shells

Fudgy Chocolate Fondue

Fruit-Glazed Cheesecakes

Banana Split Pudding Cups

Confetti Party Pie

Chocolate-Dipped Strawberries

Strawberries 'N' Cream Dessert

Mexican Bread Dessert

I love warm fruit desserts, sweet and juicy, like an apple pie or cobbler. They are easy to make and so basic and delicious.

—Betty

I have never met a bad dessert. When we travel, I remember the desserts we eat in restaurants; Betty remembers the entrées.

—Pat

IN THIS CHAPTER WE OFFER recipes for fruit desserts, cheese-cakes, mousses, puddings, and pies. All those desserts that don't fall into the cake or cookie category.

We begin with our Old-Fashioned Apple Pie for several reasons. First, apples are America's favorite fruit, and when baked into a pie, are as good as can be. Second, this recipe was the winner of a contest we held back in the 1980s. The recipe was a family favorite actually submitted by a nine-year-old girl. We don't think apple pies get any better. We hope you'll agree.

As you bake the pie crust, make sure the edge doesn't get overbrowned or burned. You can shield it with a ring of aluminum foil cut from a square of foil. Measure and cut this out before you fill the pie plate.

Kid-Friendly Desserts

Not surprisingly, a number of the desserts here are designed with kids in mind. Our Flower Pots and Shovels is a derivative of "dirt pudding." We added chocolate-coated plastic spoons, wrapped in color plastic wrap.

The Banana Split Pudding Cups, inspired by the old-fashioned soda fountain classic, have marshmallows and a cherry on top, although we omitted the nuts because most children don't like them or might be allergic to them.

The cheerful Confetti Party Pie is a refrigerated pie colorfully decorated with sprinkles and candy-coated chocolates. Easy and fun for kids' celebrations.

Cheesecakes and Crumb Crusts

Cheesecakes rank high as one of America's favorite desserts, but making a whole cheesecake frightens some folks. We came up with recipes for cheesecakes baked in foil baking cups rather than springform pans, which removes much of the mystery and makes them fun, simple desserts.

Ours are so easy, you don't have to worry about some of the normal complications like cracked surfaces and chewy textures. We don't use as much cream cheese for ours, and because they're easy to carry to a party or take for a brown bag lunch, they fit nicely into today's lifestyles.

These and other desserts in this chapter call for crumb crusts. To make the crumbs, put the cookies or crackers between two sheets of wax or parchment paper and roll them with a rolling pin. Never make the crumbs more than a day ahead of time, to prevent them from clumping or getting stale.

Elegant Desserts

Several of the recipes on these pages are fancy enough to serve at a special dinner party. For example, the Fudgy Chocolate Fondue couldn't be easier, particularly because the chocolate is melted and then served in a Reynolds Pot Lux Disposable Cookware pan. Serve the molten chocolate with strawberries, chunks of banana, pear slices, cubes of pound cake, or angel food cake, and it's always a sublime crowd pleaser.

Chocolate-Dipped Strawberries, which harden on a sheet of wax paper lining a cookie sheet, are luxurious treats on their own or can garnish a cake platter or dessert tray. Use the biggest, most perfect strawberries you can find, and if the stems are still on them, all the better!

Made in a Pot Lux pan, the Chocolate-Raspberry Mousse is one of our favorites for a party or neighborhood get-together. It's smooth, rich, and lusciously creamy. The same can be said of the Strawberries 'N' Cream Dessert, which is a little lighter and delightfully refreshing.

Words of Wisdom

Rely on plastic wrap for desserts that require no cooking but which do need time in the refrigerator. The plastic wrap stretches to fit over the bowls or dishes to form a tight seal to maintain freshness and all the great flavor.

We like using color plastic wrap to cover dessert dishes, because it brightens up the refrigerator and gets us in the party mood. And because we both just love desserts, we're always looking for an excuse to have something sweet!

we're always looking for

an excuse to have

something sweet

Old-Fashioned Apple Pie

PREP TIME
25 minutes

COOK TIME
45 minutes

MAKES
8 to 10 servings

Pastry for 9-inch deep-dish double crust pie

4 to 5 cups tart cooking apples, peeled, cored, and sliced (about 3 pounds)

1¼ cups sugar

⅓ cup flour

1 teaspoon ground cinnamon

2 tablespoons butter or margarine, cut into pieces

2 teaspoons milk

½ teaspoon sugar

1 Preheat the oven to 350°F.

2 Prepare the pastry. On lightly floured parchment paper, roll out half of the pastry to a ⅛-inch thickness. Transfer to a 9-inch deep-dish pie plate. Gently fit the pastry into the dish.

3 In a large bowl, toss the apples, sugar, flour, and cinnamon until the apples are coated thoroughly. Spoon the apples evenly into the pie crust and top with the butter.

4 Roll the remaining pastry on lightly floured parchment paper to a ⅛-inch thickness. Drape over the apples. Trim the excess pastry along the edges of the pie dish and fold the edges under and crimp the edges. Using a small, sharp knife, cut a small design in the center of the pastry to allow steam to escape. Brush the top of the pastry lightly with milk and sprinkle with sugar.

5 Bake for 45 to 50 minutes or until the crust is golden brown. Serve warm.

REYNOLDS KITCHENS TIPS

- *Golden Delicious apples make great pies. As they bake and soften, they also hold their shape and are never mushy.*

- *To decorate the pie, roll out scraps of pastry and cut designs with a cookie cutter. Lay these on the pastry before brushing the pastry with milk. Some ideas for shapes are leaves, stars, and flowers.*

Apple Cobbler

1 cup sugar

¼ cup flour

1½ teaspoons ground cinnamon

2½ pounds Golden Delicious apples (about 6 large apples), cored and thinly sliced

2 tablespoons butter or margarine, cut in pieces

One 6-ounce can refrigerated flaky buttermilk biscuits

Ice cream (optional)

PREP TIME
20 minutes

COOK TIME
50 minutes

MAKES
5 to 6 servings

1 Preheat the oven to 350°F for at least 20 minutes and arrange an oven rack so that it is in the center of the oven. Put a 1½-quart disposable plastic cookware pan on a cookie sheet so that the pan does not hang over the sides.

2 Combine the sugar, flour, and cinnamon on a sheet of wax paper.

3 Put the apples in a large bowl and sprinkle with the sugar mixture. Toss to coat, transfer to the pan, and top with the butter.

4 Bake on the cookie sheet for about 35 minutes. Use the cookie sheet to remove the pan from the oven. Let stand for at least 2 minutes before lifting the pan by the handles. Stir the apples.

5 Spread sugar on a sheet of wax paper. Separate the biscuits and coat both sides with sugar. Use a 2-inch star-shaped cookie cutter to cut stars from the biscuits and arrange the stars over the center of the hot apple mixture.

6 With a small, sharp knife, cut through one side of the leftover rings of biscuit dough remaining after the stars are removed. Arrange 4 of these strips around the edge of the pan to make a scalloped border.

7 Return the pan on the cookie sheet to the oven and bake for 15 to 20 minutes longer or until the biscuits are golden brown. Use the cookie sheet to remove the pan from the oven. Let stand for at least 2 minutes before lifting the pan by the handles.

8 Serve warm with ice cream, if desired.

REYNOLDS KITCHENS TIP

By using wax paper to protect the counter and for spreading out sugar, it's an easy task to coat biscuit dough with the sugar. Cleanup is a snap!

Quick Apple Crisp

2 medium apples, cored and sliced

2 tablespoons packed brown sugar

2 tablespoons raisins

2 tablespoons chopped nuts

Ground cinnamon

Ground nutmeg

2 teaspoons butter or margarine

2 Oatmeal-Raisin Cookies, crumbled, page 290

Frozen yogurt or ice cream (optional)

PREP TIME
10 minutes

COOK TIME
8 minutes

MAKES
2 servings

Quick Apple Crisp

1 Divide the apple slices between 2 microwave-safe individual-size baking dishes. Sprinkle each with brown sugar, raisins, nuts, and a pinch of cinnamon and nutmeg. Top each with the butter.

2 Cover each dish with a sheet of wax paper. Microwave each dish separately on high power for 2 to 4 minutes, or until the apple slices are tender. Stir the apples.

3 Top each dish with a crumbled cookie. Serve immediately with frozen yogurt or ice cream, if desired.

REYNOLDS KITCHENS TIP

Wax paper makes a terrific lid for many microwaving jobs. Because it does not fit snugly, it naturally vents the steam, yet it holds in enough moisture for even cooking.

...

Chocolate-Raspberry Mousse

PREP TIME
20 minutes
CHILL TIME
3 hours
MAKES
6 to 8 servings

10 chocolate sandwich cookies, crushed (about 1 cup)

2 tablespoons butter or margarine, melted

One 3.9-ounce package instant chocolate pudding mix

3/4 cup milk

One 12-ounce container frozen whipped topping, thawed

3/4 cup raspberry or strawberry jam

Milk chocolate candy bar shavings

Fresh raspberries or strawberries (optional)

1 Put the crushed cookies and melted butter in a 1½-quart disposable plastic cookware pan. Using a fork or your fingertips, press the mixture over the bottom of the pan to form a crust.

2 In a large bowl, whisk together the pudding mix and milk. Stir in a third of the frozen whipped topping. Spoon this evenly over the crust.

3 Spoon the jam into a mixing bowl and stir until smooth. Fold in the remaining

whipped topping and spread evenly over the pudding layer. Cover with the pan's lid and refrigerate for at least 3 hours or overnight.

4 To serve, sprinkle with chocolate shavings and garnish with fresh raspberries and strawberries, if desired.

Chocolate-Raspberry Mousse

Cherry-Apple Crisp

One 21-ounce can cherry pie filling

One 21-ounce can apple pie filling

$\frac{1}{2}$ teaspoon vanilla extract

$\frac{1}{2}$ teaspoon almond extract

$\frac{1}{2}$ cup quick-cooking oats

$\frac{1}{3}$ cup flour

$\frac{1}{4}$ cup packed brown sugar

3 tablespoons butter or margarine

Ice cream (optional)

PREP TIME
20 minutes

COOK TIME
25 minutes

MAKES
6 servings

1 Preheat the oven to 400°F for at least 20 minutes and arrange an oven rack so that it is in the center of the oven. Put a 1½-quart disposable plastic cookware pan on a cookie sheet so that the pan does not hang over the sides.

2 Put the cherry and apple pie fillings, vanilla, and almond extract in the pan and toss to mix.

Cherry-Apple Crisp

3 In a bowl, mix the oats, flour, and brown sugar. Using two knives or a pastry blender, cut in the butter until the mixture resembles coarse crumbs. Stir half of the topping into the fruit mixture. Sprinkle the remaining topping over the fruit.

4 Bake on the cookie sheet for 25 to 30 minutes or until the topping is golden brown. Use the cookie sheet to remove the pan from the oven. Let stand for at least 2 minutes before lifting the pan by the handles.

5 Serve warm with ice cream, if desired.

> **REYNOLDS KITCHENS TIP**
>
> *Disposable plastic cookware pans cannot withstand oven temperatures higher than 400°F. It's easy to calibrate your oven for accuracy. Use an oven thermometer, sold in supermarkets, hardware stores, and houseware stores, to gauge the temperature. If the thermometer registers a temperature higher or lower than the thermostat setting, adjust the dial up or down. For instance, if thermostat setting is set at 350°F and the oven thermometer says the temperature is actually 325°F, set the dial at 375°F to compensate.*

...

Flower Pots and Shovels

½ cup premium white morsels

8 white plastic spoons

Multicolored sprinkles

Eight 12-inch chenille stems

Eight 9-ounce clear plastic cups

2½ cups cold milk

One 5.9-ounce package instant chocolate pudding mix

32 chocolate sandwich cookies, crushed

Caramel popcorn, crushed

Gummy worms

PREP TIME
20 minutes

CHILL TIME
1 hour

MAKES
8 desserts

1 Put the white morsels in a microwave-safe bowl and microwave on high power for 1 minute. Stir and then microwave on high power for 30 to 45 seconds longer. Stir until smooth. Dip each plastic spoon into the softened morsels to coat and let the excess drip off. Sprinkle with colored sprinkles. Place spoons on wax paper and refrigerate until hardened.

2 Wrap the tops of the spoons with clear or color plastic wrap; twist at the base of spoon to secure. Wrap handles of spoons with plastic wrap; twist plastic wrap at

base of the spoons to secure. Fluff and trim the ends of the plastic wrap, if needed.

3 Make 2 small holes near the top in opposite sides of the plastic cups. Insert the ends of the chenille stems through the holes and twist to secure handles.

4 In a large bowl, whisk the milk and pudding mix for 2 minutes. Stir in 1 cup of crushed cookies.

5 Spoon 1 tablespoon of the remaining crushed cookies into each cup and top with pudding mixture. Insert the handle of a spoon in center of the pudding in each cup. Top with the remaining crushed cookies to look like dirt, crushed caramel popcorn for rocks, and gummy worms. Refrigerate for 1 hour until ready to serve.

Flower Pots and Shovels

Party Cheesecakes

25 chocolate sandwich cookies, crushed

¹/₃ cup butter or margarine, melted

Two 8-ounce packages cream cheese, softened

¹/₂ cup sugar

2 eggs

¹/₂ teaspoon vanilla extract

³/₄ cup mini chocolate morsels

I teaspoon vegetable shortening (do not use butter or margarine)

PREP TIME
15 minutes

COOK TIME
20 minutes

CHILL TIME
2 hours

MAKES
16 cheesecakes

1 Preheat the oven to 350°F. Place 16 foil baking cups in muffin pans.

2 In a bowl, toss the cookie crumbs with the butter. Press a rounded tablespoon of the crumb mixture into the bottom of each baking cup.

Party Cheesecakes

3 In the bowl of an electric mixer set on medium speed, beat the cream cheese, sugar, eggs, and vanilla extract until smooth. Remove the bowl from the mixer and stir in ½ cup of the chocolate morsels with a wooden spoon or spatula. Spoon the mixture into the baking cups, filling each about three-quarters full.

4 Bake for 20 to 25 minutes until set. Remove the baking cups from the pan and set the cheesecakes aside on wire racks to cool completely.

5 To make icing, put the remaining ¼ cup of chocolate morsels and the shortening in a microwave-safe bowl. Microwave on medium power for 1 to 2 minutes or until the chocolate turns shiny and soft. Stir until smooth.

6 Drizzle the chocolate icing over the cheesecakes. Refrigerate for at least 2 hours before serving.

. . .

All-American Ice Cream Cups

Approximately ten 2-inch round coconut macaroon cookies

½ gallon vanilla ice cream, slightly softened

¼ cup apricot preserves

18 maraschino cherries

½ teaspoon almond extract

½ cup sliced almonds

PREP TIME
10 minutes

FREEZE TIME
1 hour

MAKES
18 desserts

1 Place 18 foil baking cups in muffin pans.

2 Crush the cookies in a food processor or by putting the cookies between sheets of wax paper and rolling them with a rolling pin to make crumbs. You need 2 cups of loosely packed crumbs.

3 Put the crumbs, preserves, and extract in a large bowl and stir with a fork until the

crumbs are coated with preserves. Press a rounded tablespoon of the crumb mixture into the bottom of each baking cup.

4 Working quickly, spoon 1 scoop of ice cream into each baking cup. Top each with a cherry and sliced almonds.

5 Freeze for at least 1 hour or until ready to serve. For longer storage in the freezer, cover the muffin pan with heavy duty aluminum foil.

All-American Ice Cream Cups

Caramel Cream Dessert

One 3-ounce package cream cheese, softened

2 cups frozen whipped topping, thawed

One 12¼-ounce jar caramel ice cream topping

2 cups cubed pound cake

¼ cup chopped pecans

Two 15-ounce cans sliced peaches in juice, drained

½ pint raspberries or strawberries

PREP TIME
20 minutes

CHILL TIME
2 hours

MAKES
6 to 8 servings

Caramel Cream Dessert

1 In the bowl of an electric mixer set on medium speed, beat the cream cheese until smooth. Add the whipped topping and ¾ cup of the caramel topping and beat until well blended.

2 Put the pound cake cubes in a 1½-quart serving bowl. Drizzle with the remaining ¼ cup of caramel topping. Spread half of the cream cheese mixture over the cake in an even layer. Sprinkle with 2 tablespoons of chopped pecans.

REYNOLDS KITCHENS TIP

Cover glass containers with color plastic wrap to brighten up your boring refrigerator. The colors let you color code meals or leftovers, and the superior stretch and cling of the wraps—regardless of color!—allow you to seal bowls and platters with no worry of messy spills.

3 Top with the peaches and half of the raspberries. Spread the remaining cream cheese mixture over the fruit. Sprinkle with the remaining 2 tablespoons of chopped pecans and the rest of the raspberries.

4 Cover with plastic wrap and refrigerate for at least 2 hours or overnight.

. . .

Chocolate-Mint Cups

PREP TIME
15 minutes

FREEZE TIME
1 hour

MAKES
12 desserts

21 chocolate sandwich cookies

3 tablespoons butter or margarine, melted

One 7-ounce jar marshmallow creme

½ teaspoon peppermint extract

1 teaspoon milk

2 to 3 drops green food coloring

One 12-ounce carton frozen whipped topping, thawed

1 Place 12 foil baking cups in a 12-cup muffin pan.

2 Set aside 6 cookies. Crush the remaining 15 cookies in a food processor or by putting the cookies between sheets of parchment paper and rolling them with a rolling pin to make crumbs.

3 In a mixing bowl, toss the crumbs with the butter until coated. Press a rounded tablespoon of the crumb mixture into the bottom of each baking cup.

4 In a large bowl, combine the marshmallow creme, peppermint extract, milk, and food coloring, and stir until blended. Gently stir in the whipped topping.

5 Spoon about ¼ cup of the marshmallow filling into each baking cup, filling it nearly to the rim. Freeze for at least an hour or until ready to serve. For longer storage, cover the muffin pan with heavy duty aluminum foil.

6 To serve, cut or break each of the remaining 6 cookies in half. Insert a cookie half into each dessert as a garnish.

. . .

Chocolate Dessert Shells

Four 4- to 5-inch-wide baking shells

¾ cup semi-sweet chocolate morsels

2 teaspoons vegetable shortening (do not use butter or margarine)

Ice cream or sherbet

Fresh fruit, such as strawberries, peaches, raspberries, or bananas, cut in bite-sized pieces (optional)

PREP TIME
15 minutes

CHILL TIME
1 hour

MAKES
4 servings

1 Line a cookie sheet with non-stick aluminum foil, non-stick (dull) side facing up.

2 Wrap the rounded side of the baking shells with non-stick aluminum foil so that only the outside of the shell is covered. Tuck the excess foil under the edges of the shells. The non-stick (dull) side should be facing out. Set the wrapped shells on the cookie sheet.

3 In a small microwave-safe bowl, combine the chocolate and shortening and microwave on high power for 1 to 2 minutes or until the chocolate is soft and shiny. Stir until smooth.

4 With a spoon, carefully spread the melted chocolate over the foil-covered side of

the shells. Do not spread the chocolate over the edges. Refrigerate for
1 to 2 hours or until firm.

5 Carefully remove the baking shells
from the foil, leaving the chocolate
on the foil. Put the chocolate shells
on serving dishes and gently peel
off the foil.

6 Fill the chocolate shells with ice
cream or sherbet. Garnish with
fresh fruit, if desired. Serve immediately.

. . .

Fudgy Chocolate Fondue

**One 12-ounce package semi-
sweet chocolate morsels**

**¹⁄₂ cup butter or margarine, cut
in pieces**

**One 7-ounce jar marshmallow
creme**

¹⁄₂ cup half-and-half

**Fresh strawberries, banana
chunks, pear slices, pound cake
cubes, or angel food cake cubes,
or any combination of these**

PREP TIME
5 minutes

COOK TIME
1 minute

MAKES
2¹⁄₄ cups

1 Combine the chocolate morsels, butter, marshmallow creme, and half-and-half in a
1½-quart disposable plastic cookware pan.
Microwave for 1 minute on high power. Stir
until nearly smooth. Microwave for 10-second
intervals, stirring after each, until smooth.

2 Serve the fondue immediately. Dip the fruit or
cake, or both, into the chocolate.

Fruit-Glazed Cheesecakes

PREP TIME
15 minutes

BAKE TIME
17 minutes

CHILL TIME
2 hours

MAKES
12 cheesecakes

CRUST

1 cup graham cracker crumbs

2 tablespoons sugar

1/3 cup butter or margarine, melted

CHEESECAKE

Two 8-ounce packages cream cheese

1/2 cup sugar

2 eggs

1/2 teaspoon vanilla extract

1/4 teaspoon orange extract

Fresh fruit, such as strawberries, blueberries, raspberries, grapes, kiwi, or mandarin orange segments

1/3 cup apricot preserves

1 teaspoon lemon juice

1 Preheat the oven to 350°F. Place 12 foil baking cups in a muffin pan or on a cookie sheet.

2 To make the crust, toss the graham cracker crumbs and sugar in a large bowl and then stir in the butter until the mixture holds together. Press a rounded tablespoon of the crumb mixture into the bottom of each baking cup.

3 To make the filling, in the bowl of an electric mixer set on medium speed, beat the cream cheese, sugar, eggs, vanilla, and orange extract until smooth. Spoon into the baking cups, filling each about three-quarters full.

4 Bake for 17 to 20 minutes until set. Transfer the muffin pan to a wire rack to cool completely. Refrigerate for at least 2 hours or until thoroughly chilled.

5 Top each cheesecake with fresh fruit.

6 In a small bowl, stir the apricot preserves with the lemon juice until smooth. Spoon evenly over each cheesecake.

> **REYNOLDS KITCHENS TIP**
>
> *To make graham cracker crumbs, put crackers between two sheets of wax paper and crush by rolling with a rolling pin.*

Fruit-Glazed Cheesecakes

Banana Split Pudding Cups

PREP TIME
15 minutes

CHILL TIME
1 hour

MAKES
6 desserts

2 cups low-fat milk

One 3.4-ounce package vanilla-flavored instant pudding and pie filling

2 medium bananas, sliced

1 cup miniature marshmallows

1 cup chocolate bear-shaped graham snacks

1 cup frozen non-dairy whipped topping, thawed

6 maraschino cherries

Colored sprinkles

Chocolate bear-shaped graham snacks

1 In a large bowl, whisk together the milk and pudding mix for 1 to 2 minutes, or until blended. Stir in the banana slices, marshmallows, and bear-shaped graham snacks.

2 Spoon into 6 dessert dishes or custard cups. Top with whipped topping.

3 Cover with plastic wrap and refrigerate for at least 1 hour or until ready to serve.

4 To serve, remove the plastic wrap and top each dessert with a cherry, colored sprinkles, and a graham snack.

...

Confetti Party Pie

PREP TIME
20 minutes

BAKE TIME
8 minutes

CHILL TIME
4 hours

MAKES
8 to 10 servings

CRUST

2¼ cups chocolate bear-shaped graham snacks, crushed

1 tablespoon sugar

⅓ cup butter or margarine, melted

FILLING

One 8-ounce package light cream cheese, softened

2 tablespoons sugar

One 8-ounce carton light frozen whipped topping, thawed

½ cup toffee chips (optional)

3 tablespoons candy-coated chocolate candies

2 tablespoons colored sprinkles

1 Preheat the oven to 375°F.

2 To make the crust, in a bowl, toss the crumbs, sugar, and butter until well blended. Press evenly into the bottom and up the sides of a 9-inch round glass pie plate.

3 Bake for 8 minutes or until set. Set the pie plate on a wire rack to cool completely.

4 To make the filling, beat the cream cheese and sugar in the bowl of an electric mixer set on medium speed.

5 Remove the bowl from the mixer and fold in the whipped topping and toffee chips, if desired. Pour into the crust. Cover with plastic wrap and refrigerate for at least 4 hours before serving.

6 Remove the plastic wrap and decorate with chocolate candies and sprinkles before serving.

Confetti Party Pie

Chocolate-Dipped Strawberries

24 large strawberries

1 cup semi-sweet chocolate morsels

2 teaspoons vegetable shortening (do not use butter or margarine)

PREP TIME
15 minutes

CHILL TIME
15 minutes

MAKES
24 servings

1 Line a cookie sheet with wax paper or parchment paper.

2 Rinse the strawberries and pat them dry with paper towels.

3 In a small microwave-safe bowl, combine the chocolate morsels and shortening, and microwave on high power for 1 to 2 minutes or until the morsels are soft and shiny. Stir until smooth.

4 Dip each strawberry halfway into the melted chocolate. Place on the prepared cookie sheet. When all the strawberries are dipped, refrigerate for 15 minutes or until the chocolate sets.

REYNOLDS KITCHENS TIP

The chocolate-dipped strawberries will not stick to the wax paper or parchment paper used to line the cookie sheet.

Chocolate-Dipped Strawberries

Strawberries 'N' Cream Dessert

PREP TIME
15 minutes

CHILL TIME
2 hours

MAKES
14 servings

One 10-ounce packaged pound cake, cut in ½-inch-thick slices

¼ cup orange juice

One 14-ounce can sweetened condensed milk

¼ cup fresh lemon juice

1 teaspoon grated lemon peel

One 8-ounce carton frozen whipped topping, thawed

2 pints strawberries, hulled and sliced, or two 10-ounce packages frozen sliced strawberries, thawed and drained

Sliced strawberries for garnish (optional)

Lemon slices for garnish (optional)

1　Arrange the cake slices to fit in a layer in the bottom of a 1½-quart disposable plastic cookware pan. Reserve the remaining slices for the second layer. Brush the cake slices with orange juice.

2　In a mixing bowl, stir together the condensed milk, lemon juice, and lemon peel until thickened. Stir in the whipped topping until blended. Spread half of this filling mixture over the cake and then layer half of the strawberries over the filling.

3　Arrange a second layer of cake over the strawberries. Brush with orange juice and repeat layering with the lemon filling and strawberries. Cover the pan with its lid and refrigerate for 2 hours or until set and ready to serve.

4　Garnish with sliced fresh strawberries and lemon slices, if desired.

REYNOLDS KITCHENS TIP

Snap the lid on the disposable plastic cookware pan and refrigerate the fruit dessert. The lid keeps odors out and freshness in. Plus, if you want to carry this to a picnic, potluck, or neighbor's house, it's ready to go.

Mexican Bread Dessert

PREP TIME
25 minutes

COOK TIME
25 minutes

MAKES
6 to 8
servings

I pound white bread, cut in 1-inch pieces

3 cups packed dark brown sugar (I pound)

2 cups water

2 cups apple juice

¼ cup butter

I cinnamon stick

4 whole cloves

I cup pecan pieces, toasted

I cup raisins

2 cups grated queso fresco or Monterey Jack cheese (5 ounces)

1 Preheat the oven to 350°F. Line a 10½-by-15½-by-1-inch pan with non-stick aluminum foil, non-stick (dull) side facing up.

2 Spread the bread cubes in a single layer on the baking pan. Bake for about 15 minutes, turning the bread several times, to dry out the bread without browning.

3 In a large saucepan, combine the brown sugar, water, apple juice, butter, cinnamon, and cloves, and bring to a boil over medium-high heat. Reduce the heat and simmer for 15 to 20 minutes, stirring occasionally until the mixture turns into a light syrup.

4 Line a 9-by-13-by-2-inch pan with non-stick aluminum foil, non-stick (dull) side facing up.

5 Put the bread cubes in a large bowl. Add the pecans and raisins and toss to mix. Strain the syrup though a fine-mesh sieve over the bread. Let the mixture stand for a few minutes to allow the bread to absorb the syrup. Stir in the cheese.

6 Spread the bread mixture in an even layer in the prepared pan.

7 Bake for 25 to 30 minutes or until the top is crisp. Serve warm.

> **REYNOLDS KITCHENS TIP**
>
> *The non-stick foil makes this easy to serve. Nothing sticks!*

Mexican Bread Dessert

Holiday Desserts

The recipe for
Snowman Cupcakes
is on pages 271–272.

During the holidays, I sometimes bake pound cakes and wrap them in color plastic wrap to give as gifts. Or I cut a pound cake in half and wrap it up.

—Betty

Last year I bought really pretty plates that were crying out for cookies. I baked holiday cookies, arranged them on the plates, covered the plates with plastic wrap, and gave them as gifts. Even if it's easy, a gift is lovely if you make it yourself and wrap it nicely.

—Pat

EVERYONE WANTS THEIR DESSERTS TO turn out perfectly every time, but never more than during the holidays. To help you achieve this goal, we have gathered eighteen recipes that illustrate all that is sweet and glorious about holiday desserts.

We make no claim that these are classic Christmas desserts—you won't find plum pudding or bûche de Noel—but you will find lots of ideas for desserts, special treats, and gifts from the kitchen. Coming from the Reynolds Kitchens means that they are easy, relatively fast, and so thoroughly tested, you should have no problems.

As confident as we are, it still pays to heed sound culinary principles. Read through the recipe first, make sure you have all the ingredients and that they're fresh. Don't use eggs that have been in the fridge since October, and make sure your baking powder and baking soda are no more than four months old (it's a good idea to date these products when you buy them, just as you should date dried spices and herbs). Check that you have the right size pan, enough aluminum foil, wax paper, plastic wrap, and parchment paper.

Assemble, measure, and prep the ingredients. This means sifting the flour if necessary, chopping chocolate and nuts and letting butter soften. Allow the oven 20 minutes or so to preheat, so that it reaches the correct temperature.

Finally, set aside time for holiday desserts. Making these treasures should be a pleasure—not something you squeeze in at the end of a harried day. We appreciate the luxury we have of working in a test kitchen every day, and we urge you to find time to turn yours into a sweet-smelling, happy holiday dessert kitchen.

Traditions

We adore colorful desserts during the holidays, which explains our elegant, fresh tasting Cranberry-Orange Layered Dessert and the Cherry-Coconut Trifle. Both are made in clear glass bowls to show off their colors and layers.

The Toasted Pecan–Cranberry Bark, Mocha Walnut Truffles, and Peanut Butter Bonbons are easy-to-make candies (you don't even need a candy thermometer!), and are wonderful to have in the house when holiday guests drop by or when you need a special gift.

Try our White Chocolate Party Mix or the Orange-Coconut Chess Tarts for your next holiday party. Display Festive Cream Cheese Cookies and Santa Snack Cakes on a dessert tray wrapped in rose plastic wrap.

Make your own traditions with our recipes. No one will be disappointed.

Food as Gifts

We think food makes a great gift. Something you take the time to make is part of you, and you can't get more personal than that. Pat's teenage daughter and her friends make cookies for one another every year and wrap them in pretty paper or boxes. What a lovely tradition.

We have great ideas here for gifts for loved ones, teachers, neighbors, soccer coaches, or anyone you want to remember. Mocha Walnut Truffles and Peanut Butter Bonbons, for instance, are irresistible nestled in scrunched up color plastic wrap and tucked into pretty boxes.

Our Chocolate-Dipped Spoons are thoughtful gifts for the coffee lovers among your friends or accompanying the Double-Chocolate Cocoa Mugs.

We've seen scores of gingerbread men in recent years, and while all are charming, we think our Gingerbread Boys and Girls take the prize. Pat came up with the idea for a gingerbread decorating kit, which is a thoughtful gift to give to a family with young children. Decorating them is so much fun—create gingerbread kids with expression and attitude!

Gift Wrapping

Color plastic wrap was one of the most innovative new products Reynolds ever introduced and, while it first appeared in the markets almost twenty years ago, it's still a marvel. Using it adds that finishing touch that elicits all those appreciative smiles.

Additionally, color plastic wrap is inexpensive and versatile. Use it to over-wrap platters, to wrap loaves of Spicy Sweet Potato Bread, or to bundle packets of cocoa mix for our Double-Chocolate Cocoa Mugs. Bunch it into fluffy bows and showy sprays.

We like to line tins with holiday printed wax paper as well as color plastic wrap during the holidays. We also use holiday baking cups when we bake muffins and cupcakes. Taking this extra step is effortless but adds to the festive spirit of the season.

Words of Wisdom

Stock up on color and holiday printed plastic wrap, holiday baking cups, holiday printed wax paper, and other Reynolds products before the holidays. Our extra large foil cups are great for the Blueberry Crunch Muffins, and it's super-easy to roll dough with wax paper or parchment paper. Don't forget to line pans for baking with non-stick aluminum foil for easy cleanup.

When you glaze the Santa Snack Cakes or any other cake, set a wire rack on top of a piece of wax paper to catch the drips. Line cookie sheets with parchment paper or non-stick aluminum foil and let candies harden and set on them. Wrap sticky popcorn balls in plastic wrap to make Frosty Snowmen.

These products truly are the home cook's best friends. It's comforting to have your "friends" nearby when you're creating special treats for the holidays.

Cranberry-Orange Layered Dessert

PREP TIME

30 minutes

CHILL TIME

5 hours

MAKES

12 servings

1½ cups boiling water

Two 4-serving size packages cranberry-flavored gelatin

Two 11-ounce cans mandarin orange segments, drained, juice reserved

One 16-ounce can whole-berry cranberry sauce

2 teaspoons grated orange peel

⅛ teaspoon ground cinnamon

⅛ teaspoon ground cloves

One 8-ounce package cream cheese, softened

⅓ cup sugar

One 18-ounce container frozen whipped topping, thawed

¼ cup chopped pecans or walnuts (optional)

1 Pour the boiling water into a large bowl and then stir in the gelatin until completely dissolved. Add 1 cup of the reserved mandarin orange juice, the cranberry sauce, 1 teaspoon of the orange peel, the cinnamon, and the cloves, and stir to mix.

2 In another bowl, mix together the cream cheese, sugar, and remaining teaspoon of orange peel. Add 1 cup of the gelatin mixture and stir until blended.

3 Cover the bowl holding the gelatin and the one holding the cream cheese mixture with plastic wrap. Transfer the mandarin oranges to a small bowl or container and cover it with plastic wrap. Refrigerate all three for about 2 hours, or until the cranberry gelatin is thickened and a spoon drawn through it leaves a definite impression.

4 Remove the cream cheese mixture from the refrigerator and stir half of the whipped topping into it until well blended. Spoon half of this mixture into a 3-quart dessert dish or bowl, spreading the layer evenly.

5 Top with half of the cranberry gelatin, spread into an even layer. Spread half of the remaining whipped topping over the gelatin. Arrange half of the mandarin orange segments on top.

> **REYNOLDS KITCHENS TIP**
>
> *Make dessert ahead of time—when you have the time. Cover with plastic wrap and refrigerate. The plastic wrap stretches to seal tight to keep food fresh and tasting great even when eaten later.*

6 Repeat to make another layer of cream cheese, cranberry gelatin, whipped topping, and orange segments.

7 Cover with plastic wrap and refrigerate for at least 3 hours and up to overnight, or until set. Sprinkle with nuts, if desired, before serving.

. . .

Spicy Sweet Potato Bread

PREP TIME
10 minutes

COOK TIME
50 minutes

MAKES
1 loaf

¼ cup old-fashioned oats, uncooked

2 tablespoons packed brown sugar

1 teaspoon butter or margarine, softened

One 15¼-ounce package nut bread mix

½ cup cooked, mashed sweet potato

½ cup raisins

½ cup water

¼ cup vegetable oil

1 egg, lightly beaten

1 teaspoon ground cinnamon

½ teaspoon ground nutmeg

Color plastic wrap

1 Preheat the oven to 350°F. Line a 4½-by-8½-by-2-inch loaf pan with non-stick aluminum foil, non-stick (dull) side facing up.

2 In a small bowl, combine the oats, brown sugar, and butter.

3 In a large bowl, stir together the nut bread mix, sweet potato, raisins, water, oil, egg, cinnamon, and nutmeg until the dry ingredients are moist. Spoon into the loaf pan. Sprinkle the oat mixture evenly over the batter.

4 Bake for 50 to 55 minutes, or until a toothpick inserted in the center comes out clean. Put the pan on a wire rack to cool for 15 minutes. Invert the pan and remove the loaf. Let the loaf cool completely on a wire rack.

5 Put the loaf on a cutting board lined with a paper doily. Overwrap the board and loaf with color plastic wrap until ready to serve.

6 To wrap for gift giving, tear off a sheet of color plastic wrap that is approximately 3½ times the length of the loaf.

7 Set the loaf of bread lengthwise on the sheet of plastic wrap.

8 Gather the ends of the plastic wrap and bring up to the top of the bread. Tie the ends of the plastic wrap together with curly ribbon. Trim the ends of plastic wrap and fan out.

Spicy Sweet Potato Bread

Gingerbread Boys and Girls

PREP TIME
20 minutes

CHILL TIME
2 hours

COOK TIME
10 minutes

MAKES
2½ dozen cookies

¾ cup butter or margarine

¾ cup packed brown sugar

1 egg

½ cup molasses

1 teaspoon vanilla extract

3¼ cups flour

1 teaspoon baking soda

1 teaspoon ground ginger

½ teaspoon ground cinnamon

½ teaspoon ground cloves

½ teaspoon salt

Decorating icing

1 In the bowl of an electric mixer set on medium speed, cream the butter and sugar for 3 to 4 minutes, or until light and fluffy. Add the egg and beat until well blended. Add the molasses and vanilla and blend.

2 Combine the flour, baking soda, ginger, cinnamon, cloves, and salt on a sheet of parchment paper. With the mixer on low speed, add the flour mixture gradually to the bowl. Beat until blended and the mixture forms a crumbly dough.

3 Turn the dough out onto a lightly floured sheet of parchment paper. Divide the dough in thirds and form each into a ball. Wrap the balls in plastic wrap and refrigerate for at least 2 hours or until firm.

REYNOLDS KITCHENS TIP

To make a Gingerbread Cookie Decorating Kit, assemble the following supplies to accompany the Gingerbread Boys and Girls cookies.

- Tubes of decorating icing in different colors

- Packages of fruit roll-ups

- Miniature candies

- Color plastic wrap

Assemble this kit and give it to children or anyone else who would like to decorate gingerbread boys and girls. Wrap stacks of plain, baked cookies in color plastic wrap and tie with ribbons. Put the cookies, decorating icing, fruit roll-ups, and miniature candies in a basket or tin. Include some written tips on how to cut the roll-ups to make fashionable outfits, which can be attached to the cookies with frosting. The candies are used to make the eyes, nose, mouth, and buttons.

4 Meanwhile, preheat the oven to 350°F. Line a cookie sheet with parchment paper.

5 Roll each ball of chilled dough between 2 lightly floured sheets of parchment paper to a thickness of ¼ inch. Using 4- or 5-inch gingerbread boy or girl cookie cutters, cut out cookies. Put the cookies on the cookie sheet, leaving about 1 inch between them.

6 Bake for 10 to 11 minutes or until the edges are barely browned. Let the cookies stand on the cookie sheet for 1 minute before transferring to a metal rack to cool completely.

7 Decorate as desired with icing.

8 Wrap each cookie in rose or green plastic wrap to give as gifts. Twist the plastic at the top of cookie and tie with a ribbon. Fluff the ends of plastic wrap and trim with scissors.

· · ·

Mocha Walnut Truffles

PREP TIME
20 minutes

CHILL TIME
6 hours

MAKES
24 truffles

8 ounces bittersweet or semi-sweet chocolate, finely chopped

½ cup heavy cream

1 tablespoon instant coffee powder

2 teaspoons vanilla extract

1½ cups ground walnuts

1 Put the chocolate in a medium bowl.

2 In a small saucepan, heat the cream just until it boils. Stir in the coffee powder until dissolved. Pour over the chopped chocolate, let stand for 30 seconds, and whisk until smooth. Stir in the vanilla.

3 Put a sheet of plastic wrap over the top of the chocolate and press it gently against the surface of the chocolate to prevent a skin forming. Refrigerate for at least 6 hours or overnight.

4 Line 2 cookie sheets with wax paper or parchment paper. Spread the walnuts on one of the cookie sheets.

5   Shape rounded teaspoons of the chocolate truffle mixture into balls. Roll in nuts until coated.

6   Put the truffles on the second cookie sheet. Cover with plastic wrap and refrigerate for at least 1 hour or until serving.

REYNOLDS KITCHENS TIPS

Truffles, a delicious gift, can be dressed up or down, depending on the container in which they are presented.

- *Line a gift box or tin with holiday designs printed plastic wrap or color plastic wrap. Use small pieces of plastic wrap to make an individual nest for each truffle. Arrange the truffles in the gift box.*

  - *Fill a special gift coffee mug, crystal candy dish, or pretty stemware with truffles. Overwrap with holiday designs printed plastic wrap or color plastic wrap. Gather and twist the plastic wrap at the top and tie with a ribbon.*

Mocha Walnut Truffles and Peanut Butter Bonbons

Peanut Butter Bonbons

1½ cups powdered sugar

⅓ cup smooth peanut butter

3 tablespoons butter or margarine, softened

1 tablespoon milk

6 ounces semi-sweet chocolate

2 teaspoons vegetable shortening (do not use butter or margarine)

PREP TIME
30 minutes

COOK TIME
2½ minutes

CHILL TIME
90 minutes

MAKES
2 dozen bonbons

1 Line a cookie sheet with wax paper.

2 In the bowl of an electric mixer set on low speed, beat the powdered sugar, peanut butter, butter, and milk until smooth and blended.

3 Using 2 teaspoons of the mixture for each, shape into 1-inch balls. Lay the balls on the cookie sheet. Cover with plastic wrap and refrigerate for at least 1 hour or until firm.

4 Meanwhile, put the chocolate and shortening in a 1-quart microwave-safe bowl and microwave on medium power for 2 to 4 minutes, stirring every minute. When the chocolate is softened and shiny, stir until smooth.

5 Let the chocolate cool slightly. Dip the peanut butter balls in the chocolate to coat. Put the balls on a cookie sheet lined with wax paper and refrigerate for at least 20 minutes or until firm. Reserve the remaining chocolate.

6 Microwave the remaining chocolate on medium power for 30 to 45 seconds or until fluid. Drizzle over the chilled bonbons. Refrigerate for at least 10 minutes until the drizzled chocolate is firm.

7 Nestle each bonbon in an individual nest of color plastic wrap. Arrange in a decorative box or cookie tin.

REYNOLDS KITCHENS TIP

To make individual nests for candies, place your thumb in the center of a 6-inch-long sheet of color plastic wrap. Mold the plastic wrap around your thumb to form nests. Place the bonbons in the nests and arrange in a decorative box.

Rudolph Cupcakes

One 18-ounce package white cake mix

One 16-ounce container chocolate ready-to-spread frosting

24 large red gumdrops

48 green candy-coated plain chocolate candies

24 miniature pretzels, broken in half

Additional broken pretzels

PREP TIME
30 minutes

COOK TIME
cake mix package directions

MAKES
24 cupcakes

| Preheat the oven to 350°F. Place 24 holiday baking cups into two 12-cup muffin pans.

Rudolph Cupcakes

2 Prepare the cake mix following the package directions for 24 cupcakes. Spoon the batter into the baking cups, filling each about two-thirds full.

3 Bake as directed on the cake mix box, or until a toothpick inserted in the center of a cupcake comes out clean. Set the muffin pans on wire racks to cool.

4 Frost the cooled cupcakes with chocolate frosting.

5 Decorate each with a red gumdrop for a nose, 2 green candies for eyes, 2 pretzel halves for antlers, and a broken pretzel for a mouth. With the tip of a toothpick, put a dot of chocolate frosting in the center of the green candy eyes, if desired.

> **REYNOLDS KITCHENS TIP**
>
> *Line a basket for gift giving with color plastic wrap. Use it generously so it overlaps the sides and looks festive and lush. Arrange cupcakes in the basket and then loosely overwrap the basket for transport. Attach a gift card.*

...

Toasted Pecan–Cranberry Bark

PREP TIME	10 minutes
COOK TIME	10 minutes
MAKES	about 3 dozen candies

1 cup pecan halves

One 20- to 24-ounce package white candy coating

¾ cup dried cranberries

¼ teaspoon ground nutmeg

1 Preheat the oven to 325°F. Line a cookie sheet with parchment paper or non-stick aluminum foil, non-stick (dull) side facing up.

2 Spread the pecan halves in a single layer on the cookie sheet.

3 Bake the pecans for 10 to 15 minutes or until lightly toasted and fragrant. Stir the nuts once during toasting. Transfer the cookie sheet to a wire rack and let the pecans cool.

> **REYNOLDS KITCHENS TIP**
>
> *Use either parchment paper or non-stick foil for the bark. It will release easily from either—and cleanup is a breeze. To give the bark as a small gift, wrap several irregularly shaped pieces in color plastic wrap and tie with a ribbon. To give the entire recipe, line a holiday tin with color plastic wrap and lay sheets of holiday decorated wax paper between layers of bark. You can also put a few pieces in holiday foil baking cups and wrap these with color plastic wrap.*

4 In a microwave-safe bowl, melt the candy coating according to package directions. Remove the bowl from the microwave and stir in the cooled nuts, cranberries, and nutmeg.

5 Spread the candy mixture on the lined cookie sheet so that it is ¼-inch thick. Refrigerate until set and cool. Break the bark into 1½-inch pieces.

Toasted Pecan–Cranberry Bark

Festive Cream Cheese Cookies

1 cup (2 sticks) butter or margarine, softened

One 8-ounce package cream cheese, softened

1 cup sugar

$\frac{1}{2}$ teaspoon vanilla extract

$2\frac{1}{2}$ cups flour

$\frac{1}{2}$ teaspoon salt

$\frac{1}{2}$ cup pecans, finely chopped

Red and green sugar crystals or colorful sprinkles

PREP TIME
10 minutes

CHILL TIME
6 hours

COOK TIME
15 minutes

MAKES
8 dozen cookies

1 In the bowl of an electric mixer set on medium speed, cream the butter and cream cheese until smooth. Add the sugar and vanilla and beat until light and fluffy.

2 Combine the flour and salt on a sheet of parchment paper. With the mixer on low speed, add the flour gradually to the bowl. Remove the bowl from the mixer and stir in the pecans.

3 Lay 4 sheets of non-stick aluminum foil, non-stick (dull) side facing up, on a countertop.

4 Shape the dough into four 6-inch-long rolls, each about $1\frac{1}{2}$ inches in diameter. Lay each roll on a sheet of foil and wrap each in foil. Refrigerate for at least 6 hours or overnight.

5 Preheat the oven to 325°F. Line a cookie sheet with non-stick aluminum foil, non-stick (dull) side facing up.

6 Lay a sheet of wax paper on the countertop and sprinkle it with sugar crystals.

7 Remove 1 roll of dough from refrigerator. Unwrap and roll in the sprinkles to coat. Cut the roll into $\frac{1}{4}$-inch-thick slices and place on the cookie sheet.

8 Bake for 15 to 18 minutes or until the bottoms of the cookies are lightly browned when lifted. Transfer the cookies to a wire rack to cool.

9 Repeat with the other 3 rolls, working with 1 roll at a time.

REYNOLDS KITCHENS TIP

To decorate and give these cookies as gifts, stack several together and put the stacks in holiday baking cups. Overwrap the baking cups with color plastic wrap and tie with a ribbon.

Merry Santa Cupcakes

One 18-ounce package white
cake mix

One 16-ounce container vanilla
ready-to-spread frosting

Red sugar crystals

Miniature candy-coated plain
chocolate candies

Miniature marshmallows

PREP TIME
30 minutes

COOK TIME
cake mix package
directions

MAKES
24 cupcakes

| Preheat the oven to 350°F. Place 24 holiday baking cups in two 12-cup muffin pans.

Merry Santa Cupcakes

2 Prepare the cake mix following the package directions for 24 cupcakes. Spoon the batter into the baking cups, filling each about two-thirds full.

3 Bake as directed on the cake mix box, or until a toothpick inserted in the center of a cupcake comes out clean. Set the muffin pans on wire racks to cool.

4 Frost the cupcakes with vanilla frosting.

5 Decorate a cupcake to look like Santa. For the hat, sprinkle the top third and halfway down one side of the cupcake with red sugar crystals. Put the chocolate candies on the frosting for eyes and the nose. Cut 2 marshmallows in half lengthwise and place at the edge of the red sugar to make a hat brim. Place a marshmallow at the end of the red sugar for the hat's tassel. For a beard, arrange 10 marshmallows over the bottom third of frosting. Repeat with the rest of the cupcakes.

6 Wrap the cupcakes in holiday designs printed plastic wrap or put the cupcakes in a gift box lined with color plastic wrap.

> **REYNOLDS KITCHENS TIP**
>
> *When you use baking cups, there's no need to grease the muffin pans, and cleanup is fast and easy.*

. . .

Orange-Coconut Chess Tarts

PREP TIME
30 minutes

COOK TIME
35 minutes

MAKES
12 tarts

One 15-ounce package refrigerated pie crust, divided into 2 pieces

3 eggs

⅔ cup sugar

¼ cup milk

1 tablespoon cornmeal

4 teaspoons orange juice

2 teaspoons grated orange peel

¾ cup flaked sweetened coconut

1 Preheat the oven to 350°F. Place 12 foil baking cups in a 12-cup muffin pan.

2 On a lightly floured sheet of parchment paper, roll out one of the pieces of pie crust to a 14-inch round circle. Lightly flour the rolling pin to prevent sticking.

3 Using a flattened foil baking cup as a guide, cut out 6 pastry circles with a small, sharp knife. Insert a pastry circle in 6 of the foil baking cups. Repeat with the

remaining pie crust to make 6 more pastry circles and insert these into the remaining 6 baking cups.

4 In a large bowl, whisk together the eggs, sugar, milk, corn-meal, orange juice, and orange peel. Stir in the coconut. Divide the filling evenly among the baking cups, spooning it on top of the pastry circles.

5 Bake for 35 to 40 minutes or until the rim of the crust is light brown. Transfer the muffin pans to wire racks and let the tarts cool completely.

REYNOLDS KITCHENS TIP

Foil baking cups can stand without support on a cookie sheet or in a shallow baking pan, or you can insert them in muffin pans. They hold up well for serving, too.

. . .

Blueberry Crunch Muffins

PREP TIME
15 minutes

COOK TIME
20 minutes

MAKES
12 servings

TOPPING

$^1/_2$ **cup flour**

$^1/_2$ **cup sugar**

$^1/_4$ **cup butter or margarine, softened, cut in pieces**

MUFFINS

3 cups flour

1 cup sugar

4 teaspoons baking powder

1 teaspoon salt

2 eggs, beaten

1 cup milk

$^1/_2$ **cup butter or margarine, melted**

2 teaspoons vanilla extract

2 cups frozen blueberries, rinsed and drained

1 Preheat oven to 375°F. Place 12 extra large foil baking cups on a cookie sheet. If the cookie sheet is dark or non-stick, preheat the oven to 350°F.

2 To make the topping, use a fork to mix together the flour, sugar, and butter in a small bowl.

3 To make the muffins, mix together the flour, sugar, baking powder, and salt in a large bowl.

4 In another bowl, whisk together the eggs, milk, butter, and vanilla. Stir into the

flour just until the dry ingredients are moistened. Stir in the blueberries. Spoon the batter into each baking cup, filling it about two-thirds full. Sprinkle the topping over the muffin batter.

5 Bake for 20 to 25 minutes or until lightly browned and a tooth-pick inserted in the center of a muffin comes out clean. Transfer the muffins to a wire rack to cool.

6 When cool, wrap each muffin in color plastic wrap. To do so, tear off a 12-inch sheet of color plastic wrap for each muffin and wrap it around the muffin. Tie with a narrow ribbon. Gently fluff out the ends of the plastic wrap and trim with scissors, if desired.

> **REYNOLDS KITCHENS TIP**
>
> *Do not overmix the muffin batter. Stir only until the dry ingredients are moistened. A few lumps are acceptable.*

...

Chocolate-Dipped Spoons

PREP TIME
15 minutes
CHILL TIME
30 minutes
COOK TIME
5 minutes
MAKES
10 to 12 spoons

½ cup semi-sweet chocolate morsels

¼ cup milk chocolate morsels

¼ teaspoon ground cinnamon

10 to 12 plastic spoons

Multicolored sprinkles, chocolate-flavored sprinkles, or melted white candy coating

Color plastic wrap

1 Line a cookie sheet with wax paper.

2 In a small heavy saucepan, combine the chocolate morsels and cinnamon. Set over low heat and stir constantly until the chocolate begins to melt. Remove the pan from the heat and stir until smooth. Or, put the morsels and cinnamon in a microwave-safe bowl and microwave on high power for 1 to 2 minutes, stirring every 30 seconds, or until the chocolate softens and looks shiny. Stir until melted.

3 Dip a plastic spoon in the smooth, melted chocolate to coat its bowl. Tap the handle of the spoon against the edge of the pan to remove excess chocolate. Lay the spoon on the cookie sheet.

4 Immediately sprinkle the spoon with sprinkles or drizzle with melted white candy coating. Repeat with all the spoons.

5 Refrigerate the spoons for at least 30 minutes or until the chocolate sets.

6 Wrap each spoon with color plastic wrap. Tie with a ribbon. Store in a cool, dry place. The spoons will keep for up to a month.

REYNOLDS KITCHENS TIP

For a great gift idea, assemble our Coffee-Lover's Gift Basket.

Line a basket with several sheets of scrunched up color plastic wrap. Arrange Chocolate-Dipped Spoons and Blueberry Crunch Muffins in the basket. Also include coffee mugs and a sack of coffee beans.

Tear off 2 or 3 sheets of plastic wrap, each about 3 times the height of the basket. Crisscross the sheets of plastic wrap on a flat surface and set the basket in the center. Bring the plastic wrap up and over the basket and twist the plastic wrap at the top. Tie a wide ribbon around the twist. Gently fluff out the ends of the plastic wrap and trim the ends with scissors, if desired.

To make a bow, tear off 4 sheets of color plastic wrap. Pinch each sheet in the center and twist in the center to make a small stem at bottom with ends of plastic wrap on top. Gather the four stems together, like a bouquet of flowers, and tie with florist wire or a strip of plastic wrap. Gently fluff out ends of plastic wrap and trim the ends with scissors, if desired. Tie the bow onto the basket.

Double-Chocolate Cocoa Mugs

PREP TIME
15 minutes

MAKES
12 servings

2 cups instant non-fat dry milk powder

2 cups miniature marshmallows

¾ cup powdered sugar

¾ cup powdered non-dairy creamer

½ cup mini semi-sweet chocolate morsels

¼ cup unsweetened cocoa powder

Peppermint candy canes

1 In a large bowl, combine the milk powder, marshmallows, powdered sugar, non-dairy creamer, chocolate morsels, and cocoa. Whisk with a wire whisk to blend.

2 Lay a 12-inch-long sheet of color plastic wrap on the countertop. Spoon ⅓ cup of the cocoa mixture in the center of the sheet. Gather the ends of the plastic wrap and tie with ribbon to make an individual bundle. Repeat for each bundle.

3 Fill a holiday mug with several bundles of cocoa mix. Attach a peppermint candy cane to the mug.

4 Add a gift tag with the following heating directions: *To make Double-Chocolate Cocoa, unwrap one bundle of cocoa mix and put it in the mug. Add 1 cup of boiling water. Stir with the candy cane.*

> **REYNOLDS KITCHENS TIP**
>
> *Let your children help with the mixing and wrapping to create special holiday memories and traditions they can share. Double-Chocolate Cocoa Mugs make great gifts for teachers, coworkers, and other special people on your holiday list.*

Cherry-Coconut Trifle

PREP TIME
30 minutes

CHILL TIME
6 hours

MAKES
14 servings

One 10¾-ounce frozen pound cake, thawed

¼ cup strawberry jam

2 teaspoons almond extract

One 8-ounce package cream cheese, softened

½ cup powdered sugar

Two 4-serving-size packages coconut cream instant pudding and pie filling

3¼ cups milk

One 8-ounce carton frozen whipped topping, thawed

One 20-ounce can cherry pie filling

¼ cup flaked sweetened coconut

1 Slice the top crust from the pound cake. Slice the cake horizontally into 3 even layers.

2 In a small bowl, stir together the jam and 1 teaspoon of the almond extract. Spread over the cut sides of the cake and stack the layers. Slice the cake crosswise into ½-inch-thick slices. Arrange the cake slices around the sides and over the bottom of a trifle bowl or a straight-sided 3-quart glass bowl. Reserve any leftover slices of cake.

3 In the bowl of an electric mixer set on low speed, beat together the cream cheese and powdered sugar until smooth.

4 In another bowl, whisk together the pudding mix and milk until blended and thickened. Add this and the whipped topping to the sweetened cream cheese and beat on low speed until blended.

5 Pour the mixture into the cake-lined bowl until even with the top of the cake slices. Reserve the remaining mixture.

6 In a small bowl, stir the cherry pie filling with the remaining teaspoon of extract. Spoon half in a ring around the edge of the bowl, on top of the pudding.

7 Cut any remaining cake slices into ½-inch cubes and put in the center of the cherry ring. Top with the remaining pudding mixture. Spoon the remaining cherry pie filling on top of the pudding. Sprinkle the coconut in the center. Cover with plastic wrap and refrigerate for at least 6 hours or overnight before serving.

REYNOLDS
KITCHENS TIP

Put a sheet of wax paper over the open pages of the cookbook when you cook. It protects the book from splatters and smudges and you can read through it.

Sugar-and-Spice Cookie Pops

PREP TIME

20 minutes

COOK TIME

10 minutes

MAKES

18 cookie pops

1 teaspoon ground cinnamon

½ teaspoon ground ginger

⅛ teaspoon ground cloves

One 18-ounce package refrigerated sugar cookie dough

18 lollipop sticks

One 16-ounce container vanilla ready-to-spread frosting

Tubes of decorator icing, several colors

Sugar sprinkles

Color plastic wrap

1 Preheat the oven to 350°F. Line a cookie sheet with parchment paper.

2 In a small bowl, mix together the cinnamon, ginger, and cloves.

3 Slice the cookie dough into ¼-inch-thick pieces. Lightly sprinkle the pieces with the spice mixture. Shape each piece into balls and insert a lollipop stick in the center of each one. Lay on the cookie sheet.

4 Pat each ball into 2-inch-wide circles, each about ¼-inch thick, without disturbing the lollipop stick.

5 Bake for 10 to 12 minutes or until the edges are golden brown. Transfer the cookie sheet to a wire rack to cool completely.

6 Frost the cookies with vanilla frosting. Decorate with decorator icing and sprinkles. Let the frosting set and dry.

7 Wrap each cookie in a sheet of color plastic wrap. Gather the plastic wrap on top of the cookie and tie with a ribbon.

REYNOLDS KITCHENS TIP

To make a cookie pop flower bouquet or centerpiece, place a Styrofoam base in a gift basket. Insert the sticks of the cookie pops into Styrofoam to make flower arrangements.

Frosty Snowmen

One 3-ounce bag microwave popcorn, popped

One 10-ounce package regular-size marshmallows

¼ cup butter or margarine

1½ cups vanilla ready-to-spread frosting

6 chenille stems

Invisible or clear tape

Candy-coated chocolate candies, multiple colors

Color plastic wrap

PREP TIME
30 minutes

MAKES
6 snowmen

1   Pour the popcorn into an extra-large mixing bowl. Discard unpopped kernels.

2   Put the marshmallows and butter in a large microwave-safe bowl and microwave on high power for 1 to 2 minutes. Stir. Microwave on high power for 30 to 60 seconds longer and stir until smooth. Pour over the the popcorn and toss until coated.

Frosty Snowmen

3 Spray your hands generously with cooking spray. Shape the popcorn into six 3-inch balls and six 2-inch balls. Stack the smaller balls on top of the larger ones to form six snowmen.

4 Put ½ cup of the frosting in a microwave-safe bowl and microwave on high power for about 20 seconds or until liquid. Drizzle and spread the frosting over 2 of the snowmen. Press on candy-coated candies to make eyes and buttons. Cut 2 candies in half and press them into the frosting to form nose and mouth. Repeat to make the remaining snowmen. Let stand for at least 30 minutes or until frosting is set and hardened.

5 Wrap each snowman in a 10-inch sheet of clear plastic wrap. Overlap it at the back and press to secure.

6 Center a chenille stem on a 12-inch-long sheet of color plastic wrap. Fold the plastic wrap over the chenille stem and roll into a thin strip. Wrap the strip around your finger and gently pull up the center. Place on a snowman's head to form a stocking cap; secure in back with a small piece of invisible tape.

7 Fold a 6-inch sheet of color plastic wrap into a thin strip. Tie around the neck of a snowman to form scarf. Trim the ends. Repeat for remaining snowmen.

> **REYNOLDS KITCHENS TIP**
>
> *To display festive holiday creations, line a large tray or wrap a sheet of white cardboard with color plastic wrap.*

. . .

Santa Snack Cakes

PREP TIME
20 minutes

MAKES
16 snack cakes

One 16-ounce frozen pound cake, thawed

One 16-ounce container vanilla ready-to-spread frosting

Red and green food coloring

Sprinkles (optional)

Holiday plastic wrap

1 Slice the top crust from the pound cake. Cut the cake in half horizontally.

2 Use 2-inch holiday-shaped cookie cutters to cut 8 miniature cakes from each half of the pound cake.

3 Lay a sheet of wax paper on the countertop and set a wire rack on the wax paper. Put the miniature cakes on the rack.

4 Put ½ cup of the frosting in a microwave-safe bowl and microwave on high power for 10 to 20 seconds, or until melted. Stir food coloring into the frosting to tint it.

5 Spoon the frosting over the miniature cakes, letting excess drizzle down the sides of the cakes. Top with sprinkles, if desired. Repeat until all the cakes are frosted. Let set until the frosting is dry.

6 Arrange the cakes on a platter. Cover with holiday designs printed plastic wrap. Gather the plastic wrap at the ends of the platter and tie with ribbon. Fluff the ends and trim.

Santa Snack Cakes

White Chocolate Party Mix

PREP TIME

15 minutes

MAKES

8 cups

2 cups miniature pretzels

5 cups toasted cinnamon crunch cereal

2 cups salted peanuts

2 cups candy-coated chocolate candies

One 12-ounce package premium white morsels

3 tablespoons vegetable oil

1 Line 2 cookie sheets with wax paper or parchment paper.

2 In a large bowl, mix together the pretzels, cereal, peanuts, and chocolate candies.

3 Put the white morsels and vegetable oil in a microwave-safe bowl and microwave on high power for 2 minutes, stirring after 1 minute. Stir and then microwave for about 10 seconds longer. Stir until smooth.

4 Pour over the cereal mixture and mix until evenly coated. Spread onto the cookie sheets. Let cool and then break apart.

5 Store in an airtight decorative container, lined with wax paper.

REYNOLDS KITCHENS TIP

Use holiday decorated wax paper to line the decorative tin or container.

Index